SOUTHERN AFRICA

SOUTHERN AFRICA

OLD TREACHERIES AND NEW DECEITS

STEPHEN CHAN

YALE UNIVERSITY PRESS
NEW HAVEN AND LONDON

For information about this and other Yale University Press publications, please contact:
U.S. Office: sales.press@yale.edu   www.yalebooks.com
Europe Office: sales @yaleup.co.uk   www.yalebooks.co.uk

Set in Adobe Caslon Pro by IDSUK (DataConnection) Ltd
Printed in Great Britain by TJ International Ltd, Padstow, Cornwall

Library of Congress Cataloging-in-Publication Data

Chan, Stephen, 1949
    Southern Africa: old treacheries and new deceits/Stephen Chan.
    p.cm.
ISBN 978–0–300–15405–4 (cl:alk. paper)
1. Africa, Southern—Politics and government—1994–2. South Africa—Politics and government—1989–1994. 3. South Africa—Politics and government—1994–4. Zimbabwe—Politics and government—1980–5. Zambia—Politics and government—1991–6. Mandela, Nelson, 1918–7. Mugabe, Robert Gabriel, 1924–8. Mbeki, Thabo. 9. Zuma, Jacob. I. Title
    DT1182.C43 2011
    968.0009'0511—dc22

                                                                    2010045379

A catalogue record for this book is available from the British Library.

10 9 8 7 6 5 4 3 2 1

For Ali, Steve, Angelo and Justin – who became refugees from it all; for Ranka who was the older sister to them all; and for Sydney – who tried to put it all back together.

CONTENTS

ACRONYMS

ANC	African National Congress (South Africa)
BBBEE	Broad-Based Black Economic Empowerment
BEE	Black Economic Empowerment
COPE	Congress of the People (South Africa)
COSATU	Congress of South African Trade Unions
DA	Democratic Alliance (South Africa)
DRC	Democratic Republic of Congo
FRELIMO	Frente de Liberacao de Mocambique
GEAR	Growth, Employment and Redistribution Programme
MDC	Movement for Democratic Change (Zimbabwe)
MPLA	Movimento Popular de Liberacao de Angola
NCA	National Constitutional Assembly (Zimbabwe)
NEPAD	New Partnership for Africa's Development
PAC	Pan-Africanist Congress (South Africa)
RDP	Reconstruction and Development Programme
RENAMO	Resistencia Nacional Mocambicana (Mozambique)
SACP	South African Communist Party
SADC	Southern African Development Community
SADCC	Southern African Development Coordination Conference
SWAPO	South West Africa People's Organization
UNITA	Unicao Nacional para a Independencia Total de Angola
ZANU-PF	Zimbabwe African National Union – Patriotic Front

INTRODUCTION

Johannesburg 2008

'Sold into slavery, but he rose to become the right-hand man of Pharaoh.' Joseph was thinking about his biblical namesake. The great Pyramids must have seemed like the towers of Johannesburg to him. He trudged among the towers as he had done every day for weeks, pleading for work, not rising to become the right-hand man of anyone. He would have to lower his sights and try in the suburbs and then, like everyone said he would, scavenge a job in the outlying townships. He had his heart set on not having to steal, but he had a family to support back in Zimbabwe and he knew that, if push came to shove, he could always find odd jobs as an enforcer, a debt collector and muscular repayer of debts. A deserter from the Zimbabwean military, he knew a thing or two about how to repay those who forgot their obligations.

If it was as an enforcer then at least he wouldn't have to work in the townships long minibus rides away. The collection industry was hardest at work in the inner city suburbs, where tens of thousands of people like

Joseph looked for jobs and borrowed funds to finance their search. You move in groups of three, kick down a door, rough the guy up, issue last warnings, and take whatever's of value in the grubby room. It wasn't exactly a noble profession, thought Joseph, but he wouldn't have to move from the edge of Hillbrow – where thousands of Zimbabweans had 'settled', mostly without papers, and had somehow established both a community of their own and stilted relations with the locals. The Mozambicans nearby were not always so successful, and were more conspicuous when they chatted to one another in Portuguese.

Joseph had deserted his military unit in the southern provinces of Democratic Republic of Congo. He had fought in the battles for Kinshasa as the new millennium began, when the Zimbabweans helped Laurent Kabila consolidate his power as Congolese President – providing the throne for him that even the legendary Che Guevara, in his ill-fated African adventure of 1963, could not. Before Kabila had been assassinated he had effectively ceded control of much of his country's southern mineral wealth to the Zimbabweans. Joseph had stood guard as the senior Generals and henchmen of Robert Mugabe helped themselves to the spoils. It was designed to reinforce their loyalty to Mugabe. Disgusted, not willing to risk his life for such people, Joseph deserted and now watched the daily newspapers in Johannesburg for signs that Thabo Mbeki might persuade Mugabe to give up at least some of his power. All the while Mugabe resisted, and his Generals backed him up – men who, on television, appeared even more self-satisfied than when Joseph had seen them, behaving furtively before they became self-confident in their plundering of southern Congo. 'I would not want to be the right-hand man of such a Pharaoh,' thought Joseph. But, as he watched the limousines cruise by in Johannesburg, read in the newspapers about corruption charges brought against Jacob Zuma, he realised how merciless even South African politics could be and thought, in a no-smoke-without-fire sort of way, that corruption was laying down its foundations amidst the tall buildings. 'We can teach them a thing or two about that,' Joseph muttered as he knocked on another office door.

This was a one-man show. It was a fellow Zimbabwean and, yes, he had a job for Joseph – a choice of two jobs, in fact. He could be part of a small Zimbabwean labour gang that provided hod-carrying on the cheap for one of the fly-by-night South African construction companies that were throwing up housing units, quickly and badly, so that the ANC could honour its election pledges to poor communities. The company had been swiftly formed to take advantage of the empowerment regulations that privileged black businesses, and its bosses knew very little about the building trade. They knew enough to pay very low rates for illegal Zimbabwean labour. The other job was better, his countryman said, eyeing Joseph's physique. It was to provide protection for these same labour gangs. 'The local workmen have been undercut by us,' he said, 'and there are some areas where we are helping to build houses which have the rumblings of a lot of anger building up.'

Joseph got a uniform with green and red epaulettes (he had to buy his own boots), a PR24 – the standard issue police swing baton – a construction-site helmet, and a car ride to his immediate assignment. He couldn't believe his luck, but he also knew that what his new boss had told him was true. Away from the mix of Hillbrow, anti-Zimbabwean sentiments had been increasing for some time and Joseph had to run the risk of its exploding in his own face. Even the South African workers performing the more skilled tasks would look down critically upon their Zimbabwean labourers. And he knew that the security guard had to be him, had to be a Zimbabwean. A South African would think twice in the current climate before standing between a Zimbabwean labour gang and a crowd of angry unemployed fellow citizens. The Egyptians, thought Joseph, were going to turn upon the Israelites.

I begin with that story from 2008. It is reminiscent of an earlier story from 1941 when the young Nelson Mandela, fleeing the restraints of the countryside and a small university, arrived in Johannesburg – anxious for the bright lights and opportunities, but penniless and proud – and had to take a first job as a security guard, being thankful for the opportunity. The growing intimacy and integration of the Southern African region has meant that what was once a saga in one country is now a repeated saga in a connected network of countries. And, just as South Africa then was a country of vast inequalities, there are today vast differences in wealth and opportunity among the different parts of Southern Africa. There have also been vast increases in complexity since the days of the young Mandela. It is not simply a case of white despots in Pretoria having a modern counterpart in black despots in Harare. Economies, politics and expectations have grown larger and more sophisticated – and so have the way they partake in the world outside Southern Africa. This has posed certain problems in how to write this book. In particular: how to write an intelligent book for the non-specialist reader who has a newspaper and television knowledge of Southern Africa built around a small number of political leaders – whose personalities and motivations are often trivialised or turned into caricatures of good and evil?

I have concentrated precisely on a small number of countries from the region, and on a small number of their political personalities, but have tried to give them their full range of complexities and contradictions. I wanted to suggest by this that the entire region and the way its parts interact is full of complexities and contradictions. So that Nelson Mandela is not a saint, but a skiving, jazz-freak student radical, lately given to wearing stupid shirts; so that Thabo Mbeki did not fail by simple lack of effort in his 'quiet diplomacy' with Robert Mugabe, but was driven by complex and highly learned patterns of reasoning; so that Robert Mugabe himself did not become a tyrant because of a love of tyranny, but lost himself in the contradictions of his convictions, until his stubbornness became malignant and finally malevolent; so that Jacob Zuma did not gain the leadership of the ANC by sheer vulgar populism, but by harnessing an unlikely alliance of brilliant political and business minds who helped him for the sake of their own revenge. The ambition of this book is to endow what the Western media has turned into black caricatures with the same sort of life we would automatically assume was inherent in Tony Blair, Gordon Brown, David Cameron, Nick Clegg, George Bush, Barack Obama and Nicolas Sarkozy.

It is also to repay some debt to a region that helped form me. Some of my own experiences weave in and out of this book. The intention was to help further humanise the region – for it is clear I made many mistakes as a young man high on diplomatic and political adventures – but I hope I do not intrude too much on the personalities and themes of the book, particularly as they become more complex in their own right as the book develops.

Having said that, I set out to tell a story: one that links many stories, and some of these have had full-length books written about them. The industry of Southern African biography is huge, and I have contributed to it myself. But the aim here is not to recount the life of Thabo Mbeki as comprehensively as Mark Gevisser[1] or as critically as William Gumede,[2] or to give a blow by blow account of the formation of Robert Mugabe.[3] The aim is to show how, in a linked and intimate region, lives and political decisions weave in and out of one another. Agendas clash, sometimes they dovetail, and sometimes they dovetail in unexpected and perverse ways.

That explains the writing methodology I have chosen for this book. I have tried to write it as a weaving tapestry, overlapping many strands and threads in a colourful though, hopefully, still intellectually honest fashion.

It will be clear in my accounts of South African mediation in the Zimbabwean tragedy, and in the plunging of knives into backs within South African politics, that I have been informed by close participants in those events. Very often such accounts differ markedly from reported wisdom – although not always from the 'diplomatic cables' which Western governments frequently choose to ignore for their own political reasons. I cannot reveal my informants, but I hope there have been enough of them for me to make judicious choices in sometimes conflicting stories. I hope that these accounts, when tallied with agreed knowledge, can provide new ways to understand the region. I am indebted to those who have taken me into their trust and must find ways to repay their kind confidences.

The book begins with a brief historical account but, thereafter, concentrates on the 1990s and 2000s. Although Southern Africa is a vast region with ten countries in it – excluding Democratic Republic of Congo and Tanzania which are often associated with the region, and the island territories of the Southern Indian Ocean – I have concentrated on the relationships between South Africa, Zimbabwe and, to an extent, Zambia. They were the three territories most associated with Cecil Rhodes. South Africa and Zimbabwe (as Rhodesia) were the key bastions of white minority rule until decades after the rest of Africa attained majority rule. Zambia, once called Northern Rhodesia, became the exile headquarters of liberation movements struggling against minority rule, including South Africa's ANC. The patterns of interaction established over the years have never been erased – although they have changed in character and motivation. They have also changed in terms of the personalities of presidents who have driven interaction onwards.

Of those people I am able to name, I wish to acknowledge my gratitude to many who, over the years, helped me understand the region. Some are now dead, but I include them to honour their memory. In no particular order, Dan Karobia, Muna Ndulo, Gatian Lungu, Lloyd Chingambo, Kwaku Osei-Hwedie, Chaloka Beyani, Walter Mazzuki, Kebby Musokotwane, Ngande Mwanajiti, Ibbo Mandaza, Jimmy Mavenge, Hasu Patel, Brian Raftopoulos, Johnson Ndlovu, Morgan Tsvangirai, H.W. Van Der Merwe, Andre du Pisani, Greg Mills, Mervyn Frost, Sandy Johnson, Adam Habib, William Gumede, Raphael de Kadt, Sydney Mufamadi, Henry Paulse, Renee Horne and Ranka Primorac all helped me. Diplomats posted to several embassies over the years were very helpful. Of course no one is to blame for any shortcomings in this book but myself.

Map 1: Colonial Southern Africa

Map 2: Independent Southern Africa

CHAPTER 1

THE GREAT NORTH ROAD

Cecil Rhodes wanted to link Africa, south to north. He wanted a through road to facilitate his expansionism. The road he began ran through South Africa and what is today Zimbabwe and Zambia. Transport links have always bound these three nations together. But South Africa and Zimbabwe, still called Rhodesia until 1980, were bound together as well by the stubborn retention of white minority rule. Although liberation movements from both countries were headquartered in Lusaka, the capital of Zambia, it was military victory for nationalist groups in the surrounding Portuguese territories, particularly in Angola, that sparked a wave of battle and struggle, with the active involvement of many non-African countries including the superpowers of the day, that culminated in the diplomatic manoeuvres that gave independence to Zimbabwe. After that, Apartheid South Africa was isolated in the region – but far from defeated. With the independence of Zimbabwe, the Apartheid machine prepared to uncoil for one last great offensive against its black neighbours. This conflict defined the political relationships and personalities of much of what was to come, well into the first decade of the twenty-first century.

Cecil Rhodes wanted to build a road from Cape Town to Cairo. It didn't even get halfway but, even now, a Great North Road still snakes out of Lusaka, Zambia – promising much and petering out in the Congolese wilderness. It was the old fox, Henry Kissinger, who realised that Africa was too big to be encompassed by a single vision. In the 1970s he thought he could anchor US interests in three, possibly four, major states: South Africa and Egypt were there, so the Cape and Cairo still featured, only without the road; so did Nigeria in the west and, as an afterthought, Nairobi in the east. Nothing in the centre. Everything petered out in the centre. That was the heart of darkness, albeit with a dictatorial ruler friendly to the US. President Mobutu of what was then called Zaire was indulged and left alone.

The US needed rulers and regimes that were friendly. In 1976 the Cold War had become spectacularly hot, but far enough away from the West for it to be fought by proxies. Apartheid South Africa acted as the US proxy in the swathe of the continent that took in the Atlantic and Indian Ocean seaboards from the Cape to the northern tips of Angola and Mozambique, and everything in between. There was talk in Pretoria, London and Washington of forming a SATO, a South Atlantic Treaty Organisation. This never happened but South African warships began to use NATO naval doctrine, signals and contingency planning formulas.[1]

The advent of Cuban troops in Angola in 1976 had alarmed Washington. The South African military, responding to a new Angolan government with Communist leanings, had been driven back by the Cubans. Suddenly, Africa was no longer the continent of low-intensity guerrilla wars but a place where tank columns manoeuvred for position and where air superiority determined strategic planning. As the South Africans fell back, the US prepared to support its Apartheid ally in long wars.

But Kissinger realised that a tide of majority rule, of black rule, was rolling towards South Africa, where the white minority stubbornly clung to power – even as it was being steadily surrounded by black states. What he wanted to avoid was majority rule accomplished by military victory; especially Communist-assisted military victory, as had just occurred in Angola. A military fightback was, in his and Pretoria's view, unavoidable. But Kissinger also wanted a buy-out. Military might would keep Communist-aided states at bay and destabilised. Economic might would buy peaceful settlements in troublesome areas – such as Rhodesia. The Kissinger plan, highly generalised but striking the centre of the problem, was to compensate white Rhodesian farmers for giving up their land to a black majority. With a key grievance addressed, the black nationalists would negotiate a future rather than go to war for it, and not seek Communist help as they did so. The moderate government that ensued would cooperate with the huge economic might of South Africa.[2]

The South Africans had long dreamed of the surrounding states becoming part of an economic zone. It was a little like the Japanese dream of a Greater East Asian Co-Prosperity Sphere in the years before World War II – seeking to benefit economically from the surrounding region while dominating it politically and, if need be, militarily. It was naïve of the Japanese to imagine that their dream would not create resistance. Likewise, the South African dream was never going to work as long as Pretoria was the capital of white racism in a continent casting off the chains of discrimination.

This was a time of tangled history in Southern Africa, as racial divides at home were made into chess-pieces on an international board. West and East clashed over Southern Africa while, within the region, black sought to emancipate itself from white.

Today, giant rainbow-coloured lizards dance on Cecil Rhodes' grave in the Matopos Hills in Zimbabwe. It is an eerie place, rocks balance precariously on top of one another in natural columns, and local people say that ancestral spirits dance and weave in and out of the rocks. The view seems to stretch on for ever and, in the vegetation below, rhinos still roam.

It has been hard to get away from Rhodes. Born in 1853 he lived, by any standards, a great if pernicious life until his death in 1902.[3] He had an unreserved belief in the 'civilising' capacity and destiny of the white

European race, and that this sanctioned his expansion into other lands. He founded the state of Rhodesia, later Northern and Southern Rhodesia (Zambia and Zimbabwe). In the war against Robert Mugabe's guerrillas, the soldiers of the white-ruled Southern Rhodesia would be awarded the General Service Medal, bearing Rhodes' portrait. From 1890 to 1896 he was Prime Minister of the Cape Colony in what is now South Africa. Rhodes University in South Africa was named after him. He founded the De Beers Mining Company, whose diamond mines form the bedrock of Botswana's economy. His British South Africa Company had its own police force and, as one of the great multinational corporations of its day, was licensed by the British government to conduct a privatised form of colonialism. His interests stretched as far as the Congo and he tried, unsuccessfully, to obtain mining concessions there. Ironically, a hundred years later, these came to Mugabe's Generals.

But Rhodes wasn't the only man to seek to unite Southern Africa.[4] Shaka, the great Zulu Emperor, in his conquests, made unions out of disparate tribes, incorporated either into the Zulu empire or united against it. I remember in the late 1980s visiting Zambia and dining with the air force high command. Suddenly, all eating and drinking had to stop. It was time for that week's instalment of the South African television epic of Shaka. The General and his colonels sat riveted, for Shaka was their predecessor – a black man recognised even by whites as a great warrior and general.

The whole saga of Shaka is now being revisited by historians.[5] The young leader who rose to prominence by the ferocious discipline and loyalty of his impis, he seemed to bring something new to Southern Africa by way of both battle and vision of unity. Certainly his innovation of the short stabbing spear caught his adversaries by surprise. But were his battle tactics that revolutionary? Was he really so ruthless? He was certainly highly successful by the standards of his day. He lived from 1787 to 1828 and united all the Zulu sub-tribes. At his height, he ruled over 250,000 people and fielded regiments, impis, numbering 50,000 soldiers. He did more than unite the Zulus. His military conquests forced many other tribal groups to unite into stronger units, or relocate their homes. Dissident Zulus and Shaka's impis themselves set up homes in the areas they overcame, so that there is a Zulu imprint among the Ndebele people of western Zimbabwe and the Ngoni people of south-eastern Zambia. But, even after he died, Shaka's military legacy made a great impact upon the expansionist white population of Southern Africa. The Boer settlers, marching north on their great *Voortrek* to establish their own lands away from the British, defeated a Zulu army at the 1838 Battle of Blood River. On the other hand, Zulu regiments wiped out the British at the 1879 Battle of Isandlwana, and both battles entered the folklore of the region.

Until recently the region has been one of battles and confrontations. War only stopped in Angola and Mozambique in the 1990s, both having had significant Apartheid South African interventions – although the direct nature of these began to cease after the Battle of Cuito Cuanavale in southern Angola in 1988 where, once again, Cuban forces with Soviet air superiority outmanoeuvred the South African military. But the battles left their mark and gave birth to their own legends. It was an open secret in Lusaka that the young air force commander with whom I dined – General Hananiah Lungu – the fan of Shaka on television, had disobeyed President Kaunda's orders forbidding any military retaliation against the constant incursions by white Rhodesian forces, including their warplanes, to discourage Zimbabwean guerrillas operating from Zambian soil. One day in the late 1970s, indignant at the taunts of Rhodesian pilots, he took off in his own fighter and crossed the border undetected. He then dropped smoke bombs the length of the main Rhodesian air force base – just to indicate he could do it, and that the Zambians could reply more forcefully if they were let off the leash – then made it back to Zambia before the astonished Rhodesians could muster a reply. Kaunda lectured the young officer fiercely, then promoted him.

The Rhodesians had been trenchantly supported by South Africa. Rhodes was only the beginning, and the relationship between the two countries developed with ferocity as the twentieth century progressed.

* * *

In 1910 the project begun by Rhodes in South Africa had reached a level of consolidation and maturity. The fierce rebellion by Boer settlers against British encroachment on 'their' lands had been suppressed – but not before the Boer fighters had given the British a severe lesson in unconventional warfare.[6] The country was sufficiently at peace in 1910 to be given 'dominion' status: a form of independence, subject to final sanction of the British crown and its organs.[7] It was the same kind of 'independent' status, with variations, given to Canada and New Zealand. Canada only severed its final constitutional links with the British Parliament in 1982 and New Zealand continues to recognise Queen Elizabeth II as Head of State. South Africa, however, became a full-fledged republic in 1961, after many years of developing and enforcing Apartheid. It declared itself a republic when it was expelled from the Commonwealth. The increasing number of Third World countries gaining independence and entering the Commonwealth made South Africa's membership untenable. It was the only country without majority rule. The surrounding countries were all slated to receive independence in the near future. The British Prime Minister, Harold Macmillan, had visited South Africa in 1960 and made his historic 'wind of change' speech, urging the South African Parliament to move with the times and recognise the rights of the black population. It was one of the great eloquent speeches of the twentieth century, but had no effect. From that moment of refusal to listen to Macmillan, it was clear South Africa had to go it alone and, in 1960, the Sharpeville massacre – when 69 black protesters were killed and 180 injured – declared to the world South Africa's determination to preserve Apartheid at all costs. But, if South Africa had to go it alone in broad international terms, it was determined to undermine its isolation by developing strong links with Western corporations, by becoming the ally of Washington in its war against Communism, and by ensuring that the surrounding African states remained as white, or as compliant, as possible.

South Africa had been working on the surrounding states for some time. The regional protective buffers for Apartheid went hand in hand with the steady development of legalised discrimination at home. Strong links were formed with the white-ruled states and then, as independence began to come, it particularly supported the minority settler government in Rhodesia, suppressed nationalist movements in South West Africa (now Namibia), over which it had assumed disputed control, and sought to condition Botswana, Lesotho and Swaziland into becoming compliant, untroublesome states. All the while, South Africa increased the pressure on its own black population.

It was not as if the black population in South Africa took this kneeling down. The ANC (African National Congress) was established in 1912, but in 1913 the Land Acts were passed in Parliament, creating 'native reserves' on 7 per cent of the land. This was increased to 13 per cent in 1936, and such restricted voting rights as black Africans enjoyed were rescinded. It took until 1946, however, before the first mass black protest occurred. That was a strike of 100,000 miners; and, in that year, the first United Nations discussion took place on what was happening in South Africa. Again to no avail. The coming to power in 1948 of the white Nationalist Party under D.F. Malan saw a commitment to full Apartheid. As Prime Minister, Malan embodied the strict Afrikaner ideology of white racial superiority. He declared that the Afrikaners – the descendants of Dutch and other Protestant settlers who had fought the British – were the creation of God, and that the semi-barbarous blacks had only the Afrikaner standard of civilisation as an appropriate guide to a Christian life. In 1949 the Prohibition of Mixed Marriages Act was passed. In 1950 the Population Registration Act formally divided South Africans into separate racial groups. In international terms, this should have been appalling. It was only five years after the end of the Holocaust, with its own racial groupings and the denigration and genocide associated with that, but now racial grouping and discrimination came to South Africa. In 1955 the ANC with its partners adopted the Freedom Charter. The battle lines internally had begun to be drawn.

Internationally, the first trenchant criticism came with the independence of Ghana in 1957.[8] An African voice entered the UN and the first effort at an international boycott of South African goods began the following year. After the Sharpeville massacre the ANC was banned. In 1964 Nelson Mandela was among eight men sent to prison for treason. They included Govan Mbeki, the father of Thabo Mbeki, the future president. The battle lines were fully drawn, and the ANC went underground in South Africa and established bases in exile as surrounding states gained independence. The ANC went to Zambia, the old Northern Rhodesia. Thabo Mbeki travelled extensively but basically divided his exile between London and Lusaka. But, a year after Zambia gained independence in 1964, Ian Smith and the white Rhodesian Front party in Southern Rhodesia – now Zimbabwe – unilaterally declared its independence from Britain, with a promise never to allow majority rule for a thousand years.[9] This suited South Africa down to the ground. It had a key buffer state in place, and it thought it could control the other surrounding states.

Even the names in this case were revealing. 'Rhodesia' harked back to Cecil Rhodes, but 'Zimbabwe' referred to a great African civilisation which had built stone cities across the country, probably as urban centres marking a trade route that headed towards the Mozambican coast.

South Africa had an ally in Portugal. Its right-wing government was determined, until its fall in 1975, to hold on to its colonies in Angola and Mozambique. South Africa had annexed South West Africa. It had occupied the territory, then a German colony, during World War I; administered it under a League of Nations mandate between the two wars; then annexed it after World War II. The Germans had killed a significant part of the population when it rose against colonial rule and, although SWAPO (the South West African People's Organization) began a guerrilla war against South African rule, the huge land mass and small population – it is the world's most thinly populated country after Mongolia – made successful war impossible. SWAPO, like the ANC, set up an exile headquarters in Zambia. But Zambia could be kept at geopolitical distance. With Angola, Mozambique and South West Africa all under white governorship, South Africa faced only the problem of how to control neighbouring Botswana, Lesotho and Swaziland.

This was accomplished in three ways. Economically, the three states were incorporated into the Southern African Customs Union, controlled by South Africa. This gave them tangible and significant economic benefits. Diplomatically, South Africa worked to isolate these states from the growing UN consensus against Apartheid. Swaziland was forced to sign a secret non-aggression pact as late as 1982. Militarily, South Africa would demonstrate its capacity on selected occasions, and did intervene briefly with its armed forces in both Botswana and Lesotho. By and large, these three states never caused South Africa any major difficulties. The independence of Angola and Mozambique in 1975 however, and the independence of Zimbabwe in 1980, all three after vicious military conflict, led South Africa to reformulate and heighten its regional policy into one of coordinated and constant destabilisation.

That vicious conflict had been a long time coming. Portugal, under a right-wing dictatorship, had always considered her territories in Africa as part of metropolitan Portugal. They were not meant to be regarded as colonies. When surrounding states began achieving independence in the 1960s, Portugal resisted the clamour for majority rule on the grounds that Portugal could not give independence to part of herself. As violent resistance began to grow, the Portuguese responded with increased military intervention. Many young conscripts were sent to the African front, and the war became increasingly unpopular with the Portuguese population. In Angola, three pro-independence rebel factions developed considerable armed strength, and began to be assisted by foreign powers. As the intensity of the war increased, its unpopularity in Portugal also rose. In Cape Verde and Mozambique, armed struggle had also broken out. The united rebel movement in Mozambique assumed control of much of the countryside. The Portuguese government sought increasingly to quieten its citizens by restricting information about the African wars. Young conscripts had their own tales to tell, as did the number of casualties. But a sustained critique of government policy was unable to develop, and the government had the support of the senior military officers – from which its dictatorship had originated. Censorship and repression were common in Portugal. As the majority of Western Europe began the project of economic cooperation and shared democratic values, Portugal was isolated and left behind. It became one of the poorest and least advanced countries in Europe, and the African wars were an increasing drain on the economy.[10] But if an uprising were to be possible, it had to come from within the junior ranks of the army itself, from the younger officers. In 1975 this happened.

When the tanks of the young officers appeared on the streets of Lisbon, announcing the overthrow of the dictatorship, Portugal entered the modern European era. As if a huge weight had been lifted, citizens poured into the streets to welcome the coup. The full bloody truth of the African wars had been hidden from ordinary people and no Portuguese author had dared chronicle the expense caused to the Portuguese state, not to mention the extent of African suffering. From their tanks the soldiers threw hastily translated works of the English historian, David Birmingham, to explain the reality of Portuguese repression in Africa. Birmingham, whose essays had been forthright about the cost and ruthlessness of Portuguese policy in Africa, had conspired to be in Lisbon and, from within the crowds, saw his writings begin to have their effect.[11] The new government announced immediate independence for the African territories. But little had been done to prepare them. In Angola, the rebel groups were fighting against one another as well as against the Portuguese. And tens of thousands of Portuguese settlers felt abandoned by Lisbon and insecure under their new rulers. Thousands fled to Portugal and lost everything. In Mozambique, departing settlers tried to smash every working toilet in the capital city, so that the victorious rebels would have nothing. But the new Mozambican government accepted Robert Mugabe onto its territory and, once there, the Zimbabwean nationalist began to take control of the armed struggle against white rule in his neighbouring country, striking across the border from Mozambican bases. This was at times problematic. Mugabe went as a controversially elected President of ZANU (Zimbabwe African National Union). The election had been held in prison, prior to his release, and was not universally accepted. Once in Mozambique, he had to overcome a guerrilla military leadership that did not automatically accept his seniority. The Mozambican government was sometimes in consternation over the intrigues and power plays of the exiled Zimbabweans. Meanwhile, the white Rhodesian forces would strike back against the Zimbabwean guerrillas and Mozambique became a literal front-line state.

But in Angola, when it seemed that the Marxist-leaning, Soviet-supported rebel group, the MPLA (Movimento Popular de Liberacao de Angola), had won the power struggle among the three liberation groups, the government of Apartheid South Africa decided to act. It sent in its army and its tanks on the assumption that no African guerrilla force could stand in its way. However, it was not the MPLA forces they encountered but hastily despatched Cubans. The Cold War was still raging, and in Africa was turning hot. Moscow asked Havana to step in and it did. Havana did so partly because it was obliged to Moscow for its political and financial support in the face of United States sanctions, but also because it had a genuine commitment to – if not romance with – Third World emancipation. Che Guevara had gone to fight in Africa in 1963, in the Congo, Angola's vast neighbour. But Angola also allowed Moscow to turn the Cold War 'hot' – if far away from Europe. At a safe distance, it could test US and NATO resolve in the face of Soviet military interventionism and that by its allies. In some ways, Angola was a test case for the Soviet invasion of Afghanistan in 1979 where the West found it could do nothing.

Having said that, it should not be assumed that the Angolans were pawns. There was genuine idealism and much courage on the part of the liberation movements. The Marxism of the MPLA was not a simple clone of what was acceptable in Moscow or Havana, but had African conditions in mind. The colonialism of the Portuguese had lasted longer than any other, and had an extensive record of brutality towards any attempt at emancipation except on Portuguese terms. Those terms were very much to do with metropolitan Portugal retaining extensive interests and territorial rights in Africa, along with political control. Self-determination was out of the question. Now, with the downfall of the right-wing dictatorship in Portugal, the liberation struggle in Angola attracted the firepower of both Apartheid South Africa and the Eastern bloc.

It has gone down in African folklore as the first great defeat of the South African Apartheid military forces. Something like the Zulu victory in pitched battle against the British at Isandlwana. It was no such thing. There were skirmishes and minor battles but no full-scale engagement. Rather, the two forces fought a war of manoeuvre, jostling for position, and the Cubans won. When the Cuban commander contacted Pretoria and said he had surrounded a key forward part of the South African forces and could pull tight the noose just like that, and asked how many body bags Pretoria wanted to ship back to South Africa, the South Africans agreed to withdraw – at least for the time being. Disaffection back home with the forward defence of Apartheid, even among white people affected by conscription to bolster the armed forces, made discretion the better part of valour. But the psychological sense of victory in Angola and across Southern Africa was immense. The mighty Apartheid machine could be opposed and made to pull back. The MPLA secured its hold over government, and its chief guerrilla rival, UNITA (Unicao Nacional para a Independencia Total de Angola) retreated to its southern rural strongholds, vowing to carry on its own struggle for victory in Angola. Here was an ally ready for Pretoria's assistance. But all of this had taken Pretoria by surprise, and it needed time to regroup.

In Mozambique the FRELIMO (Frente de Liberacao de Mocambique) rebel group became the government unopposed. It hosted the Zimbabwean nationalist guerrillas who were led by Robert Mugabe – but only after Mugabe had won a power struggle within their ranks. These guerrillas received Chinese training, both in Mozambique and Tanzania, and some officers in China itself. Mugabe's Marxism had been influenced by the Chinese and Maoist depiction of peasant struggle, as opposed to the struggle of an industrialised working class. The Chinese were, in turn, committed to African liberation, for reasons of genuine belief in people's liberation and also to ensure that they had a countervailing voice in Africa to that of the Soviet Union.

By 1976 the guerrillas were engaging the white Rhodesian forces in battle inside Rhodesia. But, despite Chinese training, they had to make it up as they went along. The Chinese had no idea of Rhodesian battle strength or capacity and had taught classic guerrilla war as they had known it. Guerrilla commanders sent platoon after platoon to certain death as a means of finding out. Despite propaganda, the aim seemed not to liberate and govern entire areas, but to deny those areas to the white government. Minority white government was to be made difficult. The local population was to shelter the guerrillas and provide information on government patrols. However, despite the Chinese adage about becoming one with the rural population, the guerrillas were not above exemplary punishments and executions in the Zimbabwean villages they encountered, forcing the inhabitants to all-night *pungwes* or meetings where fighting songs would be sung, local spirit mediums consulted and 'traitors' executed.[12] It was not quite a 'reign of terror', but the guerrillas were determined that their areas of operation would be supportive – whether that took one form of 'encouragement' or another. They knew that, if captured or caught in a firefight, they would face no mercy from the Rhodesian forces. Rhodesian commanders ridiculed the guerrilla training. 'They can't control the kick-back, they get too excited and always shoot above our heads,' one brigadier told me. But the fighting began to take its toll and a bloody stalemate began to grip the white-ruled country.

The Soviets who, through the Cubans, had intervened in Angola, and the Chinese who had supported both the Mozambican liberation movement and Mugabe's forces, now found themselves in their own tussle for military and political leverage in Zimbabwe. The Zimbabwean liberation struggle had, from an early stage, split into two main groups.[13] Each now had a powerful international patron. War in Southern Africa had become internationalised, and the West was still committed to South Africa because of its strategic minerals and command of the shipping lanes around the Cape of Good Hope. It was embarrassed by Apartheid, but had decided firmly to support the Apartheid regime. But it cautiously watched the war develop in Zimbabwe. The key objective was to safeguard South Africa. Rhodesia was a forward line of defence, but was not the key object in the minds of Western strategists.

Mugabe, operating from bases in Mozambique, had Chinese support. The guerrillas of Joshua Nkomo's rival liberation party, with a degree of Soviet training, had begun their own operations from Zambian bases. They weren't nearly as effective as Mugabe's, but their sheer presence tied the Rhodesian army, its white conscripts and its own black riflemen down. Nkomo, a former trade union official, could lay claim to being the first great black nationalist leader in Rhodesia. He drew much of his support from the west of the country and his liberation party was extensively identified with the Ndebele people of the two Matabeleland provinces in the west.

Even with much Apartheid South African material and financial support, Rhodesia found itself stretched thin. In 1978 the minority Prime Minister, Ian Smith, desperately tried to forestall genuine majority rule by installing a power-sharing government with all roles shared by black moderate politicians – Bishop Abel Muzorewa being their leader. But it was little and late. It established a precedent in that country at a time when desperate governments would seek to forestall defeat by gerrymandering a power-share. The South Africans were far from convinced and had begun to contemplate the difficulties they would face if Rhodesia were taken by storm. A victorious black army on its borders would be an emblem for its own restive black population. If there had to be a black government, better to have one not won by force of arms. Not only that, but if Rhodesia fell to the guerrillas, it would mean that three states to its north had been won by armed struggle. It couldn't respond militarily to all three. It had to take one out of the equation so it could ponder the best military strategy for the other two: Angola and Mozambique. But the Rhodesian power-share still excluded the guerrilla parties, and neither Smith nor Muzorewa wanted them in. They in any case did not want to govern alongside a small-town racist and a small-town bishop turncoat. And, although far from controlling all the countryside as they claimed, the guerrilla armies had learnt their craft and were making life a bloody mess outside the cities. It was the advent in 1979 of Margaret Thatcher as Prime Minister of the United Kingdom that concentrated the minds of everyone.

Margaret Thatcher came to power with an impulsive streak. She wanted to transform the country and to cut loose every historical albatross hanging around her government's neck. On an early visit to Australia, in a televised speech, apparently without prior consultation, she dropped the bombshell that the United Kingdom would recognise the Rhodesian government of Ian Smith with its cosmetic power-sharing involving Abel Muzorewa. I remember the televised moment very well. It was on a small black and white screen. The diminutive Thatcher was flanked by the tall figures of the conservative Australian Prime Minister Malcolm Fraser, and her own Foreign Secretary Lord Carrington. As she made her announcement the jaws of both men dropped. It was a special television moment as, without further flinching or movement, their minds clearly ground through the diplomatic consequences – half the world would be affronted and the damage to Britain's international relations would be immense – and then the steps that would be necessary finally to settle the Rhodesian problem. Thatcher's impulsiveness had placed the issue firmly at the centre of their agenda. For that at least she is owed some thanks. But I have always wondered what Peter Carrington said to her when they were alone together some moments later.

Whatever he said he was too gentlemanly to record it in his memoirs,[14] or even to speak it in private conversations after he was no longer Foreign Secretary. But he clearly dissuaded Thatcher from immediate recognition of Smith and Muzorewa. He seems to have requested, and been given, the late spring and summer of 1979 to find an alternative way forward.

Henry Kissinger was never the only exponent of 'shuttle diplomacy'. One of Carrington's closest colleagues, Lord Harlech, traversed the

Atlantic constantly that summer, seeking a common position with
Washington. Another, Sir Anthony Duff, flew up and down Africa
sounding out the least positions with which the Africans could live. At
that stage, Carrington probably had in mind an as yet unclear form of
power-sharing, sufficient to provide some genuine inclusion of a range
of black figures, without totally sacrificing the interests of the white
minority. The form of it was vague, but it had to be more convincing,
and more tilted towards black interests, than the Smith–Muzorewa
attempt. Duff probably sounded out African leaders on the accept-
ability of a coalition that included Nkomo. At that stage, British
outlooks probably still excluded Mugabe. However, the African states
were not going to be passive recipients of whatever Carrington came
up with. Zambia's President Kenneth Kaunda had his senior aide,
Mark Chona, also create vapour trails throughout eastern and southern
Africa to achieve a united African position. Contact was made with
the South Africans by the emissaries of both Carrington and Kaunda.
'If the British convene the conference, Kaunda ensures the attendance
of Nkomo, and Nyerere of Tanzania and Machel of Mozambique
ensure the attendance of Mugabe, can you "encourage" the attendance
of Smith and Muzorewa?' The South Africans said yes.

But it was harder than it looked. Getting Nkomo and Mugabe to
attend was one thing. Getting them to work together was something
else. They had tried it before at unsuccessful talks in Geneva.
Underneath the surface unity it was a fraught cooperation. There were
clear ideological differences, Nkomo seeming pragmatic alongside
Mugabe's firebrand determination; but there were significant personality differences as well. The highly educated Mugabe contrasted with
the largely self-taught Nkomo. As the older man, Nkomo expected at
least a degree of deference from Mugabe. Something of the flavour of
dislike was caught by a flabbergasted Julius Nyerere, the President of
Tanzania. He had provided rear bases and training camps for Mugabe's
soldiers. He had hosted the Chinese instructors of Mugabe's forces.
The frontline bases were provided by President Machel of the recently
independent Mozambique. Nyerere called in both Nkomo and

Mugabe, seeking to foster a united negotiating position. He thought it prudent to begin by talking to each man separately in his own private study. Nkomo, as the older man, was given the customary courtesy of going in first. When it was Mugabe's turn, Nyerere rose to greet him and gestured towards an armchair. Mugabe said, 'If you think I'm going to sit where that disgusting man parked his fat ass you have another think coming.' Nyerere was the most revered of African leaders. He was the Nelson Mandela of his day. His mouth gaped. This was going to be harder than he thought. The Africans decided they themselves needed an external figure to help the Nkomo/Mugabe project, and to help them from being wrongfooted by Carrington. That person was Guyana's Shridath Ramphal, the flamboyant but brilliant Commonwealth Secretary-General. To this day Carrington *will* speak in a way that, while not disparaging of Ramphal, minimises his contribution to the talks that followed. But it was Ramphal who coordinated Kaunda, Machel and Nyerere, and added key figures from the non-African Commonwealth: Michael Manley of Jamaica and Australia's Malcolm Fraser. They became the quintet that Ramphal arrayed against, not Carrington in the first instance, but Thatcher.

What this meant was that the military struggle in Southern Africa, already internationalised, was giving way to an internationalised diplomatic struggle. Prime Minister Michael Manley was a descendant of the white diaspora in Jamaica, but he partook fully of the ethos of the Non-Aligned Movement that was also a core of the Commonwealth insistence that there should be a freed Third World. The joker in the pack was Prime Minister Malcolm Fraser. From the Australian political right, he had been flabbergasted at the clumsiness of Thatcher's early diplomatic intentions towards Southern Africa. He saw an equitable solution to the Zimbabwean crisis as a key necessity in maintaining any future balance within the Commonwealth – involving influence for what was left of the 'white Commonwealth', including Australia and, despite herself, Margaret Thatcher's United Kingdom. If the Commonwealth became fully dominated by its own majority, its 'black' members, then it would be another nail in the coffin of old international relations in which the United Kingdom had strongly, if persistently wrongly, featured.

Part of Carrington's summer haste had been because the biennial Commonwealth summit was to be held in the Zambian capital, Lusaka, in early August 1979. Kaunda would be the chairman. Zambia bordered Rhodesia and had suffered much 'forward defence' on the part of Smith's forces. Commando raids, air raids and attacks on infrastructure occurred periodically. Bridges became a preferred target and, in 1979, Lusaka residents were blacking out their windows at night. At all Commonwealth summits Britain had taken a hammering because of Rhodesia. There had always been a sense among the Afro-Asian majority that Harold Wilson, when British Prime Minister, had not tried hard enough to suppress the white Rhodesian regime. The idea of a 'kith and kin' relationship between the rulers of Britain and the white Rhodesian settlers was seen as explaining the British inhibition. Now the sense that Thatcher would move to recognise the power-sharing government of Smith and Muzorewa made the Lusaka summit a standoff in many ways. Diplomatic gossip suggested that, if Britain didn't budge from the Smith–Muzorewa option, the African states would leave the Commonwealth. An alternative line was that, just as the Commonwealth expelled South Africa in 1961, it might now expel Britain. The idea of recognition for what they saw as a white puppet-master hand in glove with a black puppet, masquerading as a power-share, was anathema not just to the African states but to much of the Third World membership as well. Only New Zealand's forlorn, fat and squinting Prime Minister, Robert Muldoon, stood squarely beside Thatcher. But Thatcher went into Lusaka far from convinced that Carrington had done enough that summer to set out an alternative path for her.

Ramphal knew Thatcher had arrived in Lusaka not only prepared for the fight but almost pugnaciously spoiling for it. He would greet her with cascades of charm instead. But, because he knew Thatcher found him lugubrious, he choreographed Nyerere and two of the most handsome prime ministers to lead the line of persuasion. Kaunda kept the Rhodesian issue near the bottom of the agenda paper, and all the Commonwealth heads were instructed to be sweetness and light in the opening, largely inconsequential discussions. Muldoon alone skulked in his rooms. He reminded the others of Ian Smith and was ostracised.

The early talks took place in Mulungushi Hall, a huge square copper palace atop a modest hill. The flags of the Commonwealth nations lined the gentle incline that led to the only example of grandeur in the Zambian capital. Back then, Kaunda and Nyerere still played the role of the modest African President. They had none of the conspicuous consumption or air of corrupt acquisition that now forms the archetype of African presidencies. Kaunda greeted his guests in his safari suit and cravat and chaired the preliminary sessions with gruff charm. An 'away day' interrupted the preliminary business and discussions on Rhodesia. The presidents and prime ministers were meant to relax. But it was on this day that Ramphal's procession of wise and handsome men began calling on Thatcher. There was Nyerere as wisdom. Then the two very tall prime ministers of Jamaica and Australia made visits.[15] Michael Manley, with a full head of silver hair, lean – a white man with Caribbean tan and Jamaican accent – came. He had graduated from the London School of Economics and had flown a Hurricane in the Battle of Britain. There was nothing about his pedigree that Margaret Thatcher, the grocer's daughter from Grantham, could deny. Then Malcolm Fraser came. Even taller than Manley, formerly a farmer, he had a 'gentleman's Third' from Oxford, and the laconic antipodean version of good manners. He could be raffish and played that part to Manley's elegant fighter pilot. Even now one of the most popular Google hits in Australia is the photo of Fraser and a bedazzled Thatcher dancing at the concluding ball in Lusaka, oblivious to the terrible band. It was a terrifyingly male chauvinist strategy that Ramphal choreographed. Carrington would have found it caddish. But it worked, in that Thatcher had been 'softened up' by the time the talks on Rhodesia began.

Zambia's President Kaunda, whom Carrington had disparaged on earlier occasions – and insisted on continuing to do so in his memoirs – now rose to the occasion as a skilful chairman. The inclusive Commonwealth of the future, he said, had to have an inclusive Zimbabwe – and that would not be possible while civil war was waged over matters of human rights and human principles, and while key nationalist parties were frozen out of government to the extent that they would not give up their guns. He spoke of how much damage the war had done to Zambia and how Commonwealth solidarity with both human principles – such as racial equality – and Zambia should guide the discussions. He and Tanazania's President Nyerere then said they were certain they could deliver the guerrilla nationalist parties of Nkomo and Mugabe to a negotiating table. Carrington knew the South Africans would oblige Smith and Muzorewa to attend. It would all come down to how the British, with their historical obligations in Rhodesia – Rhodes, after all, having taken the land in the name of the British crown – chaired the negotiations. That meant history was pointing its finger at Carrington himself. Every bit of steel in the former guardsman welled to the surface. He turned to tell Thatcher that she had to accept – but she had already decided to accept.

The negotiations took place in London, at Lancaster House. They began on 10 September 1979 and lasted to 21 December. Carrington played the ruthless chairman, but he was far from the only key actor in manipulating the delegations, advising them either directly or indirectly, making constant midnight phone calls to other capitals to keep friends and allies on-side. Shridath Ramphal became the nemesis of Carrington, advising the guerrilla leaders and helping them resist Carrington's pressure. Each man would claim credit at the expense of the other for the final breakthrough, but the credit should be evenly divided.

Lancaster House, an imposing neo-classical building, stands with Green Park to its west. South-west is Buckingham Palace. To its immediate east is St James's Palace – where the guard musters for its daily late-morning change at Buckingham Palace – and immediately next door is Marlborough House, built by Winston Churchill's ancestor, John Churchill the Duke of Marlborough, one of the great commanders of British history. Marlborough House was his palatial town house, all murals and chandeliers. Not a patch on his over-the-top rural seat at Blenheim Palace, but so palatial and central that Prince Charles has always sought to commandeer it for his own London residence. His mother, however, had agreed to its being made available to the Commonwealth Secretariat, and there the Commonwealth Secretary-General held court – a stone's throw from Lancaster House. Carrington had to come down from the other end of Pall Mall to reach it, and pass Marlborough House every day. He might perhaps have seen Mugabe and Nkomo, separately or together, trooping in and out – and known they were being coordinated by Ramphal who seemed to live on the telephone to Nyerere, Kaunda and Machel.

Lancaster House itself is all unsubtle grandeur. It has the typical staircase designed to make those in power feel grand, and those not in power feel like plaintiffs. Obligatory chandeliers festoon the interior, and the huge hall that became the negotiating chamber – with Carrington seated at the head like a monarch – seemed almost designed to remind all and sundry of what Britain once was. Up those steps, every morning for almost three months, Mugabe and Nkomo, Smith and Muzorewa, and various other players would climb. It would have been hard for the portly Nkomo. Once, in Lusaka, when the Rhodesian commandos had come to take him out, it was said he escaped through the toilet window as they stormed through the front door. That account of the firefight just led to incredulous laughter in Lusaka. The house had certainly been blown apart and burnt to the ground, and Nkomo had certainly escaped. But the Zimbabwean's girth could hardly have squeezed through a toilet window, and the toilet seat would have cracked under his weight as he tried to do so. Much coprophilic humour surrounded the retelling of this story – along the lines of how many times Nkomo had to put his foot in his own excrement. But I encountered him once coming into Marlborough House. He looked daunted at having to climb the stairs to Ramphal's office once again. I showed him the tiny antique lift in a back corridor: big enough to fit him alone. 'What shall we do?' asked his flustered aides. 'We have to ensure he is never alone.' 'Well,' I said, 'you're going to have to let him ride the lift alone but it's only two floors up and the lift is slow, and it will be slower now, so if you run up the stairs as swiftly as you can you will be able to usher your man from the lift to the Secretary-General's office. It's started to go up, so you'd better run.' And they did. There were few light moments in this period.

But before then the Lancaster House talks became fraught. Carrington had not fully abandoned some form of coalition as outcome – one that excluded Mugabe. Ramphal, however, helped Mugabe and Nkomo stay together and, in fact, both guerrilla leaders saw that as being in their interests; especially since all the regional presidents placed much hope in their unified front. Carrington had a simple formula, which he applied ruthlessly. It was a form of 'divide and rule' by which, on critical points, he would negotiate with one delegation only and arrive at a way forward. He would then present that 'solution' to the other delegation and lay down a deadline for agreement – adding that, after the deadline, the talks would proceed to the next point under the assumption that the 'solution' had been adopted. Usually he talked to the Smith/Muzorewa delegation first and then presented their 'solution' to Nkomo and Mugabe. There was a lengthy period when Carrington didn't seem to care if Nkomo and Mugabe walked out. They could then be painted as the recalcitrant actors who had rejected the opportunity of peace. Thatcher could have her Smith/Muzorewa government and the diplomatic fallout would be much less. This was the reason why Mugabe and Nkomo were constant visitors to Marlborough House. Ramphal would advise them on how to handle Carrington and how to negotiate around his 'solutions'. In this, Ramphal considered he represented majority Commonwealth opinion. He certainly represented the interests of Mozambique, Tanzania and Zambia, all of which wanted the conflict settled. At crucial junctures, when there was no choice but to let Carrington bulldoze his way, Ramphal would have Nyerere, Kaunda and Machel on the line instructing Nkomo and Mugabe to swallow hard and accept the Carrington formula. Machel and Kaunda were beginning to anticipate how greatly peace would benefit their own countries, and wanted a solution. Gradually, Carrington began to change his views of the leaders negotiating at Lancaster House. It hadn't taken him long to detest Ian Smith, and he found no difficulty – even from Bishop Muzorewa – in marginalising him. He thought Smith tendentious and small-minded: someone whose stubbornness had cost the British much. He increasingly favoured – given Mugabe's reputation at that time as a hardline Marxist – the possibility of a coalition involving Muzorewa and Nkomo. Even so, something about Mugabe's steely intellectual and ascetic demeanour appealed to him. Carrington the aristocrat came to see Mugabe as the lone man of quality in the pack – even if he preferred Mugabe outside his vision of Rhodesia's future. Despite this, as Christmas approached and the talks drew to their close, he was found in his club one afternoon, White's in St James's Street, sitting in an armchair as the traffic thundered outside, nursing a whisky – musing that Mugabe was the only one worthy of election to White's.[16]

The agreement was that there would be a ceasefire. Rhodesian military units would be confined to base, the guerrillas would gather in 'Assembly Points' – a form of temporary and improvised 'barracks' scattered throughout the countryside – and the peace would be monitored by Commonwealth peacekeepers (whom the British would invite). A British Governor would be reinstalled and he would run an election at the end of February 1980. Before then, Mugabe, Nkomo and their parties would be legalised and they could enter the country to campaign for votes. Although the Rhodesian civil service would organise the elections they would be supervised by imported British officials with either African or local government experience, and the entire exercise would be further monitored by a Commonwealth Observer Group (selected by the Commonwealth Secretary-General), and other observers.[17]

Who was to organise and who was to police what, who was going to monitor and who was going to monitor the monitors was the subject of pitched negotiations. But most fraught was the question of how to keep armed men in small locations, both to guarantee their safety from the other side and to prevent them from breaking out of camp to attack the other side. The guerrillas feared they would be sitting ducks in known locations, lightly armed by comparison to the Rhodesian army. There had to be several leaps of trust and hope for Lancaster House to work, especially during the months of January and February when all this was meant somehow to lead to peaceful elections that would herald a transition of power away from minority rule.

And it didn't help that the British choice for Governor, Lord Soames, was a senior Eurocrat with no African or conflict-mediation experience. He was brought in because he was thought to be steely – like Carrington. With him came Eurocratic aides: hard, bright young men also without African experience. They thought the deceits and political manoeuvres they had mastered in Brussels were directly transferable to Salisbury. Their intention was to control the transition period until elections. They were meant to ensure that the Rhodesian civil service, still partly modelled on the British colonial provincial and district system of administration, remained honest and unbiased. But they also meant to ensure that the flotillas of international observers about to descend on their violent new parish were controlled and saw only what Soames could depict as the success of his mandate. In modern terms the observers were to be 'embedded' in the Soames machinery. Ramphal would have none of that for his Commonwealth Observer Group, drawn from a wide variety of countries – including Canada as a 'white' nation, and with an Indian chairman – but he and his people had never mounted an operation in such hostile territory either. In fact, there had never been a large-scale coordinated election observation by an international group before. There had only been a small observation in Cyprus. What is now a common aspect of international politics was pioneered in the last two months of Rhodesia. It was made up as it went along, but established a lasting model. No group has departed from its foundational methodology.

In a very real sense, this was an extension of the British methodology of the most acceptable peace at the least cost. The key ingredients were the use of an existing white-dominated administration, with a superimposed directorate led by Soames; the congregation of armed forces into pre-arranged areas, but without any agreement or capacity to disarm those forces; the effort to control information as a device to delay information about things going wrong; and, all the while, the lack of a robust and provisioned Plan B if indeed things did go wrong. The British did impose a modest military presence, a small multilateral force. But it is uncertain whether all the units that made up this force would have accepted British command if an emergency had endangered the position of the guerrilla armies of Mugabe and Nkomo. The units from Third World countries might well have found any British orders countermanded by their own superiors back home.

This military presence, under the Lancaster House Agreement, was meant to control and safeguard the assembled guerrilla forces. There was no guarding of the Rhodesian army. Carrington invited peace-keeping soldiers from Fiji, Kenya and New Zealand to participate alongside British units. Green Jackets and Coldstream Guards were among the British representatives and bemused their guerrilla 'colleagues' with their upper-lip professionalism. The New Zealand Maori soldiers, conscious of their experience in Vietnam, sought to win hearts and minds by jogging Assembly Point perimeters, stripped to the waist, with local children laughing on their backs. The Kenyans flew in a planeload of Tusker beer and shared it with their charges. The Fijians brought in their preferred brew too. Assigned one particular Assembly Point that comprised guerrillas from both Nkomo's and Mugabe's armies, they (literally) sat out (if not laid out) the firefights that would erupt between the rival forces by drinking while the tracer lashed overhead. Then they would go out, ensure there were no casualties – remarkably, there never were any – and share what was left of the beer with the combatants. Unrestricted by UN protocols and procedures it was peacekeeping as organic and humanistic improvisation.

There were minor casualties caused by carelessness. I came across one Assembly Point where there was an RAF doctor. An unfortunate guerrilla had shot himself in the eye while cleaning his rifle – without having first unloaded it. 'We have no anaesthetic, Stephen. I've given him my flask of whisky. It won't be enough. It has to come out or gangrene will set in. He knows I have to take out his eye. Would you help us hold him down?' I declined with the plausible excuse of having a schedule to keep, but the young doctor smiled for I had, I am sure, visibly blanched. So much for a young man's bravado but, really, that was all the Commonwealth Observer Group had. It also had immense good luck. Parts of it came under fire and emerged. A two-person part of it just happened to be in a remote area when planes from the white Rhodesian air force dropped election leaflets, on behalf of Abel Muzorewa – the preferred black candidate of the white electorate – in defiance of the ceasefire agreement. There was some effort at style: one late addition to the Group, forced to pack at very short notice, brought to his work in militarised Rhodesia a wardrobe of exquisite lightweight Italian suits. It summed up the comprehensive naïvety of the Group.

Apart from the Commonwealth Observer Group, the exercise did need the accurate reporting the peacekeeping monitors sent back to Fortress Soames. But the real corrective to the combative young men from Brussels that Soames had assembled around him were the British election supervisors on the ground, two for each administrative district and two senior supervisors for each province. One would be seconded from British local government and the other would be a former colonial official, dragged out of retirement on the grounds that having been an administrator in Nigeria would be preparation for supervising an election in war-torn Rhodesia. They saw the absurdity of their assignments and, in joyous self-mockery, called themselves 'the old and the bold', and 'the retreads'. But they were bold. At one point Soames' advisers were on the brink of persuading the Governor to ban Mugabe from the election: they believed the carefully crafted propaganda being sent to them by diehard elements in the Rhodesian armed forces. These Rhodesian commanders had created an impression of Mugabe's guerrillas breaking the ceasefire and intimidating electors. If Soames banned Mugabe, and Mugabe tried to retaliate, it would be an absolute licence for the Rhodesians to attack the guerrillas – all now concentrated in accessible assembly points. Soames would order the Commonwealth peacekeepers to stand aside and it would be a turkey-shoot. It took an extremely impolite, won't-leave-till-you-hear-us-out delegation of 'old and bold' to berate Soames into accepting that there was a very different sense of what was happening on the ground than his young men, trying to be as tough as soldiers, had been led to imagine.

In the end, Mugabe's victory was overwhelming. Those who had hoped for a non-Mugabe victory looked toward the prospect of two minority parties – Muzorewa's and Nkomo's – together trumping one majority party. In the end Muzorewa only won three seats and, although Nkomo took all but one of the seats in the two western provinces of Matabeleland North and Matabeleland South, Mugabe won just about everywhere else. The newly enfranchised voters of the country had not been much impressed by the fears of the white minority. But they had been impressed by Mugabe. On the eve of his arrival back from exile, about to start his election campaign, the country's major newspaper, the *Herald*, ran a full-page front story that announced 'The End of Christmas'. For Mugabe was a declared Marxist, a devil – a black devil – who would abolish Christianity, Mom, Apple Pie and Christmas. That was the white fear. His first rally, shortly after he landed, attracted a million people – almost entirely black. Mugabe's tactics had often been ruthless. Liberation had not always been a merciful enterprise. 'Traitors' were shot and many young fighters sacrificed. But people were going to remember the man who had fought for them, and vote for him. Almost three decades later that memory has not faded completely. And, as in 1980, Mugabe's vote has always been strongest in the rural areas outside Matabeleland. Party organisation and conscious-raising had always accompanied guerrilla deployment from 1976 to 1980. Even though Mugabe's soldiers were concentrated in the Assembly Points, his party's cadres were active throughout most of the country. Huge queues were the hallmark of polling. The campaign itself had been largely peaceful, though not without tensions, and the white Rhodesians had actively lobbied the British to suspend the elections and its results, citing constant electoral intimidation. The size of the victory dwarfed any evidence of intimidation, and the vast majority of set-piece campaign rallies had passed by without major incident. Stadium rallies and large town hall meetings were used by the party leaders, and there was a huge leafleting campaign by all concerned. Everywhere, the sense of impending relief – that years of struggle against minority rule was about to end – was palpable. In these conditions, there had in fact been little need to intimidate.

Mugabe and Nkomo had successfully negotiated together, but they had campaigned in the election separately. Now Mugabe invited Nkomo to participate in his government. It was magnanimous but also wise. Both men's parties had power bases at opposite ends of the country. Both had ethnic affiliations that made the renamed country of Zimbabwe more than just a black and white affair. As for the white population, Mugabe went on national television and made one of the great political speeches of the twentieth century. He preached reconciliation in a quiet, understated but clearly determined manner. He appealed to higher principle and the joint future of the country. He said that, in the new Zimbabwe, there would be no black and white, no sweeping nationalisation and no sackings in the white-dominated upper echelons of the civil service.

> We will ensure that there is a place for everyone in this country. We want to ensure a sense of security for both the winners and losers . . . Let us forgive and forget. Let us join hands in a new amity.[18]

In the street, after the broadcast, I saw people crying. Almost all those in the West who have followed the fortunes of Zimbabwe, and who demonise Mugabe now, were his fervent believers on that day.

For a while everything seemed possible. But the rivalry between Mugabe and Nkomo never fully went away, and it certainly did not leave their armed men. Meanwhile, the South Africans took stock of the situation. They had completed their risk assessment. They had sized up Mugabe as no immediate threat. But they wouldn't let him become one in the future. They were beginning to finalise their military posture toward the surrounding countries. A doctrine emerged that left nothing to chance: risk nothing, dominate everything, destabilise everyone, be stronger than anyone. In July 1982, eight years before the release of Nelson Mandela, South African commandos crossed the border. The entire aerial strength of the Zimbabwean air force was parked neatly on one runway. The commandos blew up every plane.

CHAPTER 2

THE ARMED TREK

With the independence of Zimbabwe, following on from that of Angola and Mozambique, South Africa's fears of being confronted on its borders with black-ruled countries – acting as an inspiration for its own restive black majority – had come true. It retained control of Namibia on the south-west coast of Africa, and still had considerable influence in Botswana, Lesotho and Swaziland. Even so, the transition of Rhodesia to Zimbabwe meant the loss of the key strategic white 'buffer' state. South Africa prepared to unleash the full force of its 'total strategy' to subject its black neighbours to a ruthless militarised domination. Each country received a specialist variant of this domination: but the mighty Apartheid war machine was central to it all. Back in South Africa, the ANC remained banned and Nelson Mandela remained imprisoned. As the 1980s dawned, the end of Apartheid and its ill-effects at home and abroad seemed a long way off.

Zimbabwe had a peaceful first two years. Robert Mugabe gathered plaudits for what seemed like genuine reconciliation.[1] His country was held up as a model for what Apartheid South Africa might one day become. There was a majority-ruled government that observed procedures, avoided the arbitrary and did not act vindictively to earlier white enemies. It remained in the global capitalist economy and sought foreign investment. It had idealistic ministers – not all of whom knew what they were doing – but a considerable rump of white administration rolled up its sleeves to help with the transition towards expertise. The white commander of the military was retained, as was the white commander of the intelligence forces. So was the white commander of the air force.

When the South Africans blew up the air force the white commander was suspected of collusion and court-martialled. Although he was eventually exonerated, black nationalisation of security command accelerated. If that was the first palpable indication that black and white reconciliation would not always be smooth, the South Africans were at pains to drive a deep wedge between Mugabe and Nkomo. Following firefights between the armed followers of the two men, South Africa tried to recruit Nkomo's supporters, rank-and-file dissidents against the triumph of Mugabe, into an active guerrilla force. They never mustered more than a few hundred men, but other former fighters did take to the forests of the two Matabeleland provinces in the western part of Zimbabwe. It was never a large-scale rebellion, and required strong but modest policing. Mugabe's new military commanders mustered an atrocious response.

In 1982 national television showed the 'discovery' of arms caches in the west. They were paraded as evidence of a full-scale insurrection in the making. Whether these caches were left over from Nkomo's liberation war, whether they were 'insurance' against an eventual souring of relations between Nkomo and Mugabe, or whether they were planted by Mugabe's people as part of a campaign of justification for what they were about to do remains unclear. Everyone around me knew that a ferocious era was about to begin.

The Fifth Brigade was formed to suppress the 'insurrection'. It was commanded by Perence Shiri, who in the 2000s would become one of Mugabe's most senior hardline advisers. It was trained by North

Koreans. The graduation march-past in Harare was terrifying. They marched, not in goose step, but with axe kicks. These look like goose steps but the leg comes straight up until the boot is high above the head. Then it crashes down. The intent is that it should crash down on someone. It was pure Tae Kwon Do, the Korean martial art. Then the graduating brigade smashed stacks of tiles with their bare hands. They didn't sing or chant like normal Zimbabwean units: they shouted like Korean martial artists. These were not fighting soldiers: they were not trained to fight against an enemy who would fight back. They were suppressors. They were being sent to pacify a population that might support the handful of western dissidents – by simple virtue of terrifying that population; slaughtering large parts of it as a warning to others; and slaughtering in horrific ways. The sadistic ingenuity of the Fifth Brigade in their killing of defenceless people makes their work a war crime. And it was the world's first usage of a term that mutated into 'ethnic cleansing'. Zimbabwe, in very loose terms, contains three major ethnic groups. The smallest of them, the Tonga, live in the north and were divided by the enlargement of Lake Kariba when the great dam there was built. As such, they straddle both southern Zambia and northern Zimbabwe. The two larger groups are the Ndebele in the west – closely related to Zulu origins – and the Shona in the east. The Shona are further divided into several sub-groups but, by and large, these coalesce under the 'Shona' umbrella. They form much of the heartland of Mugabe's support, and the two liberation armies of Nkomo and Mugabe could be said to have comprised largely Ndebele and Shona fighters respectively. The Fifth Brigade saw themselves, and were encouraged to think of themselves, as a heightened mode of this division. They were eastern Shona unleashed upon western Ndebele people. The Fifth Brigade called themselves the *Gukurahundi*, the whirlwind: the whirlwind that cleanses the crop by blowing away the chaff.

Estimates of casualties, all after the fact, are unreliable. Tens of thousands were said to have died, but an emerging consensus suggests 10–20,000. It was not only the number of deaths, but the horrific way in which death was dealt. Burnings alive and hand-grenading of people herded into groups were common. No one in Europe or the United States uttered a word of protest: in part because no one knew.[2] The slaughter was remarkably clandestine but there was enough evidence for people to suspect the work in progress. Mugabe however was still the darling of the world. He was the embodiment of reconciliation as it was seen in black and white. When years later he seized the white farms, the world again focused first on the white farmers and only later gave much notice to the hundreds of black democrats who had been killed. It took the work of scholars like Richard Werbner[3] and then Jocelyn Alexander[4] to unveil the horrors of what occurred in Matabeleland. Death at the hands of the Fifth Brigade could be gratuitous, slow, but painstaking on the part of the perpetrators. An industry of post-mortem horror and criticism of Mugabe began in their wake. But, while all this was happening, the South African strategists were basking in their smiles. The more divided Zimbabwe became, the easier the defence of Apartheid would be.

There is a Café Palette on the Left Bank of Paris. It is near the rue de Seine off Boulevard Saint-Germain and opens on to the street in summer. It is around the corner from Les Deux Magots, where Jean-Paul Sartre and Simone de Beauvoir would drink and write. The tourists who come there have no idea of its history – nor perhaps do its staff or owners. From the late 1960s right up to the 1980s, the South African ANC (African National Congress) fighters sitting there would be watched. Like Joshua Nkomo's senior Zimbabwean commanders, the South Africans would be en route to Moscow for advanced training. Café Palette was the rendezvous. Their instructions were to go there every day; how many days was not specified. Here they would be watched by Soviet agents who, when finally satisfied that no South African agent was also watching them, would make the contact and arrange for them to be 'delivered' to Moscow and their training sites.

Pretoria knew the training was going on and that urban guerrilla war – what we now call 'terrorism' – would intensify in South Africa.[5]

They also knew that they didn't want to be like the white Rhodesian military, complaining that they never 'lost' – while a black government ruled in any case. No, the trick had to be, not to seek to win, but to control the insurgency right down to its lowest possible capacity. And the conjoint strategy had to be to starve the guerrillas of any possible regional base for meaningful operations. ANC guerrillas were one thing, but emboldened and supportive regional states something else entirely. Pretoria didn't want to conquer the surrounding states of Southern Africa. It didn't want to have to govern them. It wanted to destabilise them so they couldn't support the guerrillas or think of taking any action themselves against South Africa. But different states required different approaches. And it couldn't all be military muscle. Pretoria couldn't spread itself too thin. But all the approaches would be subsumed under a single strategic policy. It was called 'Total Strategy'.

The military theorist for the French strategy of total suppression in Algeria, in the face of the uprising for independence from 1954 to 1962, was André Beaufre. The South African academic, Deon Geldenhuys, was sometimes singled out as the architect of Total Strategy[6] – the man who laid out the principles devised by Beaufre for the white generals of the South African Defence Forces. His defenders say that he was merely describing, objectively, the options available to the South African military and was not an advocate or intellectual father of the devastation to come. In fact, the South African military had been moving towards Total Strategy ever since its retreat from Angola in 1976. And it was different from the French action in Algeria. Algeria was one country and France was its colonial power. Moreover, a very great deal of the Algerian uprising was located not only in Algiers but the old town of Algiers. The South Africans had an entire region of many states to bend to its will. In particular, it had three black governments who had fielded large liberation armies – Angola, Mozambique and Zimbabwe – and it had less militarily threatening states, like Zambia, which commanded much diplomatic support. Even so, the foundation principles were the same as Beaufre's:

put a controlling clamp upon every state's military and economic capacity; intimidate them psychologically; limit their options politically; reduce their transport and communications networks to a fraction of their capacity; demand treaties to mark their subservience; renege on those treaties and make development impossible and dependence on South Africa maximal. Let them keep their independence, let them make noise, but make them into tributary states. And drive the ANC ever northwards until they have no bases or even offices left in all of Southern Africa.[7] Cultivate links with the United States in particular and NATO in general, pointing to the Cold War and the Cuban forces in Angola. Make the West understand its need for South-African-mined strategic minerals, control of the sea lanes around the Cape of Good Hope, and the role the South African economy played in the global financial and corporate world. And how these things were of more importance to the West than the end of Apartheid, especially if black majority governments should look like those in Angola and Mozambique – Communist or Communist-inflected, militarised and themselves undemocratic. Why then should South Africa become democratic when it guarded a vast array of Western interests and, as the diplomacy and propaganda put it, Western values?

In 1981, one year after Zimbabwe's independence, Total Strategy began. It was part of the new 'forward-defence' of South African President P.W. Botha. With it he installed a State Security Council which answered to him. It bypassed the Cabinet, was not elected – even by a white minority – and was not transparent. It gave the Generals a place in government as the resources of the state were prioritised around its forward-defence. It came to be known as the era of the 'Securocrats', an inner circle where many wore uniform,[8] the same sort of inner circle that marked the fraught days of Robert Mugabe years later. Although dissidents were briefly supported in western Zimbabwe, and the air force blown up, Zimbabwe was not the main military target. Angola and Mozambique were. The idea was to make Zimbabwe and Zambia feel as if they were caught, west and east, in a pincer – so anxious that the conflicts on their borders should not overspill that they dared not look south. Just to ram the message home, occasional raids would be made into Zimbabwe and Zambia, particularly Zambia where the ANC had exile headquarters, as did SWAPO (the Namibian resistance movement). These raids could have real intent with specific targets, or they could be symbolic. SWAPO never knew which was what. But, living in Lusaka for most of the years of Total Strategy, I was caught up in the safe-houses network for the children of ANC members. When intelligence said the commandos would make their raids the parents went underground and the children would be farmed out to a pre-arranged series of Zambian homes. There seemed to be a lot of cheerfulness about this, though it was always swift and, away from the children, highly serious. The South Africans made air raids too, but these seemed largely symbolic and were never in the centre of Lusaka. But once, two days after I had bought a beautifully hand-woven scarf, I learnt that the South African weaver had been killed in her refugee camp by a South African plane. I have kept that scarf but even now, when I look at it, I think of the blood of all those years and cannot wear it.

The Namibian issue was different.[9] The South Africans never saw SWAPO as a major threat. The ANC was the target. Nevertheless the western fringes of Zambia would be used as a through route by which to outflank SWAPO units, and certainly to attack their rear bases in Angola. The Zambians threw soldiers into the western areas, but an amazing phoney war was then fought. Kaunda again wanted to make a symbolic show of defiance without risk. The two sides would patrol, having sent out signals as to where each would be, and avoid each other. If by chance they encountered each other they would fire briefly, deliberately miss, then melt away with honour satisfied.

However, the main action in Angola was not concentrated on the motley SWAPO forces but on the MPLA Angolan government forces and their Cuban allies with Soviet support.[10] These represented both a black nationalist and militarised Marxist example to others, including ANC members in South Africa; and the Cuban presence was seen by Washington as a 'hot war' outreach from Moscow. The Cubans would tend to be held in reserve and most of the frontline action in this period was between South African forces and their dissident Angolan UNITA allies on the one hand, and MPLA units on the other.

UNITA had been the larger of the two liberation factions that had lost out to the MPLA. It commanded much support in the south of the country and contested the fact that the MPLA should constitute Angola's sole government. Both the Americans and the South Africans formed alliances with UNITA as a means of holding the Cuban and Soviet-supported MPLA in check. The Chinese, because of their own arguments with the Soviet Union, had done the same – although Chinese support was withdrawn as the MPLA consolidated Africa-wide recognition for its government. Angola and, through Angola, Southern Africa was caught up in the messy international politics and rivalries of the day. But all this meant not only an internationalised conflict but one that was heavily equipped. These were the days of tank columns, of mechanised war in Africa; days of air superiority; days almost like a great European war when, if not the occupation of territory, the denial of it to the other side was a key objective.[11] The larger aim was to destabilise and weaken the Angolan state, and to set up a buffer UNITA zone in the south of the country. The war would wax and wane around the capture of certain southern cities and towns. The buffer state had to have a capital, after all. The Angolans took a beating, but their main objective was to safeguard Luanda, their own capital; still, they certainly made a show of contesting the south. And, if they lost control of the south, then they wanted desperately to preserve command of the oilfields further north. There was a point where the forward-defence of Apartheid merged into contestation around global commodities. In the end, the MPLA kept the oilfields. UNITA learnt to subsist off diamonds and the term 'war diamonds' or 'blood diamonds' crept into our guilty lexicons.

The South African strategy was different in Mozambique. After the fall of Portugal's colonial government FRELIMO (Frente de Liberacao de Mocambique) came to power unopposed. There was no opposition party like UNITA in Angola. The South Africans set about creating one. For them, Mozambique was to be a war by proxy, and the proxy was called RENAMO (Resistencia Nacional Mocambicana). The rebel movement was trained and equipped by South Africa. It received its preliminary strategic orientation and operational goals from South Africa. It had very good communications technology and, at an early stage, acquired greater operational capacity than the FRELIMO forces. It should be said that, as time passed, RENAMO did acquire a political programme of its own, not least drawn from widespread disenchantment with the performance of the FRELIMO government which was inept and clumsy, lacking in transparency and unable to bring development to Mozambique. Before then, however, RENAMO became a byword for brutality and atrocity.[12] It became one of the first movements to use child soldiers and literally blooded them by forcing them to commit atrocities against their own communities, and even their own families. It was both an initiation into RENAMO and an atrocious gesture of farewell since, having killed people who had been their own neighbours or relatives, the children could not go back. Nor was such killing done by simple bullets. Terrifyingly ingenious means of death were devised for the children to implement. If Angola became an African version of a mid-twentieth-century European war, then Mozambique was a throwback to medieval savagery – to a time when, in Europe, the casual, gratuitous and cruel slaughter of innocents became a lingering shame that no later Geneva conventions and laws of war could quite erase. Mozambique was not like the concentrated and technologised killing of the Nazi concentration camps, nor was it like the Cambodian killing fields where large numbers would be herded together to be shot, and nor was it a genocide like Rwanda would later be. It was a village-by-random-village series of mini-spectacles to drum fear into people and to make them petrified of supporting the government.

Wherever the rebels went, they ruled. FRELIMO troops, demoralised by inept command, limited weaponry and irregularity of poor pay, became unwilling to risk their lives in resistance. It got to the point when RENAMO could send a FRELIMO garrison advance notice of an attack. This was to give the FRELIMO troops an opportunity to withdraw. And when as often as not they did, the target RENAMO sought would be painlessly there for the taking. But it added to the impression that the government could not protect its own people.

By 1984, desperate for respite, Mozambique signed the Nkomati Accord with South Africa.[13] In return for Mozambique's expelling the ANC, South Africa would rein in its support for RENAMO. While the Mozambican government duly fulfilled its part in a humiliating agreement, South Africa honoured its side of the treaty only partially. It did wind down its direct support, but continued to provide the rebels with superb equipment – especially communications equipment. RENAMO could coordinate its attacks all over the country, simultaneously open up several fronts, outflank the government soldiers every time. The FRELIMO government could no longer protect the few alternative transport routes available to independent Southern African states seeking to avoid dependence upon South Africa for the shipment of their exports and imports. The most important was the Beira Corridor, the railway that led to the only great working port in Southern Africa not in Apartheid hands. It linked Zimbabwe to the sea. The corridor ran through rebel RENAMO territory. South Africa had driven the ANC further north, destabilised and humiliated the Mozambican government, and could put an economic stranglehold on Zimbabwe by denying it access to the sea. Total Strategy was working well on the eastern flank of Southern Africa. There were no Cubans there. South Africa expected no problems with its domination. There would be no Mozambican fightback. Surely there would not be a Zimbabwean effort to take on RENAMO and risk the direct wrath of Pretoria's war machine.

There was. In 1985, the leaders of Mozambique, Zimbabwe and Tanzania met. It was the old triumvirate that had stood against Ian Smith. The enemy was different now. It was a black rebel movement, but sponsored by the Apartheid government. It was causing military chaos in Mozambique but also economic disruption in Zimbabwe.

And rebel strongholds were close to the northern border of Mozambique with Tanzania. They decided to reply to the rebels militarily, but not throughout Mozambique. They concentrated their efforts on the Beira Corridor and, to a lesser extent, a smaller northern transport link called the Tete Corridor. Tanzanian and even some Malawian troops entered Tete, largely guarding trains. But it was the Zimbabweans who marched in force into the areas around the Beira Corridor. It was the first full-scale African military reply to Pretoria without the help of outsiders like the Cubans. It was only five years after independence, three years after the destruction of the Zimbabwean air force – so it was done without air cover and on the assumption that Pretoria would not escalate the conflict from a proxy war to a direct involvement with warplanes and attack helicopters. The Mugabe government had achieved most of its terrifying objectives in the Matabeleland provinces and the Fifth Brigade remained there to 'pacify' an intimidated and butchered population. The soldiers who went into Mozambique were veterans of the liberation struggle with combat experience. They were very successful in sweeping the rebels before them, capturing bases and documents that incriminated Pretoria.

But it came at a price. The first was that the Zimbabwean forces were strung out over a long corridor and, once having won it, were in stationary guard positions and themselves vulnerable to attack. The second was the effect on Zimbabwean morale when the soldiers realised they were mowing down children. In one such action, a Zimbabwean unit had relieved a FRELIMO force holding a strategic location. They received one of the RENAMO advance notices, announcing the time of the attack. The RENAMO fighters thought the outpost was still garrisoned by FRELIMO, and fully expected a withdrawal. The Zimbabweans did not withdraw and, when the attack came, destroyed the entire RENAMO force. Then they went out to inspect the casualties and were appalled to find that they had killed a large number of child soldiers. The Zimbabweans were hardened soldiers, but they had never before slaughtered children, and actions like this did have an effect on morale. Even so, the Zimbabwean incursion into Mozambique accomplished its military objectives of creating a breathing space for FRELIMO, and securing the transport corridor for Zimbabwe.

Even though the ability of the FRELIMO army did not improve, its morale did. There was still no response from Pretoria. Then, in August 1986, the Third World's Non-Aligned Movement held its summit in Harare. The world's post-colonial leaders came to Zimbabwe. India's Rajiv Ghandi thundered about the need for a huge Third World army to confront the Apartheid government. In October 1986, flying home at night from Harare to Maputo, in an aircraft piloted by Soviet personnel who had flown the route before, following a beacon that had somehow been moved so that the aircraft would plunge into a hill, the Mozambican President Samora Machel died in an air crash. He left a widow, Graca Machel, who would reappear on the Southern African scene in a very non-militarised manner – playing a part in the healings of the region as the wife of Nelson Mandela – but he also died as a symbol of what Pretoria could do by way of revenge. The South Africans vehemently denied the assassination.[14]

But it was almost 1987. Outside Africa, the world was changing. In 1985 Mikhail Gorbachev had become General Secretary of the Communist Party in the Soviet Union. Reform was in the air. The expense of Soviet support for Africa was being reappraised, not just in Africa but in places like Afghanistan. Pretoria fully expected the Cuban presence in Angola to be scaled down. Machel's death would keep enough pressure on the eastern side of the region for South Africa not to increase its own expenditure there. Even Zimbabwean analysts were beginning to discern that RENAMO had developed a political agenda that was independent of Pretoria and concerned misrule by FRELIMO.[15] This was echoed by other scholars.[16] Initially the misrule had been manifest in administrative incapacity, then in strategic developmental choices that jarred with peasant aspirations, and finally in corruption. RENAMO said it stood against this kind of centralisation, ineptitude and corruption. In 1987 the Catholic Church began tentative overtures to introduce some dialogue between RENAMO and FRELIMO. Pretoria expected to win: in early 1986 it had put a huge effort into its destabilisation programme, attacking not only Zambia and Zimbabwe but even the normally untroublesome state of Botswana, and playing a role in the downfall of the government in Lesotho; it thought it was bludgeoning its way to a peaceful, even if a militarily pacified region; and that it would enjoy the prospect of a winding down of Soviet support for radical governments. It also believed that notwithstanding the military reach of Zimbabwe – 'We could have wrung the Zimbabwean army's neck like a chicken,' one South African commander told me – nothing the Zimbabweans did could change Apartheid at home.

But, just to make sure of a pacified region, Pretoria decided to anchor its rebel allies firmly and formally in control of southern Angola. It still wanted its buffer zone. It decided to consolidate a geopolitical space that could be ruled by UNITA, and to capture the southern city of Cuito Cuanavale to be the headquarters of a rebel government. This was an ambitious and dangerous move. It meant a transition from supporting a guerrilla movement to installing that movement almost as a territorial government – one that acted also as a proxy for Pretoria. Total Strategy had been conceived as an instrument of destabilisation. As such, it meant South Africa had constant operational access to the countries it destabilised. But South African units entered and withdrew. They denied territory to the recognised government, but did not seek to end that government's pretence to rule its country. Now Total Strategy was to be extended in southern Angola to be an instrument of occupation and rule. This would also allow Pretoria a fait accompli in the face of the world. The international sanctions campaign was increasing its tempo, and even Washington was rumbling against Apartheid. Establishing the rule of its guerrilla ally in southern Angola would be a signal that Pretoria could not be stopped; that it determined the fate of its surrounding nations, never mind that of its own people.

But it was hubris, a step too far. Faced with cuts in their expenditure, but also by the prospect of humiliation in Angola – a dozen years of involvement ending in victory for the other side – the Soviet Generals went to Gorbachev and asked for enough money for one last but properly equipped throw of the dice. They wanted, in particular, new aircraft. Gorbachev had been redirecting budget from the military to the civilian economy, and beginning its liberalisation. It was a daring request by the Generals, but refusal meant the risk of defeat for the Soviet effort in Angola, and the defeat of two Soviet allies: the government of Angola itself, and the Cuban forces fighting there. Gorbachev gave the Generals the funds and equipment they requested, and one year.

It was 1988 but in some ways the battle for Cuito Cuanavale was like a medieval siege – with modern technology. Aircraft, tanks, mines and surface-to-air missiles were all involved. The MPLA Angolan government and the Cubans desperate to retain control of Cuito Cuanavale, ringed the city with minefields. Within the city they massed batteries of anti-aircraft missiles. Cuban tanks took up forward positions and employed a mobile strategy. The tanks weren't going to dig in, but fight a war of manoeuvre. But it was in the air that the Soviets achieved, for the first time, superiority. They sent in latest generation MIG fighters with advanced avionics, and with Soviet pilots. Suddenly the South Africans found their fighters outflown and out-gunned. There would be no aerial attacks on Cuito Cuanavale. Instead, they envisaged a frontal assault, sending UNITA troops through the minefields almost as human sacrifices to clear the way. Then their own tanks would go in. It was an odd inversion. It was almost as if the South Africans were adopting the full-frontal Warsaw Pact strategies so feared by NATO commanders in Europe – where it was anticipated that, if war began, the armies of the Soviet Union and their East European allies would pour forwards in such strength and depth that the NATO forces would have to withdraw. By contrast, the Soviet and Cuban commanders were fighting the sort of mobile war once beloved of the Israelis.

The champions of mobility won. The Cuban command decisions and sheer speed of manoeuvre led to a decisive victory.[17] It was not a bloody victory but was greeted almost with incredulity in the hammered region – and then celebrated with delight. The Cubans, fighting their war of manoeuvre, and much as they had done at the very beginning of the war against South Africa in 1976, managed to surround and entrap a very large proportion of the South African forces. They hadn't even bothered with UNITA: the South Africans had been targeted as the principal enemy. This was the last battle of the Cold War – because this war was now also ending. Washington sent a message in answer to Pretoria's anguished pleas. It would not help. The Cuban commander, as his predecessor twelve years earlier had done, sent a message to Pretoria: withdraw your forces while they can still walk, or they will come home in bags. Pretoria asked that they be allowed to walk. It was a crucial blow for the securocrats of Apartheid and for President Botha of South Africa. The received wisdom today is that the ANC won the right to majority rule by internal heroism accompanied by a low-intensity guerrilla war. The current South African president, Jacob Zuma's singing 'Bring me my machine gun' perpetuates this account. It was won by war, certainly. It was won in Angola. The release of Nelson Mandela would not have taken place without Gorbachev and the Cubans.

Before then, Washington – realising that Southern Africa would be better secured by negotiation rather than force, and that Apartheid could no longer be an instrument which extruded benefits to the West – threw its weight behind regional negotiations. This is where Chester Crocker, Ronald Reagan's Assistant Secretary of State for Africa came into his own. Long criticised for his policy of 'constructive engagement', which many judge to have supported Pretoria while extracting few compromises over Apartheid, Crocker now led the dismantling of Apartheid's regional forward line. The buffer zones and the destabilisation were going to disappear. There would be no more Total Strategy.

Crocker is these days a bespectacled professor at Georgetown University, teaching and writing about conflict resolution. He is a very good Africanist scholar. But his own book about the conflicts and negotiations in Southern Africa is partisan to himself.[18] Even so, he is graciousness itself, having recently freely offered himself for interview – and criticism – in another scholar's book on his tenure.[19] This polite and engagingly idealistic man was very like Carrington in the choices he had to make. Carrington rescued the Zimbabwe issue from the folly Thatcher seemed determined to commit. It was an incomplete accomplishment as he studiously refused to have the ownership of land placed upon the 1979 Lancaster House agenda. Again in the 2000s, the farm invasions raging, he and I were debating in Cambridge and I said this had been a mistake. He turned and cut me dead with a withering, 'And what would you have done?' How would you have solved Zimbabwe then? The Carrington account is that he did all that was possible. Crocker's would be that, given the Cold War, there was no likelihood when Reagan assumed office that Apartheid – in its full flow towards Total Strategy and internal repression – would die away. Accept South Africa's support against the outreach of the Soviet Union and try to ameliorate the worst aspects of its discrimination. Historically, as in the case of Carrington, this was wrong. At the time, he probably had little choice. This is not to be an apologist for either man. Diplomacy is often a choice between wrong or impossible options.

The Crocker-led negotiations over Angola took in the future of Namibia[20] – since a part of Pretoria's strategic rationale had been to choke SWAPO's support at its geographical source. Angola and Namibia share a border. Take southern Angola and SWAPO cannot mobilise its guerrilla war in neighbouring Namibia. But the real reason for South Africa's wish to hang on to what was then still South West Africa was to have a buffer zone against majority rule. Now the buffer zones would go and, even within the South African Cabinet – long bypassed by the securocrats – there were mutterings about the inevitability of majority rule. It meant that the position of South African President Botha, the man who had unleashed Total Security, was no longer assured. The Cabinet realised that negotiations were inevitable within South Africa itself – just as they were about to occur over the future of Angola and Namibia. If President Botha could not countenance internal negotiations, there would be – the Cabinet whispers said – a palace coup.

Before then Crocker chaired ten rounds of formal talks, and several informal ones – in London, Brazzaville, Cairo, New York and Geneva – before, on 22 December 1988, a set of accords was signed in New York. The recognised governments of Angola and South Africa were participants in the talks, but SWAPO and UNITA were excluded from every round – as if those who fought, for good or bad cause, were only pawns. And the South Africans, anxious suddenly to depict themselves as friends of Africa, made a circus out of what they thought were good public relations: posing on camels in Egypt, and shaking hands with the African delegates with huge, forced grins on their faces. Forced or not, they agreed to the withdrawal of South Africa from Angola; the Cubans would do the same; and Namibia would be granted independence under majority rule.[21]

South Africa has now almost a tradition of palace coups. The one that toppled Thabo Mbeki in 2008 was preceded by one 19 years earlier. The signal for the palace coup against President Botha was his suffering a stroke in January 1989. Ill health could be used as an excuse for demanding he step down and, even though the stroke was not incapacitating, it did galvanise the plotters to seize the moment. The South African Cabinet realised that change was inevitable and that it would be better not to resist it but try to control it; set terms for it; protect one's interests within it; accommodate change without too much sacrifice. Forward-defence became damage control and limitation. This did not come without internal struggle and, to an extent, the rise of F.W. de Klerk, previously seen as a lightweight, struck many as a compromise after the harder men of the securocrats and the Cabinet had cancelled one another out. But the securocrats had a sting left in their tail. In April 1989, as Namibia prepared for independence, SWAPO forces unwisely crossed from their Angolan bases into their own country. This had not been agreed and was caused partly by miscalculation on SWAPO's part, and also by bad advice from the majority-ruled states fearful that, without a SWAPO military presence inside Namibia, the South African authorities would seek to sabotage independence. The SWAPO advance into Namibia was met by a ferocious South African military response. Out-gunned, the SWAPO soldiers were on the verge of decimation, and have very unorthodox Australian peacekeeping under UN colours to thank. No other UN contingent has been quite so emphatic. Dutch soldiers at Srebrenica might take note. But an Australian contingent drove like Mad Max between an armoured South African force and a largely defenceless SWAPO infantry battalion. The South African commander ordered the Australians to move aside. The laconic Australian answer is minor folklore. 'You're gonna haveta go through us, mate.' They didn't and the coda of Total Strategy faded away.

De Klerk was to serve as an interim leader and would be confirmed as President after elections in September – but he began almost immediately sending feelers into the region, particularly towards the Zambian President Kenneth Kaunda. In June, despite the misgivings of other regional presidents, Kaunda said he would meet de Klerk. At the end of August, on the Zambian side of the Victoria Falls, they met. Kaunda is a large, tall man. His smile radiates so much it seems theatrical. De Klerk did not have Kaunda's physical stature so the photos of Kaunda showing de Klerk the sights seem almost comedic. Backgrounded by damp rainforest the large black man puts his arm around the smaller bald white man – the former in a black safari suit and the latter in a grey business suit – and aiming a laser-beam smile uses his other arm to point something out. Somewhere, just out of camera shot, desperate aides were holding umbrellas in a desperate attempt to keep the spray of the Falls from their heads.

Kaunda went into the talks without a single briefing note on de Klerk. There wasn't one because neither the President's aides nor the Ministry of Foreign Affairs had a dossier on de Klerk. He had been that unexpected as a South African leader. De Klerk had devoured six ring-binders of briefing notes on Kaunda. The misgivings of the other presidents seemed real. How do you negotiate with an unknown quantity who heads the power that has thrashed you about for almost a decade and that has oppressed its people for considerably longer? Both men denied it at the time, but Kaunda told de Klerk, 'You have to release Nelson Mandela.' It was Kaunda's last great act of foreign policy. His own people would rise against him the following year, demanding democracy, and he would fall in the elections of 1991.

In February 1990, in response to regional and international pressures, and seeking to control and condition the future rather than defeat what increasingly seemed inevitable, the South African government lifted the ban on the ANC and other political organisations. It maintained a state of emergency – just in case. But, at 4 p.m. on 11 February, after 27 years in prison, amidst bright sunshine, Nelson Mandela walked out. He was tall and lean and immaculately dressed. But for those who had campaigned for this moment, and who had only seen the photographs of him 27 years earlier, his appearance was a shock. He was elderly and grey-haired now, leaner than when he had been imprisoned. The jowls and knitted brows of his youth were no longer there. A firebrand had gone in and it seemed a sage was striding out. His sagacity came to be universally celebrated. But fraught years of negotiation lay ahead of February 1990. And Robert Mugabe of Zimbabwe was only half filled with delight.

CHAPTER 3

THE RAINBOW BRIDGE

The Cold War that ended in Europe in 1989, with the fall of the Berlin Wall, ended in Southern Africa in 1990 with the release of Nelson Mandela. The West has since gone out of its way to make Mandela a saint – almost as compensation for having allowed his imprisonment to continue for so long. But he was not a saint, and neither had the Cold War been cold in Southern Africa. It had been the hot manifestation of the confrontation between the superpowers, and the nations of the region had been pawns. Some, like Mugabe, had tried to act with military might of their own. Some, like Zambia's Kaunda, had steered an uneasy line between resistance and pacific principle. Now the wave of democracy that sprang from the end of Communism would cause Kaunda's overthrow. Meanwhile, ironically in retrospect, Mugabe would bask in the limelight of democracy and human rights. Across the border, in South Africa, Mandela and Thabo Mbeki set about the vexed business of making freedom and, then, making a freed nation work. It wasn't going to be easy – just as the four years of negotiations between Mandela's release and his great election victory were not easy. Mandela made many mistakes. As President, he scored great symbolic victories and bequeathed his successor,

Thabo Mbeki, much symbolism. It was vitally necessary symbolism. But was much of it just symbolism?

Harare 1991, and the leaders of the Commonwealth gather for their biennial summit. These summits fall in uneven years, so it was as close as they could get to a ten-year anniversary of Zimbabwe's independence. The motorcades of the presidents and prime ministers swept up the tree-lined boulevards. But all had to come to the air-conditioning-free press shed where, with the sweaty crowd of journalists, the academics were confined. The press conferences of the leaders were, however, usually held in the cool of the evenings. As the revenge of the press pack, the atmosphere would still be fetid from the day's perspiration and cigarettes. The new Commonwealth Secretary-General, Emeka Anyaoku, came with Robert Mugabe to announce the Harare Declaration on Human Rights – Mugabe seeming enthusiastic and no one knowing how ironic this would seem a decade later. Indeed the various drafts of the Declaration had been the subject of intense behind-the-scenes debate between the British and the Commonwealth Secretariat – with, surprisingly, in today's context, Mugabe supporting the stronger Commonwealth draft. The British prevailed with a watered-down rendition of human rights, replacing the early document prepared by the Commonwealth Secretariat's Moni Malhoutra. Like the Americans refusing to join the International Criminal Court, the British did not want a future where they would be hoist on their own petard. That meant no one could be hoist. The Declaration had no petard. But Britain's John Major, Anyaoku and Mugabe, despite differences in the drafting process, claimed it was a great document outlining great principles to do with human rights as a prerequisite for any state's Commonwealth membership. Human rights were taken as cardinal to the Commonwealth project.

All the same, pressure groups like Human Rights Watch bombarded people with dossiers on Zimbabwean abuses – but these centred on harassments of the opposition party of the time, which had been both properly and improperly defeated in the 1990 elections.[1] Where it was improper it was heavy-handed; again a portent of what was to come. Not a word on the slaughters in the Matabelelands that had come to an end a bare three years earlier, but of which the world still seemed ignorant and content to be ignorant. Zimbabwe was, by and large, a great triumph. Blacks had not slaughtered whites and South Africa, unalarmed by Zimbabwe, was making slow but steady negotiating progress towards majority rule. In this context, the black opposition leaders of South Africa came to lobby the summit, and the leader of the PAC (Pan-Africanist Congress), the long-time rival of the ANC, even came to the press shed. Mandela, by contrast, quietly and unobtrusively 'worked' the Commonwealth leaders individually and in small groups, and almost all were charmed by the tall, dignified man who they were sure would be the next President of South Africa. Of Mandela, Mugabe said not a word. He had supported the PAC. Its sense of black consciousness and mildly Maoist inclinations – its sense of being closer to the late Steve Biko than Mandela was, even though it had not been Biko's organisation – its non-Moscow, non-trade-union-dominated history all had an appeal to Mugabe; particularly the sense of black consciousness, the black identity, its roots in a black culture. And Biko had achieved his own legendary and symbolic sacrifice, having been beaten to death by the Apartheid police, the truth of which was uncovered by the young Helen Zille, then a journalist and later the most significant opposition leader to the ANC in post-Apartheid South Africa. Mugabe was not going to obstruct Mandela and, although he had made Zimbabwe a land where black and white coexisted peacefully, events were to show that Mugabe's vision was narrower than Mandela's.

Many books have been written on Nelson Mandela, both recounting and romanticising his life, and certainly forgiving his youthful indiscretions.[2] Simultaneously, much seems to have been left unsaid about other aspects. He was a less than perfect family man and father.[3] Even that he eluded capture by the Apartheid authorities for a time by posing as the chauffeur of a gay white South African seems not to have been elevated to the vast array of legends surrounding Mandela. But perhaps some of the equalities in the rainbow nation's constitution – non-discrimination on grounds of sexual persuasion is explicitly included – owe partly to this episode. Even so, there are still undercurrents in conservative ANC quarters that are uneasy about homosexuality, so being chauffeur to a gay man is not sung as a welcome for gay people into the pantheon of liberators. But the lingering effect of such exposure to help from different people probably did find its way into the constitution just as, further north, Kenneth Kaunda's espousal of a Gandhi-esque passive resistance to Rhodesian attacks and Apartheid's Total Strategy were the result of his being sheltered by Indian migrants to Zambia when he was a nationalist leader and also on the run.

Nelson Mandela was born in 1918 in Qunu in the Transkei, near the south-eastern coast of South Africa, a little below KwaZulu-Natal. He was of aristocratic Thembu descent – the Thembu being part of the Xhosa-speaking peoples. But he was the son of his father's third of four wives, so he would never inherit his minor chieftaincy. He was named after Lord Nelson of Trafalgar. His parents hoped he would be a man of victory and agreed he should be educated. When his father died in 1930 Nelson was adopted by the Thembu Paramount Chief and this man paid for his education. He was circumcised as part of the Thembu adult-initiation rites at the age of 16 and, in 1939, went up to Fort Hare University College. This had been started by missionaries and was one of the few places in South Africa where black scholars could freely study. Robert Mugabe also went there. Nelson Mandela's best student friend was Oliver Tambo, later also a leading anti-Apartheid figure. They would skive off from class and break dormitory curfews to go dancing. Banned from Fort Hare for leading a protest, and fleeing the prospect of an arranged marriage, Mandela headed for Johannesburg and its jazz clubs and, after much effort, found work as a security guard. By chance he met Walter Sisulu, again someone who would become a great anti-Apartheid activist, and Sisulu sponsored Mandela to the completion of a law degree at the University of Witwatersrand – and match-made his first marriage. At Wits,

Mandela met the white Communist, Joe Slovo, and his wife, Ruth First – and the cast for what was to be the leadership of the ANC Youth League and later, with the addition of Govan Mbeki, the seniority of the ANC, had been gathered.

In the meantime, war was raging in Europe. After the war, South Africa posed as a champion of the brave new world that emerged, Prime Minister Jan Smuts being active in the foundation of the United Nations. But the grand statements that followed upon the birth of the UN – the Universal Declaration of Human Rights – were being flouted in an increasingly repressive South Africa. The fresh-faced, newly married, freshly minted young lawyer, Nelson Mandela, was appalled by the discrimination even he, as an educated young graduate, faced. He resisted having a special cup set aside for him at the law firm where he worked – so that he would not sip from the same cup a white lawyer might later use – and simply gave up taking tea breaks altogether. Outside his office, racialism was increasing. Even so, the discriminations under Smuts were to look mild when, in 1948, D.F. Malan led the National Party to power in South Africa. This was the official advent of Apartheid and all its major legislative instruments. The savagery of repression increased as non-white resistance increased, culminating in the Sharpeville massacre of 1960, and the banning of the ANC and the newly formed PAC. The ANC set up a military wing, Umkhonto we Sizwe, the Spear of the Nation, in 1961. This was expressly to fight fire with fire: to be an instrument of violent resistance even though, at the time, there was little sense of how this resistance could be strategically and effectively enacted. As commander of Umkhonto, Mandela instructed that sabotage should not lead to loss of life. Sabotage of symbolic or economic targets, such as post offices and electricity pylons, was to drive the government to the negotiating table. Mandela slipped out of South Africa and toured other parts of Africa to drum up support. He himself undertook sabotage and firearms training in Algeria. In June 1962 he slipped back into the country and, for more than two months, he eluded capture – earning the nickname, the 'Black Pimpernel', after the then-famous Hollywood film, *The Scarlet*

Pimpernel, set in the French Revolution – but, in August, he was captured while posing as a chauffeur. The police had finally seen through his disguise. He and other ANC leaders were sent to prison after what came to be called the Rivonia Trial (named after the Johannesburg suburb in which the courthouse was located) in 1963.

When Nelson Mandela walked out of the gates of Victor Vester Prison in 1990 he was tall, lean, unbowed and elegantly dignified. He was also an old man. He had been born in 1918. Robert Mugabe of Zimbabwe and Kenneth Kaunda of Zambia were only a little younger, both having been born in 1924. They were the grand old men of liberation in Southern Africa. In 1990 Robert Mugabe was celebrating a decade of independence, with no signs of a rupture between black and white. Kenneth Kaunda, however, was facing unrest in Zambia – a country where race relations had been good throughout his 26-year tenure.[4] The long and vexed question of racism in Southern Africa was about to be transformed by a transition to democracy. This would take place in South Africa after four years of negotiation. In Zambia, democracy was about to explode in Kenneth Kaunda's face. All three countries were to learn what choice meant. Only in Zimbabwe would choice be ruthlessly suppressed.

1991 at the Commonwealth summit in Harare: Mandela worked the room; Mugabe basked in the approval of many presidents and prime ministers; Kaunda appeared briefly and flew back to Zambia. He looked pale. He had elections in just a few days' time. What might he have been thinking? All those years of patient and pacific resistance to Ian Smith's white-minority government, and all Mugabe does is name a street after him in the boondocks by the railway station? Mandela, already walking with a permanent halo, wowing all in sight? But it was Kaunda who told de Klerk to free him. The Zambian people whom he had led with patience and humanistic philosophy, had now turned against him? A cloud of preoccupation hung over him.

Kaunda turned Zambia into a one-party state in 1973. He said it was to maintain national unity in the face of the Rhodesian threat and, after

Zimbabwe's independence in 1980, to resist the destabilisation of Apartheid. But Mandela was free now and Zambians saw the prosperity of Mugabe's Zimbabwe and asked why the economic mismanagement of Kaunda's government should be allowed to continue. There was something else. The events of Eastern Europe had caught the imagination of Zambians. One-party states were falling. People smashed the Berlin Wall. It was possible to rise up. In 1990, university students in Lusaka rioted. It had happened before, but this time it was the match that lit the tinder. Demonstrations against Kaunda's rule swept the nation. If cameras had caught the events for television, as they had at the shipyards of Gdansk, at the Wall in Berlin, then the day almost all the adult population of Kabwe took to the streets to march and shout for democracy would become part of international folklore. Kaunda had to agree to elections and scheduled them for 1991. He hoped the opposition to him would not coalesce and stay together. Instead, the new Movement for Multi-Party Democracy (MMD) proved as solid as a rock. Everywhere people flashed the MMD symbol: the fingers of one hand held at as if they were a watch signalling one o'clock. An hour past midnight. 'The Hour Has Come' was the party motto. The symbol looked like a victory sign; in Harare, Kaunda seemed visibly worried. And, unlike earlier summits, no one lionised him. Other men were garnering the attention and adulation. He seemed a shadow from the past.

The MMD took the election by a landslide. But it was Kaunda's concession speech, standing down quietly and wishing the new President well, that became the event. Its dignity set a standard for Africa. Then the cameras showed him personally guiding his successor, Frederick Chiluba, around the presidential offices in State House. Afterwards he went to leave in his official car. He was about to get in when he noticed the presidential pennant still flying from it. He walked back from the door, gently removed the pennant, put it in his pocket – almost as a keepsake – and only then drove away. It is a strange thing to witness a nation rising against one man's rule, and then forgiving him in an instant. If Robert Mugabe, some years later, had been half the man Kaunda was that day, history would remember him more kindly.

Altogether in 1991, a Declaration on Human Rights was adopted in Zimbabwe, an opposition party triumphed in free elections in Zambia, and Nelson Mandela began his long list of diplomatic victories. He would be part of the change in a region that was changing fast.

Both Mandela and the ANC were on a steep learning curve. The original ANC position was to push for elections within a year of being unbanned, and Mandela argued for a first-past-the-post electoral system. He wanted a clean, uncomplicated majority by which to govern. De Klerk's National Party wanted the election to be delayed as long as possible. It sensed that, against its own expectations, de Klerk had become a popular figure: he was a known quantity who had taken huge worthwhile risks, whereas Mandela was a charismatic stranger who had suddenly reappeared. The contrast between de Klerk and his more strident, stubborn predecessors was startling. He gave the impression of reasonableness and of wanting only to prevent disruption and dislocation by his agenda of continuity. De Klerk's popularity could be turned, his advisers felt, into electoral support, and the National Party was polling well even in some black areas. And it pushed for proportional representation – hoping that, if the worst came to the worst, it could form a coalition with small parties who had crept into Parliament. The ANC realised it did not have the organisational structure to fight an immediate election and, as it began to build one, both the ANC and the National Party commissioned polls and they played a game of cat and mouse, delaying negotiations when polling was bad, moving swiftly when electoral advantage seemed possible. The ANC misjudged several times. In 1992 it mobilised mass demonstrations to pressurise the National Party but, one by one, Mandela had to withdraw the ANC demands. As the negotiations stretched into 1993, eking out progress, the National Party realised that such polling gains as it had achieved were beginning to slip away. It had to be soon or never. Finally, the election was set for April 1994. The most simple form of proportional representation was agreed, both parties were organisationally ready, and the final campaigns began.[5]

On the hustings, Mandela rose to his remarkable charismatic best. In terms of public appearances he blew de Klerk away. That amazing smile and that tall frame that should have been bent by prison, but wasn't, and the clenched fist raised under a banner that promised 'Jobs, Peace and Freedom', swept doubt and hesitation away.[6] The past was gone. De Klerk now had no reassurances that could take the nation into the future. Mandela saw the future and promised a rainbow.

This is to summarise much that has already been forgotten, and to omit much detail. But it wasn't just a triumphant march to freedom. That was when Mandela came out of prison. The years of negotiation were a crawl. And the labour of building an electoral machine was something Robert Mugabe did not have to do in 1980. By comparison to Ian Smith's backwater Rhodesia, de Klerk's South Africa was a huge country where government had, when it wanted, First World capacity. The National Party could have beaten the ANC to an organisational pulp if elections had been held immediately after Mandela's release. And, in a very real sense, the long negotiations prepared the ANC for the tedium of politics – where a government is successful mostly by carefully balanced incremental steps. The negotiations let the ANC technocrats – people like Trevor Manuel – come to the fore at complex moments. And they instilled perhaps Thabo Mbeki's sense of caution – as he watched frontline negotiators like his rival, Cyril Ramaphosa, making sometimes daring mistakes. But if Mugabe never had to do this, and never learnt from having to negotiate in protracted good faith with a formidable opponent, he did have one final great achievement up his sleeve, one final contribution to help seal peace in Southern Africa. To Mugabe, in 1992, belongs much credit for peace in Mozambique. The man who had sent in the troops now brought the RENAMO and FRELIMO leaders together.[7] It wasn't just that Mandela was in some way the symbol that the effects of the Cold War had ended in South Africa. Other people worked to ensure it was the case in the wider region, and Mugabe was remarkable in this.

Even after the release of Mandela and the beginning of the end of Apartheid, RENAMO had continued fighting. For some time

Zimbabwean military intelligence had been reporting that the rebels had a cause, and they were fighting – it seems – for this cause. And, for the past few years, the Catholic Church – led first by the Santo Egidio monastery in Italy – in concert later with the Italian government, had been mediating the conflict.[8] Peace talks had begun in Rome between RENAMO and the FRELIMO government. The Italian preparations were ingenious and very Italian. The rebels would delay the talks by insisting that they had to return to Mozambique for consultations and instructions. In the days before cellphones Italy gave them a jet plane and intercontinental radio links. Then, to keep them even longer in Rome – on the grounds that while they were there they would actually periodically negotiate – Italy treated them to Armani suits and Serie A football matches. It was impeccable – but the talks were stalled. On 10 January 1992, having been helped secretly by the US State Department and CIA to set up the meeting, and in the manner of Kaunda without the knowledge or help of his foreign ministry, Mugabe flew to Malawi and met the RENAMO leader, Afonso Dhlakama. Almost no one even knew what Dhlakama looked like. A rare photo of him, published in a 1990 book by Paul Moorcraft, and taken by Moorcraft himself, had not reached Mugabe.[9] But he looked exactly like the young Mugabe. When the two men met there was an immediate affinity. They spoke to each other in Shona and Mugabe took to him almost like a wayward son – even though his soldiers had been battling against the insurgents led by the younger man.

This was something that re-emerged in later considerably more frustrating talks with his Zimbabwean opponents. Mugabe can talk to an opponent, even an enemy, if he can adopt that person as a son. The son doesn't have to believe what Mugabe believes, or even do what he wants. He doesn't have to be a political bondsman. But he does have to allow himself to be the son. He has to acknowledge social and cultural seniority. And he has to be intelligent to the point of intellectual. He has to be like the young Mugabe graduating from Fort Hare University College. In that sense, perhaps the breakthrough was Dhlakama's – for he accepted being patronised in this manner. Even so,

Mugabe gained the plaudits for this critical meeting that allowed progress in Rome and, even though the talks remained laboured, a peace agreement was signed on 4 October 1992 and, at the Roman ceremony, Mugabe gave his second great speech about reconciliation.[10] This wasn't, as in 1980, about black and white, but about the reconciliation of black and black. It was about the future, not the past. The Mozambican peace has lasted, but Mugabe himself was never to live up to his own stirring rhetoric. Nelson Mandela, by contrast, did.

Nelson Mandela has been made into an icon of righteousness, forbearance and perseverance. His personality and charisma, even his phraseology, have been lumped into the manufacture of him as the saint for our times. In an awful twentieth century of one huge war or slaughter after another he seemed to allow humanity a moment of self-belief and exoneration. There is some indecency about all this. He was actually not a good president. The work of running the country was left to Deputy President Thabo Mbeki. He was a *symbol*, an image that bound people together and made them believe they could, even grumpily, move forward.[11] And, because he forgave 27 years of imprisonment, it became a moral requirement that everyone else should forgive. Desmond Tutu's Truth and Reconciliation Commission could not have worked without the exemplary moral image of Mandela. But the ANC did not become the authoritarian party and fractious agglomeration of factions that it did simply from Day One of Thabo Mbeki, who finally inherited the presidency from Mandela but who had effectively run the government for years before that. Mandela, with the other elderly veterans of the ANC, is to blame for at least part of that slide from victorious cockiness to a deadly conceit. There was the installation of unfit people in high positions, simply because another form of symbolism – black direction of institutions – was required and certain people were 'owed'. The beginning of corruption, although minor by comparison with other African countries, allowed many in power also to become 'equal' swiftly with rich white elites. This is a trend that has continued and increased throughout the years of majority rule. Nor has the 'politics of identity', which has backgrounded so many appointments to the civil service and government, always been ill-meaning. Not everyone moved towards corruption. But, often, highly educated ANC personnel were appointed to positions in which they had no technical competence and no technocratic expertise or strategic conceptions. And the number of people who have materialised, suddenly, claiming ANC liberation histories or, at least, sympathies, has meant the expansion of patronage to fellow travellers as well as those who actually took a stand. To this day, few have management training, and the public administrative templates they have inherited are clumsy, often designed to deliver benefits to a minority and, when expanded for majority provision, often slow down delivery. Different levels of government meant different levels of incompetence and different avenues for corruption. The binding glue that developed among all these levels was patronage, developed within the ANC and used to cement its control in all parts of South Africa. It was not a situation which encouraged bold management. There was a clear drift towards a 'steady as she goes' steering of the ship of state through international liberal economic waters, working hard not to alarm the world of capital, leaving those who were poor to believe all would be well one day because the image of Mandela said it would.

But, having said all that – which, even now, is something not said, or said meekly – the accomplishment of Mandela was magnificent. It wasn't just the image of reconciliation he brought. It was the sense of seamlessness. It was the sense that everybody could do something positive in their own time – even in their own way. They just had to do *something*. They didn't have to lose anything. This was Mandela's message to the whites. It was, in some ways, more important than the sense of hope he gave to the blacks. It led to genuine efforts at accommodation – if not always successful reconciliation. In some ways also, the limits of these efforts were well reflected in the daily cartoon strip, 'Madame and Eve', in which Eve is the maidservant of an elderly, cantankerous and condescending white woman. But Eve is the one with street-smarts. Without Eve, her employer would flounder. As the years passed, Eve evolved in the cartoon strip to a curious form, not of equality but of superiority to her employer. And the old white woman has become, grudgingly and still cantankerously, accepting and even supportive of the equality agenda. The evolution of the characters has reflected, to its avid fans, the evolution of social relations in South Africa as a whole. And so it has – because Eve is still the maidservant. Very much has changed, but the economic situation has not kept up.

To be fair, many of the early efforts to change personal habits and attitudes were impressive. In 1992, midway through the negotiations that finally led to Mandela's government of 1994, there was one such. In the class I taught at what was then the University of Natal, there were black students who had fought in Angola with the MPLA. There was also a former white soldier who had fought with the invaders, it was said, with some savagery and intensity. All term, the black and white fighters avoided each other, but cast suspicious sideways glances. Then, one day, at the outdoor coffee bar, I saw the white man get up from his lone stool and walk over to the young black veterans. Not a word. And they just made room for him – as if the timing and intent had been perfect – and finished their coffees together.

But, while the world concentrated on black–white relations, reconciliation wasn't necessarily permeating the black and black divide. And KwaZulu, in which Durban sat, was the epicentre of an intense political rivalry between the ANC and Buthelezi's Zulu-based Inkatha party. The Zulu sense of exceptionalism had waxed large in the days of Shaka, and Buthelezi was extremely reluctant to allow what he saw as political domination by other groups. His reluctance was reflected in feelings on the ground. Tensions were inflamed between Zulu and ANC groups.[12] In 1992, blood ran in the hills of KwaZulu. Inkatha maurauders would attack a village with ANC sympathies, using exactly Shaka's methods: the bullhorn, as Shaka called it, or the pincer movement – enveloping the village from two sides. Then the Zulu women would move through the middle and loot what was left. Sometimes guns were used, sometimes clubs and machetes.

There was also an element of white–white reconciliation. Throughout the struggle against Apartheid the white community was divided, with large numbers of people taking a stand of some sort against it. The principle of inequality was offensive to many and, even for some who condescended towards the non-white communities, there was a recognition that suppression and enforced discrimination could not bode well for the political future. Although the number of white liberals who took actual risks against Apartheid is much smaller than the chattering classes would maintain,[13] some certainly did lay it all on the line. One of these was the jurist, Albie Sachs, who survived a failed assassination attempt.[14] The photos were terrible. He is lying in the street. His mouth is a howl of pain. He would be stretching out an arm for help – only there is no arm. He was horribly mutilated in the car-bomb attack. Years later, Sachs is an eminent judge, and a young man comes to see him. 'My name is Henry. I was the one who tried to kill you.' He had come for forgiveness. Sachs said he would shake the man's hand but he didn't have a right hand any more; instead he would invite Henry to the cocktail parties in his house. Sachs was a leading influence in the Truth and Reconciliation Commission but, ever after, he has tramped the world's lecture circuit recounting the story of Henry's visit, gesticulating with his one arm while wearing the style of informal shirt Mandela made famous. The Henry story has become Sachs' trademark presentation. It is his personal emblem of reconciliation – even with assassins. Sachs has adopted the Mandela shirt as a symbol of the non-standard-issue politician: the political figure who, all the same, disdains the limits of politics and its self-interest; the figure who puts the interests of others above his or her own. It was a curiously potent image – although Mandela would not have wanted its commodification as the must-have souvenir of a visit to South Africa. But, if the world has crafted Mandela into a saint, the shirt is the collectible relic.

Thabo Mbeki couldn't stand those shirts. He was overheard once complaining of his 'stuffy' image: 'What do I have to do? Spend 27 years in prison and wear ridiculous shirts?' But in post-Apartheid South Africa he never could escape his reserved, carefully tailored image. This was partly because he had become a reserved and tailored man. Spontaneity and looseness of body had been crafted out of him. Watchfulness and control took their place. The contrast between Mandela and Mbeki was at its greatest at rugby matches. Before the 1995 Rugby World Cup, Mandela came on to the field dressed in a pastiche of a rugby outfit, incongruously topped off with a colour-coordinated baseball cap. He walked the line of the predominantly white Springbok players and shook their hands, smiling into the eyes of each man. He set them on fire. When they sang the multilingual anthem – that compromise everyone called reconciliation – they sang the carefully memorised and rehearsed Xhosa lyrics to 'Nkosi Sikelel'iAfrika' as if it meant the world to them. Some were crying. And all because a tall but doddery old man had stood before them and shaken their hands.[15] Jacob Zuma tried to emulate that trick. He couldn't do it on the field because Mbeki was still President but, before the final of the 2007 Rugby World Cup, he was in the Springbok dressing room doing his best to stoke up a storm. Even he did not have Mandela's panache – wearing a suit and not the Springbok jersey Mandela sported. Mandela went to the lengths of having his jersey tailored, so determined was he that his presence at the match should be a symbol. In 2007, Mbeki was sitting in the stadium's VIP box, having made the concession of wearing a Springbok windcheater over his suit. I don't think he understood the game or enjoyed it. But, afterwards, when his players had won it, he had no choice but to venture on to the field to congratulate them. The muddy and bloodied Springboks, still more white than black, spontaneously thrust the golden trophy into his hands and hoisted him on to their shoulders. It took him by such surprise that there have been few other photographs of him as President looking so delighted. But it was the players reaching out to him. It was not the President reaching out to the most burly of his citizens.

It was not always so. There is something called a gumboot dance. It was developed by black miners living in dormitories away from home. It involves slapping down on the gumboots as percussion while the wearer dances. There is a delicious 1971 photograph of the young

Mbeki, lean, beard still black, performing at an East German student event. He is wearing dark grey trousers but is stripped to the waist. And he is ecstatically performing the gumboot dance. He knows the moves and he is not afraid. He is not aloof and stubborn, and has not retreated into his head. His smile beams as he dances, flexes his back, slaps down and springs upright, coiling and uncoiling like a young man of the people.[16]

Two years into the Mandela presidency, on 14 June 1996, Deputy President Thabo Mbeki made the move that shoved the history of post-Apartheid South Africa into a realm unencompassed by Mandela's stirring rainbow rhetoric. To that extent, pretty much all that is tangible and measurable about post-Apartheid South Africa is Mbeki's. Mandela will be left as a great image, a great symbol – Moses who did enter the promised land but who sat on mountains while abdicating the future of the kingdom to Joshua. What Mbeki did, in concert with finance minister Trevor Manuel, was to launch GEAR (the Growth, Employment and Redistribution Programme). This was about growth in the first instance. Redistribution was secondary and dependent. Not only was it Mbeki's masterplan for South Africa, but – just as Mandela was a moral image and exemplar – Mbeki wanted GEAR to be the technocratic exemplar for all of Africa: this is how you run a modern state; this is how you integrate with global capital as a performing partner, not as a servitor or client; this is how you establish the modern platform upon which all else depends. Upon which welfare and justice depend.

As if this was not enough, the non-negotiable manner of Manuel's announcement of GEAR in his budget speech immediately raised hackles throughout the trade union movement and the South African Communist Party. Two of the key pillars of the ANC, previously uncon- sulted about GEAR, were alienated at a stroke. In June 1996 Mbeki did three things: he pushed through a neo-liberal economic future for the country; he established policy without full prior consultation and narrowed the possibility of dissent; and he prioritised international, i.e. Western approval over domestic equity. The political kingdom had been won, but Mbeki was prepared to narrow its inclusiveness by neglecting to consult key actors who had fought against Apartheid. And though Mbeki was prepared to ameliorate poverty to an extent, he was also prepared to leave intact – until the golden age of fiscal prosperity – the huge economic inequalities of Apartheid. It would be macroeconomics all the way. Even before the end of Mandela's presidency, the South African revolution had been steered away from the image of a rainbow nation and towards a fiscally balanced nation. Mbeki also, of course, at the same time inadvertently but unavoidably prepared the ground for a backlash. This would later personify itself as Jacob Zuma. Mbeki, as the years unfolded, tried to put many knives into Zuma's back to accompany Zuma's self-inflicted wounds. But it was to be Zuma who plunged the fatal knife into Mbeki. In this way also, South African politics – and ANC politics in particular – turned from its mission to the people into a soap opera of personalities and vendettas.

CHAPTER 4

THE FORMATION OF THABO MBEKI

If Nelson Mandela was crafted into a saint and knowingly played the role – understanding 'spin' was a potent political weapon – Thabo Mbeki was curiously more old-fashioned. Despite his studies in economics at Britain's Sussex University and his military training in the Soviet Union, he was in many ways the last of the African 'philosopher kings' in the lineage of Zambia's President Kenneth Kaunda and Tanzania's Julius Nyerere, men who wrote learned books and were at pains to demonstrate their intellectual skills[1] – almost as a deliberate riposte to the white settler condescension towards black people in Southern Africa; a riposte to the view that black people had limited intellect. South Africa was in fact the last outpost of such thinking, and the end of Apartheid did not mean that such attitudes disappeared overnight. The interesting thing about Mbeki, however, was that his thinking was heavily influenced by black American writing. He didn't, like Kaunda and Nyerere, aspire to be authentically 'African' in his thought, but to be 'black' – and this was an exile's thought, derived from the diaspora on the other side of the Atlantic. Mbeki, who had lived more years outside than inside South Africa, thought like a foreigner. He had come 'home', he understood the ANC, but he understood

'home' through the learning of an exile who had imbibed the thought of
those who considered themselves exiles. It was thought about pride – about
black pride. In some ways, it could have been applied anywhere.

It is easy to contrast Thabo Mbeki's sober and tailored image as President, all dark suits and grey ties, with the gumboot-slapping younger man – stripped to the waist and grinning his head off while he danced. But even the sober and tailored Mbeki was a highly complex man. He was a true intellectual – more so than Mugabe, who prided himself on being the most learned person in any company. With Mugabe it became a self-fetishisation and, in his old age, he has taken to belittling people and finding fault with their education or manner of expression. Even when the room was full of superbly educated and thoughtful people, Mugabe needed to be respected – if not as the intellectual superior – as the elder man, the elder intellectual, the revolutionary sage before whom all others were merely technocrats. Mbeki never had such problems. His idea of private pleasure was drinking with friends and, even as President, he drank most of them under the table; having gotten 'down and dirty' with them, he was back at his desk the next morning, sober and tailored again, before them.

When Jacob Zuma became President of the ANC at the end of 2007 he took over from Mbeki the task of writing a weekly column for the ANC Newsletter. The contrast with his predecessor's often voluminous meditations was startling. Zuma's had no intellectual content at all. This might have been just as well. The number of readers who could digest Mbeki's essays – for they became full-length literary and political essays – must have been small. Even those who fought their way to the end would have been hard put to claim familiarity with the wide range of African and Afro-American literary sources he cited. The Afro-American affiliations were the interesting ones – the writings of an African diaspora. It was almost as if Mbeki's years of exile had made him more attracted to those outside rather than inside Africa. No other world leader of his generation could have penned such erudite work: a French prime minister or president here and there, no postwar American president, and no British prime minister since Churchill. I want to look at a handful of these writings from a 20-month period, at a time when Robert Mugabe was under severe international pressure. In a way there was never any increase in the nature of pressure – just more of the same thing from the Western world, coupled with more internal degeneration. It was at the end of 2003 and the beginning of 2004 that the West threw what it had at Robert Mugabe. Both Kenneth Kaunda, by now playing an elder statesman's role in Zambia, and Thabo Mbeki defended Mugabe by way of criticising his enemies.

The felt need to defend Mugabe came in the wake of the December 2003 Commonwealth summit in Abuja, Nigeria. There, the assembled leaders agreed to continue the suspension of Zimbabwe's membership. This suspension had begun the year before, following the Commonwealth refusal to accept the declared results of the 2002 Zimbabwean elections. But, at that time, the flurry of diplomatic initiatives was still in full swing, so outright expulsion was not on the cards. It was after those elections that Thabo Mbeki proposed for the first time a power-sharing government with Mugabe as President and opposition leader, Morgan Tsvangirai, as Vice President. At the end of 2003, however, no progress had been made on the Zimbabwean issue. At the Abuja summit Tony Blair masterfully outmanoeuvred Thabo Mbeki by garnering the support of the black Caribbean and South Pacific leaders, the Asian leaders, and the Presidents of Ghana and Kenya for continued Zimbabwean suspension. Mbeki was furious but, in a real sense, he had only himself to blame. Not as pompous as Mugabe in his aura of intellectual gravitas, he nevertheless assumed that the quiet statement of continued South African efforts at mediation would win over the Commonwealth leaders. He didn't work the room or lobby. Blair moved like a master of this game, and encountered no opposition. It would not be the last time Mbeki made this mistake and, as he stormed back to Pretoria, he was as angry with himself as with Blair and the majority of the Commonwealth. Kenneth Kaunda, who did not attend the summit, but who had worked hard to position himself as an *éminence grise* of Zambian and African politics, supported Mugabe's statement that the suspension had been forced through by 'the ugly faces in the Commonwealth', and argued the justice of a post-colonial nationalisation of land.[2] The Zimbabwean government itself refused to accept continued suspension. It just declared it was leaving the Commonwealth outright and for good. But in the midst of the sort of minor tempests that buffet the Commonwealth, Mbeki re-gathered his intellectual sensibilities and penned an amazing letter to the ANC. It was entitled, 'We'll resist the upside-down view of Africa'.[3]

The first half of this essay was a legalistic exposition on why the Commonwealth had acted against its own instruments, resolutions and principles. It was very much a lawyer's argument, but one which set the tone for what also emanated from Harare – as moderates in the Mugabe government tried to put forward a reasoned defence of Zimbabwe, partly to balance the shrillness of their harder-line colleagues who attacked all and sundry involved at Abuja. There is a bridge, briefly discussing the issue of land nationalisation. The second half of the essay is, however, a combination of striking intellectual statement and a side-swipe at diplomatic values and practice. The diplomatic commentary first: it is based on an extrapolation from Henry Kissinger's book on *Diplomacy*[4] – an odd choice, at first glance, given Kissinger's support for Apartheid South Africa, putting Cold War values above human ones. Nevertheless, the passage Mbeki cites relates to Kissinger's exposition of US President Ronald Reagan's championing of human rights as a Cold War instrument to undermine the Soviet Union. For Reagan, human rights were a political instrument in a strategic contest for political gain. Perhaps the choice of Kissinger wasn't wrong after all. Human values as instrumental in a contest between governments. The old fox, Kissinger, could never leave his world chessboard alone, or accept that pawns also had their own sense of self-determination. Mbeki uses this exposition to accuse the West – this, in the Commonwealth context, meant Tony Blair – of using human rights as an instrument to overthrow Robert Mugabe. Mbeki thows the old 'kith and kin' herring in here too, so that the diplomatic commentary mixes trite throwaway lines with a real statement on what is of human value and what is merely instrumental, but fails finally to justify anything of human rights value in Robert Mugabe's Zimbabwe. Only to say there is no real value in the West continuing its historic practice of undermining Africa. This is polemic. The interesting part of the essay is his rendition of work by the Kenyan novelist (and, ironically, human rights activist), Ngugi wa Thiong'o.

Ngugi remains one of Africa's great novelists. Once imprisoned by the Kenyan government and in self-exile for many years, he is noted for two things. The first is his amazing corpus of novels and plays in which repudiated Mau Mau fighters and marginalised members of the Kenyan underclass heroically resist and petition an unresponsive elite.[5] The second is that, at the point of his greatest international acclaim, he declared he would no longer write in English but henceforth only in his native language, Gikuyu. (Subsequent novels have been translated into English.) This was a protest against international hegemonies which, to Ngugi, seemed reminiscent of the colonial practice that marginalised indigenous thought. International practice now marginalised indigenous language, the wellspring of thought. Ngugi has stubbornly maintained his position and it is best expressed in his book, *Decolonising the Mind*.[6] This book has become something of a leitmotif for politically correct Westerners who hesitate to criticise African leaders or governments, in case criticism is seen as a kind of recolonisation. The same people have not tried to learn Gikuyu, however. The difficulty of Ngugi's position is that communities in different parts of the world, and at opposite ends of history – those who colonised and those who were colonised – become hermetically sealed units.[7] It is not only language that becomes non-transactionable. Even the United Nations is not going to have a Gikuyu translator on hand, especially as the official languages of Kenya are English and Swahili – not Gikuyu – and Swahili was itself part of a much older 'globalisation' than today's, when the Arab and African worlds coincided intimately, if sometimes violently. The danger of Ngugi's position is that communities in different parts of the world become isolated in terms of normal and moral behaviour. The logic of Ngugi's position is that linguistic autonomy and freedom lead on to political autonomy and freedom. And it is this logic that Mbeki uses in his essay. First he quotes Ngugi:

> It was almost as if, in choosing to write in Gikuyu, I was doing something abnormal. The very fact that what common sense dictates in the literary practice of other cultures is questioned in an African writer is a measure of how far imperialism has distorted the view of African realities. It has turned reality upside down: the abnormal is viewed as normal and the normal is viewed as abnormal. Africa actually enriches Europe; but Africa is made to believe that it needs Europe to rescue it from poverty. Africa's natural and human resources continue to develop Europe and America; but Africa is made to feel grateful for aid from the same quarters that still sit on the back of the continent. Africa even produces intellectuals who now rationalise this upside-down way of looking at Africa.

This is the sting: that heeding the 'normal' injunctions of the West is to sell out; that it is not 'African' and not 'normal'. Mbeki is not one of those 'intellectuals' cited by Ngugi. He is the political leader of South Africa but the intellectual disciple of a Kenyan. He immediately follows this quote from Ngugi with his own application of its logic to Zimbabwe at the end of 2003:

> For example, those who fought for a democratic Zimbabwe, with thousands paying the supreme price during the struggle, and forgave their oppressors and torturers in a spirit of national reconciliation, have been turned into repugnant enemies of democracy. Those who, in the interest of their 'kith and kin', did what they could to deny the people of Zimbabwe their liberty, for as long as they could, have become the eminent defenders of the democratic rights of the people of Zimbabwe.

There is a leap in logic here. Not everything carried out by Africans is necessarily democratic, liberating and 'normal'. Ngugi was as fierce a denunciator of African tyranny as he was of the global pillage and marginalisation of Africa.[8] The 'act in itself' can be wrong, whether committed by Africans or Europeans or Chinese. Mbeki is here labouring a justification for why the land seizures in Zimbabwe could be understood and, indeed, accepted. He deflects criticism of seizure with violence and without compensation by apportioning blame to the British for not funding compensation despite a protracted diplomatic campaign to persuade them to do so – some of this led by Mbeki himself. But Mbeki's real complaint is as much against himself as Blair and the British at Abuja. He accuses Blair's delegation of lobbying and spinning and leaking disinformation to the media to create an impression that the Commonwealth was moving to Blair's side. Blair's people really did this. Mbeki, by contrast, did not. 'We deliberately avoided engaging in any of these activities. We fed no stories to the media. We did not campaign. We lobbied nobody.' He should have. But the sense of dignity Mbeki harboured quite easily elided into an aloofness, a disdain for the dirty business of glad-handing politics. He wouldn't soil his beautiful suit in a gumboot dance, and he wouldn't cheapen his moral convictions by behaving like a salesman of correct 'African' behaviour. This aloofness and disdain characterised his presidency at critical junctures. At moments of crisis when he himself had much to lose, he could not bring himself out of his withdrawn dignity and move. Right or wrong, he did not move at Abuja and afterwards used Ngugi wa Thiong'o as an ideological escape clause for his sense of disdain.

The second letter to the ANC I want to look at came in September 2004. This is a shorter essay, but an essay all the same. And it is even more extraordinary than his peroration on Abuja, Blair and the Commonwealth. This was an essay for 'Heritage Month' and the South African government theme was 'Celebrating our Living Heritage ("What we Live") in the Tenth Year of our Democracy'.[9] Even this laboured title bore Mbeki's imprint – with its didactic subclause that explains that 'what we live' is the same as 'living heritage'. It is a tenth anniversary for South Africa, but also a fifth anniversary for Mbeki's South African presidency. It should be an essay full of references to South African heritage. It's not. It's an essay on Afro-American literature. Three-quarters in, it suddenly veers into a disquisition based on the British writer, R.H. Tawney – who had an immense influence on the British Labour Party, but also on nationalist leaders like Kenneth Kaunda.[10] Tawney emphasised that moral relationships were above economic relationships. And then Mbeki is back to Afro-American literature and talking about James Baldwin. The upshot is that the essay becomes a moral fable: the story, the intangible, matters as much as the reality; the poems and songs of heritage are as important as the blood; the naming of the act as important as the act.

But, apart from an almost grudging one-line acknowledgement of Nelson Mandela, not one of the six others named is South African – or even African, except in the diasporic sense.

Mbeki begins with the diaspora, with the condition of black slaves in America. He takes the title of James Baldwin's book, *Nobody Knows My Name*, as his theme. The recovery of black identity becomes everything. He finds a 'Negro spiritual' which uses a strapline like Baldwin's title: 'O, nobody knows who I am, a-who I am . . .' These 'spirituals' contained lines of longing. Longing for release. And release meant escaping American slavery and going to Heaven: 'go home to my Lord and be free'. The finding of name, of identity, of freedom – these three things are all synonymous one third of the way into Mbeki's essay – is taken a critical step further in the Harlem poetry of the early twentieth century. Claude McKay's poem, 'The Tropics of New York', speaks of an overwhelming longing for 'the old, familiar ways' when he happens across tropical African fruit being sold in the shops.

But there are problems with Mbeki's examples. The trouble with the 'spiritual', 'Nobody Knows Who I Am', is that freedom is associated not only with going to Heaven, but going there 'All dressed in white'. Freedom meant achieving equality with the (white) master, and was not a quality in itself. And Claude McKay's poem is quite definite about his longing. He is not pining for Africa. He'd never been to Africa. He wouldn't know what 'the old, familar ways' were like. What he is pining for are 'dewy dawns, and mystical blue skies'. He is creating a mysticism which will act as a 'benediction'. In the absence of a name, the poets created an identity. The power of this identity was staggering.

The identity was a generalisation. That's why it was staggering. It wasn't burdened by difficult details. That's why so many Afro-American or 'Africana' university courses are taught by faculty who have never been to Africa – and couldn't survive there if they went.[11] What they do, while dressed in borrowed West African regalia, is take random examples of African culture. A bronze sculpture from Benin assumes the same rhetorical weight as a mask from Mali. The giant harp-like Senegalese and Malian kora plays the same music as the Zimbabwean finger piano. The Pyramids of Egypt, the stone ruins of Great Zimbabwe and the great mud palaces of Timbuktu all express the same architectural capacity. The great cavalry armies, armed with swords and rifles defending their cities against the French in Dahomey, are the same as Shaka's short-spear wielding infantry in South Africa. It's lovely. It's evocative. And it's poetry.[12]

But the result is, in my own experience, black American students who think everyone in Africa speaks 'African' and that, as Sarah Palin believed, all 53 states in Africa are one big country.

It was Ali Mazrui who traced a pattern.[13] In isolation from Africa, black Americans in places like Harlem created a modern, urban culture of their own. Some of this was drawn from the echoes of African music, as mutated through 'spirituals', the blues, and the creation of jazz as a modern pyrotechnical music on industrialised instruments. The saxophone did not come out of Africa. Some of this culture was a response to isolation, not only from Africa, but from mainstream America. Harlem was black territory – because other parts of New York were not. However, another phenomenon was occurring on the other side of the Atlantic, and that was the Negritude of Senghor and Césaire – a Senegalese and a Martiniquan – which was a highly intellectualised rendition of the artistic value of blackness. Insofar as Senghor was an intellectual in the highest French tradition, he moved comparatively easily among the philosophical and artistic communities of Paris. They had already absorbed some African influences. The brief period of Picasso's work using West African mask motifs partly drew on this. So Senghor was accepted and associated with the outskirts of Breton's surrealist movement. He was known to Sartre. The Negritude of Paris and the urban-industrial culture of Harlem, as globalisation reached out, found their way back to Africa and superimposed upon Africa an entry point to engagement with forms of modernity and more embracing forms of identity. Pan-Africanism became possible with modern communications. But it also makes the grand and poetic idea of an overarching Africanness a modern invention. It is not in itself indigenous.

What Mbeki takes from this is precisely the idea of the cultural equivalence of black to anything that is white, and the moral imperative of equality. What is created is what Tawney called, and Mbeki espoused: a moral economy. This is greater than a fiscal economy. It is both a greater achievement and something worth defending more than financial capacity. The latter is meaningless without the former. As it turned out, this belief was greater – but also more simplistic – in Robert Mugabe than in Thabo Mbeki. But it also helps explain why Mbeki could never quite bring himself to repudiate Mugabe – despite not infrequent fury with him.

Mugabe and Mbeki shared the sentiments expressed in Mbeki's last quote from James Baldwin: 'The reason that it is important – of the utmost importance – for white people, here, to see the Negroes as people like themselves is that white people will not, otherwise, be able to see themselves as they are . . . And this long history of moral evasion has had an unhealthy effect on the total life of the country.' Given the history of Apartheid South Africa, Mbeki could echo that with huge conviction. Mugabe would say that, given the history of white ownership in Zimbabwe, he was also within his rights – as a moral person – to echo Baldwin's views. It was of utmost importance.

The black/white binary did indeed resonate most with questions of entry, ownership and entitlement to place – to a foot on the land. The last Mbeki ANC newsletter I want to look at was published more than a year after the others: in October 2005.[14] Here the point that Mbeki is making is that, after centuries of dragging black people to Europe as slaves, Europe is now becoming a fortress with razor wire at the borders and naval ships in its seas to prevent any further Africans from coming in – treating illegal immigrants inhumanely; the implication is that this is merely a continuation of such treatment from days gone by. But the essay is extraordinary for two reasons. The first is the extensive use of quotes from T.S. Eliot and Walter de la Mare, who both wrote poems about the unknown visitor. This is Mbeki dipping back into a very English school curriculum. But, for him, the unknown visitor who fills the European with foreboding is the African. Mbeki does not say there is no need to feel this way. He launches into a history on precisely why the European *should* feel this way. He launches into Hannibal's invasion of Rome, and the Moorish conquest of Spain. Suddenly this is not an Arab conquest. The armies, according to Mbeki – using W.E.B. Du Bois as his only authority – were composed of Africans. Tamely, at the very end of this essay, Mbeki says that the illegal immigrants of today do not want to be conquerors. They want legal entry and humane treatment. And they wouldn't attempt entry if the West was helping properly with African development. But the message is unavoidable: you cannot guarantee your possession of land. We will enter the white citadels on black terms. Mbeki wrote that essay six months after Robert Mugabe stole the 2005 Zimbabwean elections and was completing his entry and seizure of the remaining white citadels.

It wasn't meant to be Thabo Mbeki. Originally Mandela's successor was thought to be Chris Hani, the charismatic young leader of the South African Communist Party which was part of the alliance that made up the ANC. But shortly after Apartheid, Hani was assassinated by white extremists while mowing his lawn. It seems a banal image. I drove past his house shortly after it happened. Modestly middle class, Hani was doing it himself – not a gardener. Many people hoped it would be him. Mbeki was a second choice, almost a compromise. But, when he saw his chance, he moved savagely and crushed his rivals – who never forgave him.

There is almost a dynastic sense of politics in the new South Africa. This is partly because the core leadership of the ANC in the struggle against Apartheid was very small. Tight. Sometimes it seemed hardly a mass movement except in name and aspiration. It was a group led by exiles and prisoners. Outside this group there were others of course, but there were many fellow travellers who identified themselves with the ANC, called themselves ANC, performed heroic deeds for the ANC, but who were involved in almost no way in deciding the direction of the ANC. Core ANC was exclusive. Sons followed after fathers. This was thought to be the case of one critic of Thabo Mbeki, William Gumede, who seemed of impeccable ANC stock. He was described by commentators as being of third-generation liberation lineage. In this supposed line his grandfather, Josiah Gumede, was a founder member of the ANC and its President from 1927 to 1930. He was identified with Communism, but was also an admirer of Marcus Garvey, the Caribbean-born American activist who influenced generations after him, and who established the idea of a black person in America as African. William's father, Archie Gumede, was charged with treason for his stand against Apartheid. His brother, Donald, is a parliamentarian in today's South Africa, but William followed his grandfather, Josiah, into journalism. So, when William Gumede's highly critical book about Mbeki appeared in 2005,[15] claiming the soul of the ANC had been lost, all hell broke loose. A disinformation and smear campaign rampaged throughout South Africa, masterminded at the highest level of the ANC. The key reason was that William was seen as a traitor to the tight circle in which he held lineage. This was the ANC as royal family. The Gumedes were princes. Now he was attempting regicide. King Thabo and his throne were instantly defended by a host of loyalists. But William Gumede was not the son of Archie or the grandson of Josiah at all. He was unrelated. Despite this, some explained the furore as a betrayal of lineage – and it seemed a natural explanation to many who believed it or assumed it. In truth, the ANC was capable of being much less discriminating and simply lashing out at a critic, no matter what his family tree.

But Thabo Mbeki was a man of pedigree and descent. He was the son of Govan Mbeki. For years, this fact alone brought him respect, support and deference. Privilege.

Govan Mbeki was born in 1910, and completed his degree at Fort Hare three years before Nelson Mandela arrived. He became a campaigning journalist and a leading figure in the ANC and South African Communist Party.[16] He had been served with a banning order even before being charged with treason and, along with Nelson Mandela, Walter Sisulu and others, was imprisoned. In Govan's case that meant 24 years' imprisonment on Robben Island before his release in 1987. He was Deputy President of the Senate after the end of Apartheid, and died in 2001.[17] But it was his association with Mandela and their common fate at the treason trial – which effectively created the pantheon of the ANC – that rubbed off on Thabo. Not without rancour perhaps from Govan's younger son, Moletsi – perhaps even more intellectually astute than his older brother, and his consistent critic. If the younger brother had succeeded to Mandela's throne, both South Africa and Zimbabwe would be different today. But Moletsi took after the younger Govan, becoming a major journalist and public intellectual. Thabo took after the older Govan who became a giant in the ANC.

Like Kenneth Kaunda in Zambia, the Mbeki family was influenced by Gandhi. His portrait was displayed in the living room. But there was also one of Marx. So although Thabo Mbeki later came to write letters to the ANC on Tawney, it was Kaunda who ineffectually tried to realise Tawney's moral socialism in Zambia, utilising Gandhi's passive resistance, while Thabo Mbeki became a revolutionary. He was born in 1942, but was already a student leader by 1959. On the orders of the ANC he went into exile in 1962. For 28 years he was a revolutionary abroad. When he returned to South Africa, shortly after Mandela's release, he was a stranger to his own country. The first two presidents of a free South Africa were men who had been removed from the turmoil of everyday South African life and struggle. Mandela was a prisoner, but Mbeki's revolution was a jet-setting adventure. He became head of the ANC's International Department and was a familiar in New York, London and, on his visits to Lusaka – where the exiled ANC was headquartered – called the then-luxury Hotel Intercontinental his 'home away from home'. The question of just where home was could never be answered. He took a Master's degree at Sussex, lived in London, Botswana, Swaziland and Nigeria. He did military training in the Soviet Union. Perhaps he followed the old Café Palette rendezvous routine, meeting his Moscow handlers in Paris. In those days the Soviet training of South African dissidents was not unlike what happens in today's al-Qaeda camps in Pakistan. To be a fighter is to become a saboteur. In today's terms, a terrorist. It is hard to imagine the cultivated Thabo assembling bombs. Like Robert Mugabe, he was more talented at directing the struggle than fighting in it. The soft hands of Robert Mugabe never fired an AK47 in anger either.

But this meant Mbeki was imbued, by direct exposure in several African countries and the greatest Western cities, with the ideas of a pan-Africanism stretching across and beyond the continent.[18] Rival groups espoused the idea more openly than the ANC, but Mbeki – cut adrift from South Africa – saw himself as a man of Africa as well as a South African. So that, when historians come to write an appreciation of his time as President, it will not simply be his blind spots over HIV and Robert Mugabe that take centre stage. They will figure, but it will be Mbeki's commitment to what he called an 'African Renaissance'. This is what lay behind his embrace of neo-liberal economics – of global capitalism. Not just that his finance minister, Trevor Manuel, told him to; not just that he had little choice given South Africa's finely balanced place in the world economy – but that he wanted the influx of global capital to stimulate all of Africa to grow, mature, stand up alongside the West and, finally, even challenge the West. When Mbeki championed the NEPAD (New Partnership for Africa's Development) scheme between the West and Africa, it was not to embrace democracy first and foremost. This is what the West thought: money to induce democratic practice. It was to attract Western funds for African growth. The vision was not to grow out of poverty. That would happen along the way. It was to grow in order, one day, to storm the citadels. Like Hannibal, to have Rome quaking in terror before African might. To be the stranger at the door who simply had to be invited in. This is where Mbeki's mantra, 'African solutions for African problems', came from. Both within and eventually without the continent, Africa needed to lay terms for itself.

This was hardly the vision of those who had not left South Africa, those who had stayed to struggle within the country. Trade union leaders had a very different view of what liberal economics meant. And a very different experience of what South African poverty meant. The exiled ANC leadership imagined it in hotels from afar. The prisoners on Robben Island imagined it from their enclosures. The mineworkers wanted to dig their way out of it hundreds of metres underground. They would emerge from their shifts, even their eyes blacker than when they went down, and they imagined a South Africa that differed from Mbeki's vision of grandeur. When, in their leisure moments, they sang and performed the gumboot dance, they scarcely imagined that in a faraway land a member of their 'leadership' – who had never worked in a mine – was showing off their steps before an enraptured audience.

When Chris Hani was killed, many thought the mantle of successor to Mandela would fall on Cyril Ramaphosa, the former trade union leader. He had been General Secretary of the National Union of Mineworkers. Brilliant, tenacious, and a highly skilled negotiator, the breadth of his grin rivalled Kenneth Kaunda's. But those who had returned from exile were deeply suspicious of the 'inziles' – those who had stayed. The inziles were not part of the tight core that had formed in Lusaka. Mbeki pulled off a series of brilliantly deft manoeuvres. Effectively, he knifed Ramaphosa and became President of the ANC in 1997. He who becomes President of the ANC effectively becomes the President of South Africa. Mbeki had secured the succession and became President in 1999.

Ramaphosa, whom Mandela himself preferred, never forgave Mbeki. A decade later, when Zuma was preparing his own knife for Mbeki, he worked hard to secure the support of the inzile base. And Ramaphosa helped sharpen the knife.

CHAPTER 5

THE DEGENERATION OF ZIMBABWE

While Mbeki contemplated 'blackness' in a wide sense, drawing from international writings and concentrating them inwards, Robert Mugabe was drawing his inspiration from Zimbabwe itself, and from the sense that land had not only an economic value, but a cultural and spiritual value. This had always been a part of his nationalist project, sidelined during the negotiations that led to independence in 1980, but reasserted in the national drought of 1992. It was the advent of opposing political forces in the late 1990s that prompted him finally to attempt his vision of a completed nationalisation – ownership, not just rulership, of Zimbabwe. The resurgence of the war veterans in 1997, although initially a grave problem for Mugabe, gave him an emblematic force to deploy in the later land seizures. The appearance of a strong opposition party in 1999, led by Morgan Tsvangirai, and its victory in the refer-endum of early 2000, made Mugabe realise that the moment to accomplish his dream had come. He had to seize the moment, or it would be seized from him. He unleashed the war veterans upon the farms. What was destroyed was not only Zimbabwe's economy but the middle-class lifestyle that had been a hallmark of the urbanised population. Mugabe was, in his justifications, making the land more 'African'. The watching international community lamented that he was making life in his country less 'European' in its comforts and facilities, as well as less assured in its legal protections of property, life and – only finally – the free expression of political opposition. For both Mugabe and his international critics, land came first. Political rights became the afterthought.

When finally Mbeki became President in 1999 he would have savoured his inheritance. The ANC was still widely popular in South Africa, and economic performance was good. The Western world wanted to invest and other players, notably the Chinese, were beginning to look seriously at his country. The Southern African region seemed stable. Enough for Mbeki's 'African Renaissance' to begin in his own neighbourhood. Take the region's five most stable economic players – Zimbabwe, Botswana, Namibia, even Zambia, with South Africa as the key – and they could become an integrated economy big enough to be taken seriously by the West. There would be a combined punching weight. It would show the world that Africa could get its act together productively and cooperatively. But, of all the players outside South Africa, Zimbabwe was critical. Its economic capacity made it strategic in ideas of a regional renaissance.

And a casual visitor to Harare would have felt confident of Zimbabwe's capacity. Whether driving up from South Africa, or down from Zambia, the road – which was once meant to stretch as far as Cairo – was lined with large working farms. The great throughway, Samora Machel Boulevard, was flanked by finance houses; Julius Nyerere Way led to the downtown commercial precinct; there, as part of a meticulously schematic town plan, First Avenue was a pedestrianised street of shops. You could buy boots made from elephant skin, books by serious Zimbabwean novelists, reasonably imitated 'Italian' suits or maple syrup. The grand Meikles Hotel offered five-star accommodation and, nearby, the Monomatapa Hotel still looked the part. A bit further out, the huge Sheraton was where the elite gathered for their drinks. As for the suburbs: the seriously rich lived in ranch houses in Borrowdale; prosperous farmers had town apartments in the Avenues; a burgeoning middle class lived in smaller clones of the ranch houses in Avondale; the lower middle class lived in rougher but clean suburbs like Warren Park. Chitungwiza, the vast commuter city, was linked to Harare by regular buses. And even in the 'rough' suburbs, Mabvuku and Mbare, the street-fighting men had impeccable manners. Only in Epworth was there anything that looked like a shanty. By and large, Harare was glossy. And, from elite dweller in Borrowdale to working-class commuter in Chitungwiza, the idea of a normal life was to go home after work – on motorised transport – take a beer from the refrigerator and sit down to watch the match on television. Giant plasma screen or cheap Asian portable, it didn't matter. The city was as one in its middle-class habits.

And there was a 'new age' fringe. There was even a Chitungwiza Buddhist Society, where the merits of killing cockroaches or letting them live were debated as matters of cosmic karma. You would snap out of your meditation with a start – wondering whether you were not in fact in Los Angeles. Even the weather felt the same. Everyone else was wearing Lycra. But, beneath the surface, the miracle already had shaky foundations.

Does a cockroach call itself a cockroach, knowing what the name means to others? That is what Ananda once asked Buddha. A cockroach is pure unto itself, the Lord Buddha replied. In 1997 a Polish-trained doctor with a white Polish wife came to prominence in Zimbabwe. Born Chenjerai Hunzvi, he took a *nom de guerre* despite, contrary to his claims, having never fought anywhere – let alone in the liberation struggle – and called himself Hitler Hunzvi. This was a name he adopted after his return to Zimbabwe. He would not have dared use such a name in Poland, where the memory of Nazi atrocities in World War II was still vibrant. But he used it to mean strength and ruthlessness. And, besides, those who had fought in the liberation war had made a practice of adopting *noms de guerre*. One of the leading female members of Robert Mugabe's ZANU-PF, Joice Mujuru – who later became Mugabe's Vice-President – had called herself Teurai

Ropa. Spill Blood. And she had – shooting down a Rhodesian heli-copter with an AK47. That was incredibly lucky. Those helicopters were so armour-plated that the bullet would have had to enter a tiny vent by the engine or rotor. Lucky or not, she had been brave enough to stand her ground. And when the Rhodesian commandos attacked the guerrilla base in Chimoio, Mozambique, she led such counter-attack as the guerrillas could muster, even though eight months preg-nant. You earned battle names. But Hunzvi needed one to seem the part when he became leader of the nation's war veterans. Weary after years of fruitless petitions to Robert Mugabe's government pointing out that their service and sacrifices had never been recognised or recompensed in proper pensions, they recruited someone they thought could organise and lead their protest in an educated and meaningful way. Once recruited, Hitler Hunzvi attacked the Mugabe record like a Panzer division. Mugabe had never been criticised so ferociously about the foundation mythology of his stature and his power – that he was the father of liberation; that he had led the struggle; that he had cared for his fighters. For the first time in 17 years of independence, Mugabe capitulated to a challenge. He greatly increased the pensions of those who had fought. It made Hunzvi a household name.[1] It put a huge strain on the Zimbabwean economy. It was one more straw being loaded on to the camel's back. But Mugabe himself then loaded a truckful of straw on to the camel. The year 1997 was one of economic difficulty. The international financial crises of the early 1990s were still being felt in Zimbabwe. The country's performance was being managed reasonably well in hard times, even though a recession had begun. People saw and felt constrictions, but life was still bearably middle-class or aspiring to be middle-class. The bourgeois land Zimbabwe had become was not ready for crisis and was not expecting crisis. No one was ready for crisis, the government least of all.

In 1998 Zimbabwe entered the war in Democratic Republic of Congo (DRC). It is hard to decipher tangible reasons, not only for Zimbabwe's involvement but that of several states without prior strategic interests there. Often dubbed Africa's first continental war, it attracted armies from as far north as Eritrea, Angola in the west, Namibia and Zimbabwe from the south, and Rwanda and Uganda in the east. The Rwandans, with their Ugandan allies, claimed just cause – pursuing the Hutu militias who had committed genocide, and who had taken refuge in DRC. But, for the others, it was a war of opportunism and cynicism. Governments and their armies changed sides. So Zimbabwe was firstly against Laurent Kabila, the new President, and then for him. The former playboy exile who had disgusted Che Guevara, when Che made a brief African foray to help him, had lost none of his extravagance.[2] For Che, it was Kabila's self-indulgence in the nightclubs of Nairobi and Dar es Salaam while his men (and Che) fought against the dictatorship in what was then called Zaire. For the Zimbabweans, there was the promise from Kabila of vast mineral concessions in the south of DRC. With growing unease at home, and having experienced his own vulnerability in the face of the war veterans, Mugabe now moved to secure the loyalty of his serving Generals. He distributed the concessions to them. They became rich – and loyal.[3] But their military operations were paid for by the Zimbabwean exchequer. It was costing US$ 1 million a day. Britain helped increase the bill by selling replacement parts to the Zimbabwean air force. Military cargo planes carried mineral ores out of DRC before the Generals, other senior officers and politicians set about the formation of companies that legally 'owned' the mines, and flotillas of other companies that laundered the proceeds. These days the spoils of war become part of the white-collar world very quickly and, as with all significant African corruption, legions of European and American accountants and lawyers finesse the trail of transactions through one company after another, laundering everything until dirt is no longer visible. Simple deposits in a Swiss bank account disappear under a blanket of multinational sophistication.

But the cost of the war, on top of existing recession and the cost of the war veterans' package, meant increased economic and political unrest at home. Strangely enough, although the civil society and civic action groups had a wide agenda of discontents, no one thought the

Zimbabwean economy would collapse. Everyone thought it would worsen if the war continued, but they thought things could be returned to how they were. Mugabe's aloof authoritarian style had not grown into suppression. People were wary but still thought they were free. Yet the key item on the protest agenda was the cost of the war. Withdraw from DRC, everybody said, and everything could be managed back to economic prosperity. It was not the land invasions of 2000 that marked the turn of an era for Mugabe. Economically, the turn came with the cost of the pensions for the veterans and the war. Everyone wanted Mugabe to change his policies but, in 1998, the agenda was not that Mugabe should step down. That agenda appeared in 1999, and the causes were as much to do with worsening economic times as political idealism. That came too but, by itself, would have not gathered the support it did.

Mugabe is a wise and wily politician. He set about a twin-track. He secured the support of his Generals – who had in any case been liberation colleagues. And he promised constitutional reform. Unfortunately what he promised also entailed greater power for the President. So that the first response of civil society was to campaign, not against Robert Mugabe as President, but that any president should have fewer powers. It was for a system of greater checks and balances. For more centres of power. The civil society groups coalesced as the National Constitutional Assembly (NCA), and one of its members was the trade union movement led by Morgan Tsvangirai.[4] What Mugabe did was to buy time with a call for debate on what constitutional reform meant. The longer the debate, the better it suited Mugabe. So that Tsvangirai, impatient by nature – impulsive if unchecked – decided to cut the Gordian knot in a way that, even now, rankles with members of the NCA. In 1999 he formed the Movement for Democratic Change (MDC). It was a political party, not a non-governmental organisation. It was not a pressure group. It was a challenge. Mugabe, still smarting from having been called into question by the war veterans, decided to meet the MDC head on.

Almost as if it were the final lever that dislodged all the stones in the dam, the sudden huge enthusiasm for the MDC in the cities of

Zimbabwe meant, for the first time, a significant challenge to Mugabe. In response, Mugabe decided to drive his constitutional proposals to the ballot, confident that his huge party machine and long years of voter loyalty would trounce the clumsy unorganised party that had suddenly appeared.

The difficulties that, even now, large parts of the NCA have with Tsvangirai lie in the belief that civil society at that time could have delivered more reform than a political party. It would have engendered greater political maturity, and discussion would have created a more mature polity. The polity came first. Without that, political parties were elite vehicles. But Tsvangirai reasoned that change had to come sooner rather than later, and the enthusiasm that accompanied the MDC's creation seemed to justify his move. The referendum on constitutional change was set for 12–13 February 2000. Against almost all expectations, Mugabe lost. The MDC, overjoyed at its success, scented blood. It was going to overpower Mugabe and ZANU-PF in the elections of 24–25 June that year. Suddenly the name of the game was Mugabe, and the old man was the quarry.

His reaction was to call in Hitler Hunzvi and the war veterans. He would show the MDC upstarts what true liberation meant. And, even if his days were numbered – in June or later – Mugabe was going to make his dreams of complete nationalisation of the land a reality. Even if it was the last thing he did. Even if it meant bringing his country to its knees. The scale of his enterprise was enormous, and even he did not grasp where it would lead. As February came to an end, thousands of war veterans and those who called themselves war veterans began to invade white farms.

Mugabe had always wanted the land.[5] The Kissinger plan of the 1970s would have bought him the land. Carrington, in 1979, sidestepped the issue of land. Tony Blair in 1997 refused to contemplate helping purchase the land. No one could say Mugabe never asked for help. He did, and was greatly offended, not only by Blair's outright refusal, but by what he saw as his air of arrogant superiority in refusing. Blair seemed like a colonial headmaster. It touched a nerve. Even now, Europeans fail to grasp just how raw remain the wounds of colonialism and racism. But Mugabe, in a rare insight into his private thoughts in 2005, confessed to an African magazine that even he still felt the slights he had endured as a youth. 'Memories do pile up, but the most remote ones, especially those which saw us suffer and the times when we were under bondage, under colonial rule, those can never fade away, they remain forever.'[6]

In 1992, as Mandela and the ANC were negotiating majority rule, drought swept much of Southern Africa. In Zimbabwe, the situation was dire. Still mourning the death of his first wife, Mugabe reviewed the figures. Since independence his government had purchased 3.3 million hectares of land. Even so, in 1992, 4,500 mostly white farmers privately owned 11.5 million hectares. This was one third of the arable country. Seven million black peasants lived on 16.4 million communal hectares. The imbalance was striking. It was the next set of figures that infuriated Mugabe. Maize was the staple food of the black majority. Responding to the needs of the drought, the peasant farms and the farms the government had purchased sent 31,000 tons of maize to the Grain Marketing Board, but the white commercial farms, despite the amount of land they covered, sent only 32,000 tons.

To be fair to the commercial farms, such maize as they produced was needed locally by their black workers. And they weren't in the business of growing maize: they were export producers of vegetables and luxury foodstuffs for the international market. As such, they were the economic backbone of the country. But the impression from the raw figures was that land was not being used to feed the people. In most years, Zimbabwe produced enough maize to feed everyone, with much left over to export to surrounding countries. But in this drought year it seemed to Mugabe that it was time to complete his long-delayed project to nationalise and redistribute the land. Even so, the 1992 Land Acquisition Act proposed to purchase – not seize – just 5.5 million hectares from the white farmers.

It never happened. The then Commonwealth Secretary-General, Emeka Anyaoku, will claim in private conversation that he dissuaded

Mugabe from proceeding in order not to jeopardise the talks Mandela was conducting in South Africa. The last thing the ANC needed was white alarm over dispossession of land. In reality, the white farmers mustered a huge international lobby. It was so successful that the World Bank and IMF advised Mugabe that, in the difficult economic times then being navigated, largely successfully by Zimbabwe, it was unwise to take the huge economic risk of a drop in commercial productivity and incur the huge economic cost of compensation. But if the international donor community had then decided to help fund the purchase of land, there would have been none of the turmoil that began in 2000. With his back to the wall politically after the loss of the 2000 referendum, Mugabe decided to complete his liberation dream. As for the impending elections in June, he would bludgeon his way to victory in them. He would not underestimate the MDC again.

But those who subscribe to Emeka Anyaoku's account say that Thabo Mbeki and the ANC knew they owed Robert Mugabe a debt for his drawing back in 1992.[7] So that, as the consequences of seizure began, as economic meltdown and political violence began, they stood by him. As we shall see, it was more complex than that.

To say, as Robert Mugabe did, that the liberation struggle had been about land, is to be both truthful and to cheapen other reasons that drove young men and women to fight. In the early 1980s, when I was teaching in Lusaka, there were Zimbabwean students who were youthful veterans of the war. One very beautiful woman sported a bullet wound: the bullet had entered her abdomen and exited through her back. She recounted her story of how, one day at her high school, every student just stood up at his or her desk, walked out, and kept on walking to the Mozambican border, and signed up. She featured on election posters 27 years later, standing for Robert Mugabe in the 2008 elections. Then the Mugabe slogan was to preserve the land that had been seized as the key part of the victory won in 1980. In 1981 her reasons were to do with human justice and dignity. During the 1980 ceasefire there were many young guerrillas who also spoke of human justice and dignity, and of freedom and equality. By 2008 Mugabe's message had morphed into freedom from the British – in case they came back to reclaim the land. He didn't talk of freedom from his rule and the corrupt domination of his party. He didn't talk about freedom as a quality.

Mugabe himself had never been a farmer. Nor had his father, who deserted the family when Mugabe was still young. The youngster was a bookworm, a student of Jesuits, someone who studied Latin. He was always an intellectual. He has never ploughed a field in his life. At Lancaster House he pleaded and argued with Carrington to have the land issue placed on the agenda, but Carrington refused. In some way it had become important to him. It was a symbol. What had to be done with it was less important than the idea of land. The ownership of land was a romance.[8] It was metaphysical. Dirt and dams were never of much interest to Robert Mugabe.

When the farm invasions began I watched the news footage obsessively. It was brazen – but more gradual than at first sight. Later on, when the invasions had spread west to the two Matabeleland provinces, I saw a purported veteran haranguing his colleagues from a soapbox. I recognised him as the street kid who cleaned the motley fleet of cars I had assembled for the Commonwealth Observer Group in 1980. Not quite a veteran, I thought; although the guerrillas did use children as *mujibas*, runners, messengers and spies. We ourselves had been eavesdropped and observed.

There was a core of actual veterans in the farm invaders, but many were recruited from the urban streets and treated the invasions as both employment and a 'striking back' against those who were better off, and white. Few in the early days knew anything about farming or had actual intentions to farm.

But the invasions took time to spread.[9] They began, without any warning, in the last few days of February 2000 – 20 years almost to the day of the independence elections in 1980. But they were confined to farms within commuting distance of Harare. The invading 'veterans' needed lines of supply and, at the beginning, often went home to Harare at night. It was clear that the government party, ZANU-PF, was supplying the transport and logistics. But it was also clear that the party was not internally coordinated or briefed on what was happening. Ministers and police chiefs promised, quite sincerely, that the law-breakers would be removed. Indeed, there are two open questions about it all. Firstly, whether or not Mugabe had intended the invasions to be nothing more than huge political theatre, stopping after a key number of invasions, but a large enough number to persuade the British to reconsider putting money on the table for nationalisation. Secondly, the extent to which Hitler Hunzvi either masterminded the invasions or, after ZANU-PF had started them, unilaterally expanded their scope and raced ahead – leaving politicians in his wake, struggling to keep up. Either way, the invasions gathered rapid momentum. They massaged a nerve that had been genuinely sore. Many, particularly the 'chattering classes' in the cities, regretted the lawlessness of the action, attributing it to Mugabe's expanding sense of being above restraint; but agreed that nationalisation was overdue. As for Mugabe, whether he had intended a grand but limited show of force, or whether he had to race to keep up with Hunzvi, he soon found himself riding the tiger: getting on top of events by encouraging them and then directing them. He wasn't going to let Hunzvi show him up twice.

It is difficult to judge whose was the shrillest rhetoric in those days: Mugabe's or Hunzvi's, or the 'ethical foreign policy' that Tony Blair's ministers – Robin Cook and Peter Hain – screamed in the direction of Mugabe. Aha, was Mugabe's response, you see they are just screaming for their 'kith and kin'; all the British want is white ownership of the land. In Zimbabwe, even those who objected to the invasions found little help in the British denunciations.

And even those who knew the invasions were wrong often found it hard to muster sympathy for the white farmers as a group. Many of the farmers had become exemplary citizens of Zimbabwe, treated their employees well and had learnt the local language and customs. Enough, however, behaved like Boers.[10] Perhaps they had some 'educated' black friends whom they would invite around for *brais*. But the arrogant superiority that came from being white and having technical skills was often manifest in the assumption that this was enough to justify having neither good manners nor empathy. People who would have made it in not a single European country lorded it over their servants and workers from the dining rooms of their ranch houses and swimming pools, making a fetish of demonstrating their 'origins' by ostentatiously dressing for dinner and arranging the cutlery just so. The invaders, true veterans or thugs, often behaved with astonishing meaness and brutality. But they did not always behave thoughtlessly. This period was not an atrocity. It was to unfold, however, like a Greek tragedy.

The character in a Greek play who overreaches himself – driven by hubris – convinced that the gods are with him or that the gods will not halt his destiny; the one who drives onwards to certain humiliation, but who struggles every inch of the way: historians will look back and say that Robert Mugabe was such a character. Along the way, he ruined his country and the lives of a huge number of his citizens.[11] In modern terms, he was someone who tried to fulfil history, convinced that the historical destination of Zimbabwe was recovery of ownership. But it was a regressive history. Ownership, as it once was. Before Rhodes. Not ownership for the sake of what will be. No one around him argued that the productivity of Zimbabwe could not bear the disruptions of land invasions and seizures. Particularly if land was seized by veterans and allocated to peasants who knew nothing of what land had to mean for Zimbabwe's economic place in the world. What was seized was an entire agro-industrial sector. It may have been the land of spirits and ancestors,[12] but it was also land that had been fertilised, irrigated and intensely cultivated, responding to the tobacco wholesalers and supermarkets of the world. It was land farmed on a macro-scale. Smallholdings were not the backbone of the economy. Mass made Zimbabwe. Against this mass Robert Mugabe pitted his revolutionary spirit. His advisers said that it was his 'Mao moment', his Cultural

Revolution. But that too had ended in catastrophe. The result in China was that the successors of Mao had to become more capitalist than at any other time in Chinese history. After the degeneration of Zimbabwe, with the key productive sector left in disarray, its regrowth will have to be like this – with huge variations in success and income. It will never be a homogeneous middle-class land again, but a stratified country with unbridgeable gulfs between elites and subsistence citizens – who may reclaim their political rights but not their prospects. The Mugabe experiment will have disinherited them.

But first, the laying to rest of some misconceptions and plain lies – told by more than one side. Mugabe blamed two things for the failure of his experiment: the lack of rain for successive years, and Western sanctions led by the British. The rains were indeed poor, or untimely, but what caused the failure of crops was the disrepair of dams, left without upkeep by new occupiers who lacked dam-maintenance skills or funds. In normal times these would have compensated for poor rainfall. The sanctions were targeted at the international lives of the political elite: they could not travel to many countries and an effort (largely unsuccessful) was made to track down and freeze their assets. The West argued that these were to punish the guilty, and could not have impoverished the mass of Zimbabweans. But along with the sanctions came major suspensions of aid, standby facilities, budget support programmes and investment. These were not described as sanctions, but Zimbabwe became an economic no-go zone. Liquidity dried up because Zimbabwe was squeezed out of the global movement of mass capital. These external factors helped degenerate Zimbabwe almost as much as the internal removal of agricultural productivity. All countries in today's world function on a mixture of such external and internal factors. The West knew this was also the case in Zimbabwe. So the blunt instruments used against Robert Mugabe also impacted on the citizens, and the West hoped the citizens would turn upon Mugabe as a result.

Finally, there is the contention that the land, once seized, was either distributed to uneducated peasants who did not know how to produce more than subsistence crops, or was acquired by hook or by crook by Mugabe's henchmen and henchwomen who, because they had been city dwellers, became gentlemen farmers without any true appreciation of agro-industry. The truth is that, despite huge instances of peasant failure on their new lands, some peasant farms – often those that pooled their resources – were a success.[13] Not enough. But it was not as if the entire programme was a failure. As for elite ownership of very large farms, this is probably important in the long run. When the gentlemen farmers learn what has to be done with their ill-gotten holdings, it will be land mass of the sort they now own that will lead the economic revival of Zimbabwe. But it will be hard going. Markets have closed up. Neighbouring countries like Zambia have seized the high-end tobacco market. They won't give it back. Selling degraded tobacco to the Chinese for death-cigarettes will not do anything for revival. This is looking to the future. The immediate aftermath of the farm invasions was not only economic chaos, but political contestation and democracy by brutality and coercion. And, increasingly, by cheating.

In the days before the economic consequences were felt, the repossession of white lands and the promise of their redistribution to the landless black majority created political momentum for Robert Mugabe. The creation of the 'war veterans' as an invasive and sometimes violent force, and their spread throughout Zimbabwe, meant a militant group at Mugabe's disposal as the 24–25 June elections neared. The ZANU-PF party machine, which had approached the referendum lightly – taking their victory for granted – was told in no uncertain terms to tighten up and return to the old ruthless vote-mobilisation days. The white population was warned not to take the MDC's side – the farm invasions being a symbol of what could happen to all white people. The invading 'veterans' were themselves an odd mixture of true veterans and young urban thugs. Most of the latter had never been on a farm in their lives. But they were the unsuccessful, the losers on the margins of the cities – for whom the middle-class dream had not gone, but was in the distance. Participation in the farm invasions gave them a sense of power and triumph. This meant that Mugabe and ZANU-PF now had a blooded force they could redeploy in the cities. By contrast, the MDC had little party organisation in the countryside, and now they were faced with thuggery in their home bases. In the face of this they came at Mugabe and ZANU-PF with enthusiasm, huge courage, and a ramshackle make-it-up-as-you-go-along campaign, in which many of their activists lost their lives; while the British ministers kept labouring the wrongs of dispossessing white people. Even the MDC looked askance at the British rhetoric. 'Where is the recognition of the hammering we're taking?' seemed to be the plea. Recognition began to appear – in postscripts. From the start the West got everything wrong. In those days, Morgan Tsvangirai was contemptuous of Mugabe, of the British, of the United Nations, of the Commonwealth. However, as an opposition leader, he never departed from his efforts to field huge demonstrations and protests. In many ways, ZANU-PF welcomed these. They were, for a party drawing upon immense governmental forces, including security forces, easy to crush. As long as the MDC tried nothing new, ZANU-PF was content with the extent of Tsvangirai's challenge.

If Tsvangirai viewed a raft of actors, great and small, as impediments – if he was single-minded to a fault – these qualities did not sit well with people he needed to impress. In the early days of the Zimbabwean political crisis of the 2000s, Nigeria's President Olusegun Obasanjo and South Africa's Thabo Mbeki were mediating. Obasanjo had been a frontline general in the Nigerian civil war, he had twice been President, he was a brilliant politician but blunt. He excused his bluntness by saying his military background had made him so. 'I would not have that man as a Junior Minister,' he said of Tsvangirai.[14] Obasanjo soon fell out of the mediatory frame. He didn't much like Mugabe either, and Mugabe certainly came to detest Obasanjo. But Mbeki liked Mugabe. More to the point, he never got over his initial distaste for Tsvangirai. He thought he was limited, unformed, a man with no qualities. None that could run a country anyway. He at least had to be placed under tutelage: a vice-president perhaps; a prime minister one day.

Having said that, it is important to recount that, although Mbeki liked Mugabe and found an intellectual resonance with him, he could also be critical of him. Early in the mediation effort, in 2001, Mbeki penned an extraordinary 29-page letter to Mugabe. This letter only reached the public eye in 2008.[15] A version of it was published in full that year.[16] The published version differs in some minor aspects from the original,[17] but the sentiments in both are the same. In some senses it is a document carefully crafted in revolutionary language – a rhetorical language almost designed to assuage ideological affiliations. ZANU-PF, for instance, is described as 'the party of revolution'. But the document makes a number of telling points within this rhetoric:

1. 'To resort to anti-imperialist rhetoric will not solve the problems of Zimbabwe but may compound them.' Mbeki questioned the wisdom of a quarrel with Britain.
2. ZANU-PF was becoming 'an opponent of the democratic institutions of governance and democratic processes', and there was now a 'clear alienation of the masses from the system of governance'.
3. The war veterans employed to seize Zimbabwean farms had been taken over by 'lumpenproletariat' – revolutionary riff-raff without class values.
4. Zimbabwe cannot afford isolation, nor distance from the IMF.

Mugabe never answered Mbeki's letter. There is no information to the effect that he even bothered to read it. Mandy Rossouw, an investigative journalist, argued that the document 'appears to clear Mbeki of the charge of being a covert admirer of Mugabe's dictatorial regime' – but this is a misjudgement. It clears Mbeki of being an *uncritical* admirer of Mugabe's regime. But he is still an admirer. More to the point, the key impulse of the letter is to warn against the MDC's rise. Mbeki warns Mugabe that the results of his actions will only strengthen the MDC and, as this happens, ZANU-PF as a party will 'begin to atrophy and to wither away as representatives of the popular will'. The thrust of Mbeki's long letter is to criticise the excesses of Mugabe in order to restore Mugabe and his party to the right path. It is almost like a pastoral letter from a church leader to a wayward member of the congregation. The right path is government as a revolutionary party – even if one that must pragmatically woo the IMF, seek no quarrel with Britain and the West, and be democratic in a way that bestows no automatic rights upon the party as revolutionary vanguard. It is a letter that is therefore also contradictory: simultaneously revolutionary in its rhetoric, pastoral in its reaching out to a wayward sheep, democratic in its concerns for governance, but determined that the opposition party should not win. Armed with these concerns, Mbeki set about his mediation in the Zimbabwean crisis. Perhaps it could be said that Mbeki did not only like Mugabe, he *cared* for him.

CHAPTER 6

HOW MORGAN TSVANGIRAI FORMED HIMSELF

Against the forces unleashed by Robert Mugabe was the new opposition party led by Morgan Tsvangirai. A blunt-talking former trade union leader, he was extremely popular among the disaffected of Zimbabwe, but he cut a consistently lacklustre figure in his international diplomatic efforts – especially with African leaders outside Zimbabwe. They thought he lacked consistency and, apart from his brave stand on behalf of political principles, did not have a coherent policy and operational sense of government. They also thought, especially alongside the cerebral Mugabe, that he was simply unintelligent. This was especially felt by the perhaps even more cerebral Thabo Mbeki – who, as the Zimbabwean crisis developed on the doorstep of South Africa, and as Zimbabwean economic refugees poured into his country, threatening the ANC's dream of an economically prosperous South Africa, entered the mediation of the crisis. For Mbeki, in light of the mistakes that Tsvangirai made – including a purported plot to assassinate Mugabe – the best that could be done would be to create for Tsvangirai some sort of senior understudy role in Mugabe's government. But Tsvangirai, despite rashness and inconsistency, was not the unintelligent man his critics took him for.

He was widely read and deeply interested in a range of intellectual and policy issues.

The first three Zimbabwean elections of the 2000s form a testimony to how Robert Mugabe and ZANU-PF approached the question of validation. For them, especially for Mugabe, validation was important. It was an endorsement of their vision and the historical struggle that underlay that vision. It was a generation seeking to use the past as a means to bypass the consequences of its present policies, looking forward to a future when the vision of nationalisation would be completed. How validation was got was less important than the fact that it was got. The means justified the end every time.

The elections of the 2000s, however, featured a strong opposition leader. The formation of Morgan Tsvangirai is often summarised only by reference to his trade union days, and his thoughtfulness and reflectiveness are given little consideration. Tsvangirai, unlike Nelson Mandela and Robert Mugabe, never went to Fort Hare University College; unlike Robert Mugabe and Thabo Mbeki, never took a Master's degree – or a degree of any sort; unlike Thabo Mbeki, never read Afro-American poetry, or poetry at all; unlike Robert Mugabe, did not look down on other intellectuals, but excoriated them for their ineffectualness and their penchant for pronouncing on reform from book-lined mansions; unlike Thabo Mbeki, never received any military training and, unlike Robert Mugabe, never had a guerrilla army under his control; never negotiated an end to Apartheid, the independence of a country, or the end to war in Mozambique; unlike Nelson Mandela, Robert Mugabe and Jacob Zuma, never spent long years in prison; unlike Thabo Mbeki, Robert Mugabe and Jacob Zuma, did not spend years in exile. He was a trade union boss as rough as a rock – and as hard. He was also younger. For many reasons the old men were vexed by him.

Of all the men he admired, Nelson Mandela was foremost. Books on Mandela lined Tsvangirai's study shelves. This study was in a small annexe to his house in Avondale. The desk faced the front door so that it always stood between Tsvangirai and his visitors. The books stood behind him. The room was small, the desk was large and the chairs on either side of the desk were brown leather. The house was surrounded by a high wall and, just beside the wall, was a huge tree that shed pollen like a canopy over the house. It gave Tsvangirai hay fever – but he loved the tree and wouldn't cut it down. At his house he was less strident than in his party headquarters. And love of political biographies was clearly his principal intellectual interest. I used to wonder, as he sat there, how much of which figure from what book he could use as a model for all he was going through. But it was Mandela – for his graciousness and dignity and forgiveness, he said. Tsvangirai already had much to forgive Robert Mugabe, and more to come. In time, he came to loathe him; but the feeling was mutual. During the fraught power-sharing negotiations of 2008–9 it was difficult to decipher who loathed whom more.

Morgan Tsvangirai was born in 1952. As a young man he idolised Robert Mugabe. The liberation hero, as he was painted, and the successful new leader of a bold young Zimbabwe, he caught the imagination and admiration of an entire generation. Tsvangirai did not fight in the liberation struggle but, in the 1980s, as Robert Mugabe exercised his new presidency, he began his rise in the trade union movement. He became Vice-President of the Associated Mine Workers' Union and, from 1988 to 2000, was Secretary-General of the Zimbabwe Congress of Trade Unions. That much was an overlap, with gaps, with Thabo Mbeki. Mbeki had never been a miner but performed the gumboot dance. Tsvangirai really had been a miner but was not as good a dancer. If he came to loathe Robert Mugabe, Tsvangirai came to view Mbeki, for a protracted period, as a cheat.

But even before he met Mbeki, before Mbeki became President of South Africa, Tsvangirai had earned the wrath of Mugabe. In 1996 he disputed Mugabe's economic structural adjustment programmes – implemented with IMF encouragement – because they impacted badly on his trade union members. In December 1997 ZANU-PF thugs beat him and tried to throw him out of a skyscraper window. The trade union movement in South Africa took note.

But Tsvangirai was not content to stay a man without education. He read voraciously. Political biographies were his favourites but along the way, in an unstructured and undisciplined manner, he acquired more intellectual knowledge than Mugabe and Mbeki ever gave him credit for. But it had to be drawn out of him. In July 2004 I visited Zimbabwe and spent many hours trying to draw it out of him. The result was a samizdat book which was circulated as an underground document on behalf of the MDC at the 2005 elections.[1] The statements by Tsvangirai that follow draw mainly upon the interviews for that book, with some from an earlier interview. In July 2004, Tsvangirai was on trial for treason and awaiting a verdict – which could have been a capital verdict. His mother had come in from the countryside to support him, and she and his wife would sit – as in the village – on the ground outside the house, legs stretched and leaning against the walls. I remember that scene for, shortly after Tsvangirai entered a power-sharing government with Mugabe in 2009, his wife died in a car accident. But with his wife and mother in the background those years before, Tsvangirai was incredibly calm. Ever since the formation of the MDC Tsvangirai had been hounded by Mugabe's people. The treason charges were only the latest in a line. The lawyer who had defended Mandela would come up from South Africa to defend Tsvangirai. In a way, there was a symbolism there. It linked Tsvangirai with his hero, being defended by the same man, and being tried for treason.

It was an obdurate process, both of prosecution as persecution, and defence. The chief objective, on the part of ZANU-PF, was psychological. In a way, the process was a charade; almost a protocol in which both sides knew their parts. In another way, it was deadly serious – in that Tsvangirai never knew when ZANU-PF intended to move from game to actuality. He was kept hanging in suspense wondering if, at the end of it all, he might be hanging on an executioner's rope. The objective was to put him under stress. To make him crack. The secondary objective was simply to have an excuse to confiscate his passport and thereby curtail his international travels. It was hoped this would reduce his influence and his campaign for support from Western capitals and, above all, the funds that sympathetic governments could provide his party in the name of support for democracy. The combined objectives were to reduce his scope and reduce the man. In a way, it is easier to be in prison knowing you will die than to be outside – waiting in case they take you to prison to die. On this occasion the family thought the game might be over, so the mother had come in to be with her son. It was a touching but almost flimsy protection in the face of the state. Flimsy like the makeshift armour with which Tsvangirai's people had lined the cab of his red van. The first time I grabbed a ride in this the driver saw me looking aghast at the armour. It would have just stopped a low-calibre pistol bullet. 'Better than nothing,' he said nonchalantly. Tsvangirai's critics, echoing Mugabe's conceit as an intellectual, would say that Tsvangirai had almost nothing by way of thought. I came to understand that this was wrong. It was not disciplined thought. But there was a lot of thought.

The thought was least in the field of agriculture, of agronomy and the nature of agribusiness. This he shared with the ideologues and shakers of ZANU-PF. Being middle-class in Zimbabwe, whether by birth or achievement, seems to induce almost total ignorance of what agriculturally based development actually means. Both great political parties, ZANU-PF and the MDC, are urban formations. ZANU-PF may have huge rural strongholds, but its epicentre of thought and motivation is urban. Tsvangirai was a trade union leader. He had a much more manual background than Mugabe, but he had never ploughed a field either. He kept telling me that the MDC was bringing on board the best agronomic brains – but agriculture was always far down the list of manifesto concerns.

Where he was far more convincing was his concern for the effects of HIV/AIDS. The epidemic had been largely ignored and, until the twenty-first century, officially denied by the Mugabe regime. Its incidence was low, according to the government, and efforts to suggest otherwise were simply a neo-colonial, white supremacist plot to paint Africans as promiscuous, undignified, dirty and deserving of a slow death. On that and a whole range of social issues and issues of political morality there was stark clear blue water between Tsvangirai and the Mugabe regime.

I had wanted to test him, however, on his views of international involvement in the Zimbabwe crisis. When I had first met Tsvangirai in 2000 he had excoriated both Don McKinnon, then the Commonwealth Secretary-General, and Kofi Annan, the UN Secretary-General. The root of this dissatisfaction was the lack, on the part of both men, of a magic wand. All they had were declarations, 'bits of paper' according to Tsvangirai, and the slow-motion plod of step-by-step diplomacy.[2] Four years later he was more accommodating. His ire was now reserved chiefly for the African Union and Southern African Development Community, both of whom – with a single exception with which he was satisfied (a Mauritian criticism of the lack of governmental change in Zimbabwe) – had been reticent to condemn Mugabe.

MDC diplomacy has always been 'primitive'. If not Tsvangirai, then a line of other international spokespersons have lectured the international community rather than negotiated with it. But purity of motive, no matter how desirable, cuts little ice in the constraints imposed by international law and the restraints imposed by caution, politesse and sectional interests. The dominoes have to line up and not be toppled by a man with a careless mouth. Tsvangirai never lost his style of negotiating with his moral face forward – even if this face was often contradictory. For in the maze of choices advanced during complex negotiations a moral stance on one issue will compromise a moral stance on another. But, more importantly, he never lost his essential naïvety about the limits of diplomacy. Long after our series of interviews in 2004 was over, and as the country lurched through the elections of 2008 and the vexed 'settlement' of 2009 (all described later in this book) he was sure that US pressure on Mugabe and South Africa would finally ensure he became the rightful ruler of Zimbabwe. In the protracted negotiations he would drive the South African mediators to despair, maintaining a position he was sure would be somehow forced through by the US – and changing his position when its shortcomings were pointed out by the US. But, even for the US, the need for a friendly South Africa was far more important than the need for a democratic Zimbabwe. The Americans were only ever going to press Thabo Mbeki so far. For Tsvangirai, diplomacy was Zimbabwe-centric. He never gained a view of international relations.

But he gained a view of Mbeki, and it was this I wanted to discuss with him. In particular, I wanted to go over Mbeki's essay which examined the Kenyan novelist and playwright, Ngugi wa Thiong'o, and his book *Decolonising the Mind*.[3] Tsvangirai knew of the book, though he had not read it. In fact, the book is more 'known' than read – so Tsvangirai was being honest here. But reports and 'knowledge' of the book have infiltrated and helped shape a very great deal of African debate on what it means to be African. And how this distinguishes the African, African thought, and African action to defend African values from those of the West. Ngugi, as received, is a first-line defence against having to be Western. *Decolonising the Mind* establishes, in the minds of its protagonists, the contemporary *heroic* intellectual *and* political African.

Tsvangirai was having none of that. His view was immediately practical. 'This is a very narrow concept. I mean, it is once again . . . it is trying to say that in an age of globalisation the African alone must go back to the basic African concept. And yet the world is not going to wait for the African. It is the African who must catch up. To me, that is the challenge – the African must catch up. There are new influences of technology, information, so many other influences, and the African simply cannot exclude himself from that.'[4] In fact, Mbeki certainly meant that the African had to 'catch up', but on his own terms – not those imposed from the outside. The problems come in Mbeki's conflation of Ngugi's terms for catching up with a defence of Mugabe's project of going back. Mugabe, who had never expected such degeneration, would say that it smoothed a foundation for regeneration. A Zimbabwean Ground Zero. A Year Zero. Tsvangirai would say that only an intellectual who did not live in the real world could think and act like that. Tsvangirai was a moderniser. He wanted the future immediately.

'My whole philosophy is about the future. And the future cannot continue to harp on about the past. We learn from it. I think there are lessons, there are mistakes we have made, but I think that any leader must be able to define the future in terms of the modern challenges. So I see myself more as somebody who is trying to put the African in a more credible light, rather than an African who is always complaining about the past. I think it's time to move on.'[5] There are several strands to this statement. The first is a genuine commitment to modernisation and entering the global world, whether on immediately equal terms or not. The second is a critique of Mugabe as harping on about the past and shirking the challenges of the future. But the third, Mugabe would himself reply, about putting the African 'in a more credible light', harks back to a white Zimbabwe – to which Tsvangirai was still responding. He was still trying to impress the white master, Mugabe would say. Still striving for the pat on the head. You're slow, but you're becoming credible.

One of the incentives to becoming academically endoctored, to wear flash suits, to rub shoulders with the political elite in expensive bars, was to create a distance between the new highly educated black person and the uncouth white farmer – who would be rich enough to drink in those bars but, even so, would stride in wearing shorts and flashing hairy legs. The contrast, the gap, allowed a reverse condescension. It was fake – while those rough white farmers owned almost all the arable land. But it was an intellectual posture which Tsvangirai deplored. He had, while still a trade union leader, published an article in which he lambasted intellectuals for 'lecturing workers and peasants through journals published from their mansions in low-density [rich] suburbs'.[6] In a way, he now lived in exactly that style: the book-lined study, the detached house with extensive gardens and tall trees, the high surrounding wall. But Tsvangirai would always claim he maintained his links with workers and peasants and was one with them. At the same time he was anxious, though largely unable, to close the gap between himself and the African thinkers and Mbekis of the world. He pointed out that there were many intellectuals in his MDC party. Although later the MDC would split and the best minds desert Tsvangirai, the split was not over how intellectual or otherwise Tsvangirai was, but about the lack of discipline in his policy formation – and this did hark back to the lack of a disciplined education. On one point, however, Tsvangirai was consistent to the point of severe discipline. It was his fundamental critique of the African intellectual – of Mugabe and Mbeki and all their thoughtful followers. The Tsvangirai critique agreed that there should be African solutions to African problems. But these solutions could not be predicated on blaming others. An entire intellectual class had done nothing else but articulate blame. 'We have not created the institutions that would be basic in taking this continent forward. We are still in the blame game, still in a denial stage, instead of accepting that it is we who have yet to deal with even the primary issues. We are still grappling others and trying to blame other people, instead of looking at ourselves and saying "what have we done wrong?" And the ones who have performed the greatest disservice, by not asking that, are the intellectuals.'[7]

Although the later split in the MDC was not an intellectuals vs Tsvangirai fallout, the Tsvangirai posture was certainly a contributing factor in the refusal of dissident ZANU-PF elements – largely clustered around the ruling party's intellectual and technocratic wing, and later led by Simba Makoni – to contemplate joining Tsvangirai's MDC. They talked instead of creating a 'third force', equidistant from both the MDC and ZANU-PF. In fact, these were the very same people Tsvangirai meant in his article on intellectuals lecturing peasants and workers from their mansions. Not only did Tsvangirai not wish to form an alliance with any 'third force', he had moved to create the MDC in the first place precisely because he saw no future in either mainstream ZANU-PF or the postures of its anxious intellectuals – who wanted all things simultaneously. They wanted to establish their critiques on blame while harvesting the benefits of Western education and lifestyles. They wanted the ZANU-PF nationalist and Afrocentric ideology, but without the extremist and unplanned manoeuvres that the party embarked upon from 2000 onwards. They wanted not so much to be a 'third force' as to be ZANU-PF-lite. Tsvangirai saw them as self-absorbed and, when the redistribution of seized farms began, the selfsame internal critics of the party lined up to receive their share of the plundered hectares. And those who were not with the 'third force' became the intellectually elegant apologists for that plunder.[8] The argument was that nationalisation was just and overdue. It never engaged with whether it was, at that moment in time, economically and agriculturally justified; nor whether the abruptness of the human cost was morally justified. The intellectuals dwelt in grandly empty landscapes and Tsvangirai never fully overcame his early contempt for them. But this did not make him an easy person with whom Thabo Mbeki could negotiate.

And there was one more major fly in the ointment for Mbeki. On the occasion when Tsvangirai was exonerated by the courts, found not guilty of treason, his international admirers assumed the charges had been trumped up in the first place. Indeed, to a large extent, the charges had been brought because ZANU-PF had set up a 'sting' for Tsvangirai – one which Tsvangirai fell for hook, line and sinker. Naïve to the point of gullible. The evidence thus gained was not enough to overcome reason-able doubt, but Mbeki would sit across the table from Tsvangirai and wonder what sort of man wanted to be the next President of Zimbabwe. The treason charges related to a plot by Tsvangirai to assassinate Mugabe.

The naivety and gullibility began early – when Tsvangirai and the MDC fell in with an international consultant of mixed reputation. The denouement was meant to be at the time of my interviews with him, but the verdict was postponed, and the psychology of the waiting game continued. After our last conversation Tsvangirai and I walked in his garden. We stopped under his hay-fever tree and I made to sit on a bench. He didn't stop me but, before I completed the process of sitting, he said very quietly, 'That is the bench where Ari Ben-Menashe sat.' I immediately stood up. 'He was my guest here.'

Ari Ben-Menashe was a 'fixer'. If he couldn't do it, he knew people who could. An Israeli, it was rumoured he had Mossad connections and links with an array of ex-Mossad operatives. He was thought to move in that half-world where shipments of arms could be arranged and private armies hired. Where very good and reliable hit men could be engaged. Whether he did or not, this is what many thought. He was the political consultant who could work 'alternatives'. The MDC never checked him out. He was really working for Mugabe.

The half-world really exists, of course. Precisely because it is a world into which little light is shone, it contains battalions of fraudsters, shysters, chancers and know-nothing dangerous braggarts. It also contains those who earn their living by double-crossing. Not that the firm for which Ben-Menashe worked, Dickens and Madson, based in Canada, was remotely populated by such people. The firm had, however, been implicated in aspects of Africa's war diamond trade: what Hollywood came to call 'blood diamonds'. It was well known that the MDC had been putting out feelers to any who would listen, seeking deserters from Mugabe's cause. These included behind-closed-door overtures to senior army officers. But the bulk of such officers had already been 'purchased' by mining and mineral benefits in Democratic Republic of Congo. It was speculated in Harare that the MDC wanted to be able to make certain officers a counter-offer: blood diamonds in exchange for the loyalty bought by Congolese copper. Ben-Menashe secretly filmed the meetings he conducted with Tsvangirai and the top brass of the MDC. Without warning, on 13 February 2002, a few days before the Commonwealth summit in Brisbane, itself held a few days before the Zimbabwean elections of that year, the film was screened on Australian television – almost certainly skilfully cut and edited – and it showed Tsvangirai saying to Ben-Menashe that Mugabe had to be got rid of. It did not show what Ben-Menashe had said to Tsvangirai to elicit such a statement. But the interpretation that seemed to arise from the film was that an assassination was being contemplated.

It was enough to thwart any agreement to suspend Zimbabwe from Commonwealth membership at the summit. That agreement was to wait upon a post-election judgement on the freeness and fairness of voting – and the troika that was to report their judgement was Australia's John Howard, Nigeria's Olusegun Obasanjo, and Thabo Mbeki. Obasanjo, although later at furious odds with Mugabe, had little time for Tsvangirai: 'I would not have that man as a Junior Minister.' Howard was seen as part of the British push for Zimbabwe's suspension. But Mbeki thought that the British and Tony Blair were being less than helpful in addressing the consequences of Mugabe's actions in Zimbabwe. The British were simply against Mugabe – at whatever cost. The South Africans invariably found themselves paying the cost, with Zimbabweans pouring across their borders, seeking work, seeking food, seeking relief. Some went to other countries, notably Botswana, but South Africa was the overwhelmingly preferred destination. Mbeki saw the film. And he believed that an assassination had been at least discussed, if not planned. It was all incredibly maladroit on the part of Tsvangirai. He had reason to feel cut to the core by Ben-Menashe's sting and betrayal. But he had also been incredibly stupid to trust Ben-Menashe, and even more stupid to say such words in front of someone whom his party had never subjected to any vetting or clearance procedures. The treason charge was almost the least of the consequences. Questions as to Tsvangirai's judgement sprang into the open. And about his integrity – his commitment to democracy without deals and 'accidents' to the other side. Up to then, Mugabe could plausibly say he had hounded Tsvangirai, physically abused him, threatened and frightened him, but never seriously tried to kill him. But perhaps Tsvangirai had tried to kill Mugabe. He probably hadn't: it was probably all hot air and frustration. But it showed that, in 2002, the formation of Morgan Tsvangirai had a long way to go before my long meetings with him in 2004.

His more temperate approach to others – mediators, conditional allies, opponents and outright enemies – had come about for two key reasons. The first was precisely the scorn of those like Obasanjo. The Nigerian President was seen by many as the politician's politician, but he had a track record of considerable accomplishment. He had been a frontline army commander in the Nigerian civil war.[9] He had restored democratic civilian rule to Nigeria.[10] With Australia's Malcolm Fraser, he had co-chaired the Commonwealth Eminent Persons Group that, in 1986, went to South Africa to plead for change from the Apartheid government and, among other things, to plead the release of Nelson Mandela.[11] He had, thereafter, helped spearhead the sanctions campaign against South Africa.[12] He always seemed grumpy, fat and without eloquence. But Obasanjo had credentials. If he scorned you it was for reason. The second was the slow realisation that change in Zimbabwe was going to take longer than Tsvangirai had first hoped. The early Tsvangirai, all naivety and haste, curmudgeonly and abrupt in his judgements, gave way to the need for strategy. When he had first seen footage of Belgrade crowds storming the Serbian Parliament and changing the government in their country, his first thoughts – which were very much thought aloud – were 'why not also in Zimbabwe?' This was partly because the Serbian police and soldiers did not shoot into the crowds and, in many cases, joined in the storming of Parliament. Mugabe still had tight control of the security forces and, although bullets were infrequent, tear gas and beatings were not. Beatings, in custody, could be terrifyingly severe. Slowly, the security forces learnt to beat 'scientifically' on the spot, inflicting exact injuries in the midst of a melee, without the need to size up a person in the privacy of their cells. The security forces, over the years, used a variety of tear gases. They began with North Korean gas, then Israeli gas, then finally a gas made either in Zimbabwe itself or South Africa. There are gradations of gas. Seasoned protesters can tell instantly what grade the police are using against them. They know how long they can stand and fight or whether they had better break and run immediately. The Zimbabweans always used the strongest-level gas. You ran right away, coughing and crying your heart out. Tsvangirai came to realise he could not keep throwing his people at police lines that would not break, but which would break all those who came at them. But, if he came to realise the need for strategy, and the need for a long process, he was not a good strategist.

His closest lieutenants would complain constantly, up to the split in the MDC and even afterwards, that Tsvangirai could not hold a straight course. He was always double-guessing both himself and decisions made in the party executive. Often, it was on the basis of the last person he talked to – and, if that made an impression, even if it flew in the face of a recent party decision, Tsvangirai would double back on both himself and his party. Whether to contest certain elections, or not – the decisions for and against could bounce back and forth until the MDC resembled a ping-pong tournament.

Even so, Tsvangirai gradually became a more restrained leader. He was no longer as rash as he had been. His own rank-and-file followers noticed that urgency had seeped from him and they themselves began to despair of change – despite all their efforts and the peril they had put themselves in. But, apart from all the factors outlined above, Tsvangirai grew more cautious and, to an extent, measured because of one large shadow and one repeated experience. The large shadow was what ZANU-PF with its treason charges had induced: the sense that he might one day have to stand on the hangman's trapdoor. The latter was Tsvangirai's almost entirely unsuccessful efforts at regional diplomacy. Wherever he went he could not, despite all his pleadings, impress the presidents of the surrounding states. They came to see him as a sincere and commited opposition leader. They could not see him as the leader of a government. This is important, in that it takes skill to be judiciously corrupt without breaking the nation. Whatever one thought of some of the regional leaders, all had that skill – although not all were corrupt. All, in short, had what they reckoned was good judgement: where lines were and when; above all, how to cross those lines. What they saw in Tsvangirai was a bull who charged at gates. What his own party executive came to see in him was a man who zigged and zagged. To the outside, he was on too straight a line. To the inside, he was moving on too many contradictory lines. Yet he was the best the country had in terms of leading a stand against Mugabe.[13] But both staunchest enemy and closest ally had fears of what a Tsvangirai government might bring. For them, Tsvangirai had to grow even more. To an extent, as we shall see, he began to do this. He also, at key and tragic moments, reverted to indecision and vacillation.

But it was not all plain sailing for one of his greatest sceptics either. In South Africa, Thabo Mbeki was sailing his ship into stormy waters – making large mistakes, alienating key sections of his own party, and becoming curiously authoritarian in the way he dealt with the ANC. And losing touch with the electorate. In a way he remained fully competent and professional. He was respected but far from universally loved. In fact, for a man who came to power upon the huge legacy left by Mandela, he seemed not only unlovable but somehow unlovely. The aloof man also commited himself to an incredibly idealistic but flawed economic policy. It was idealistic in its vision for Africa in the global economy. It was flawed in its distribution of wealth and benefits to his own people. But beside the grandeur and tragedy of Mbeki's ambitions, the cut and thrust of Zimbabwean politics seemed like those of a vexatious parish. But this parish could do enough damage on its own to compromise key elements of Mbeki's grand vision for a global Africa, and certainly cause huge restlessness among the poor in South Africa. When the great cities of South Africa became the homes of almost three million Zimbabwean economic refugees, fleeing the degeneration of their homeland and seeking economic opportunities in competition with the urban South African poor, great tensions arose and, following on from tension, episodes of violence.

CHAPTER 7

HOW CAN A CAR GO FORWARD WITH TWO DIFFERENT SPEEDS ON ONLY ONE GEAR?

While Zimbabwe slid towards economic ruin, with Robert Mugabe fixated on the importance of land, of ownership of the countryside, Thabo Mbeki set about his own project of economic betterment and greater equality of economic opportunities. He continued what he had begun under Mandela. Unlike Mugabe's rural project, it was a policy set firmly in the cities. It was also firmly set within a global economic context. Local development and economic empowerment could not be at the expense of South Africa's position in the international economy. Economic empowerment took place within a neo-liberal framework, but also within a parallel framework of positive discrimination. In this sense, Mbeki's policies had a curiously American ring to them. They were reminiscent of US positive discrimination measures as a result of the black civil rights movement. Whereas in the US this was particularly visible in terms of educational places for black students at leading universities, in South Africa it was a black preference in special fiscal facilities. The only problem for South Africa was that this type of positive discrimination led to the formation of a privileged black business class, and did not economically empower the mass of the poor black population; and it created new chains of corruption.

The acronym, GEAR, simply lent itself to car jokes, and in fact was chosen precisely to express the idea of getting into gear, of going forward – momentum, progress and, above all, increasingly satisfying points of arrival. It actually meant 'Growth, Employment and Redistribution' and was launched as a policy in June 1996.[1] Though still Deputy President, it was Thabo Mbeki who drove the policy forward – even though its first public champion was the finance minister, Trevor Manuel. But the non-negotiable nature of Manuel's announcement of GEAR in his budget speech had Mbeki's determination stamped all over it. A huge section of the ANC was affronted by what it heard and even those members who did not understand the economics involved were stung by the idea that, on the key question of growth and redistribution, there was to be neither consultation nor negotiation. It was the end of consensus already – in an organisation which had, rightly or mythically, prided itself on discussion, compromise and buy-in of all important players. In retrospect, at a stroke Mbeki began the creation of two ANCs and, more importantly, he began the replacement of a South Africa split between black and white with one split between rich and poor, between the optimistic and those praying for take-off, between those who lived in pepper-potted suburbs with tall trees, high walls and guards – and those who tried to live in the grinding poverty of the dusty townships. But GEAR was meant to lift exactly this latter group out of the dust. It just had to be done by creating wealth first. The problem came when that wealth was not created or, where it was, not redistributed.

Mbeki had two intentions in what was an ambitious but quite orthodox economic model. The first was certainly to develop South Africa. He was very sincere about that. The second was to make a key point to the international community – particularly the West: that a part of Africa could grow, could successfully implement a neo-liberal economy, could generate both wealth and sufficient surplus to finance a huge community programme, create enough growth to ensure a self-perpetuation of investment and employment, and pull it all off without the time-honoured need to beg from the West. GEAR was to be the cornerstone of his African Renaissance. From this great example, the entire continent would begin its self-transformation. Africa would create a vision of a day to come when it would challenge the West and, in turn, be emulated by it. GEAR was Mbeki's economic poetry.

To be fair to Mbeki, and to the steady course which Manuel was intent on steering amidst choppy international waters, GEAR accorded with the prevailing Western orthodoxy of the time.[2] In Britain, a New Labour government was set to become as neo-liberal as any of its Conservative predecessors – and more technocratically so. Investment was generated by deregulation. Capital was created by risk. Momentum would create more momentum. The corporation became the king of cars. The poor would be dragged along and empowered in its wake. It wasn't the old 'trickle down'. Everyone would move forward. It wasn't 'catch up'. There was always going to be a gap. But the faster the car went forward, the faster would be those being towed behind. Those in the car would be more comfortable, but everyone would be further forward at journey's end; and, if the model worked, the journey would never end. One day the poor would be middle-class and the rich would be oligarchs.

What the Mbeki/Manuel vision also did was to create, for the first time, an actual economic strategy. The Mandela years were coming to an end. Mbeki not only was going to seize power, but knew what he wanted to do once he got it. It wasn't going to be the informal consultations, the 'fireside chats' that Mandela conducted with the so-called 'Brenthurst Group': the senior businessmen convened by the hugely influential Oppenheimer family, the owners of De Beers and the economic heirs to Rhodes. In fact, the Oppenheimers had moved a huge distance from Rhodes, and theirs was a very socially conscious commitment to capitalism and its responsibilities. Mandela's own vision of social harmony chimed with theirs and their advice to him was pragmatic; neo-liberal certainly, but not aggressively so. There was never any question, whether under Mandela or Mbeki, or under Ramaphosa, that South Africa would abandon or even significantly ameliorate capitalism. It was a series of questions, however, of how to secure buy-in, to guarantee immediate benefits to the poor, and how to ensure that black 'take-off' involved a large swathe of the black population. Mbeki never abandoned these questions. He tried to address them all. But GEAR ensured he would address them in a certain way and that the drive forward would create not only movement behind, but a lot of contradictions and casualties – and the other policies that followed upon GEAR simply widened the corporate elite, so that it was black and white, and still very much elite. Crossing the gap to join that elite became a major reason for serving the ANC. The hope of preference, or the benefits of patronage – even corruption – were all possible in the intimacy with which, under Mbeki, political and corporate worlds cohabited.

Mandela had tried to avoid these contradictions. The private corporations certainly had their part to play – that was why there was a Brenthurst Group – but it was the state that was to be the main provider for the newly emancipated nation. The trick had been how to restructure, without further trauma, a state that had been brought to the economic brink by Apartheid. For Mandela therefore, the rebuilding of the nation as a cooperative society of equal partners – in short, the distancing of the state as rapidly as possible from both Apartheid and its own traumas – was key to establishing the conditions in which the state could provide for its people. There had to be an environment in which the corporations could function, not just nationally but as international players. What they provided the state, and what the state gleaned from foreign direct investment in the rejuvenated private sector, would be the source of economic benefits for the population. Mbeki's vision, by contrast, was to bring the private sector into direct participation with the project of economic benefit for all. The key contradiction was that, in exchange for licence to behave in a neo-liberal fashion, the corporations had to accept a modest menu of conditions. This meant that it was not a pure neo-liberalism – but it was far more neo-liberal than the ANC left wing, the Congress of South African Trade Unions (COSATU), and the South African Communist Party (SACP) would have wished. It meant that welfare depended directly on the performance of the market and the corporations within the market.

If the market and the corporations failed, the state had either to gerry-mander a response or have no prepared response of its own.[3]

Failure meant a growth rate significantly below the 6 per cent annual economic growth envisaged by GEAR. Throughout the Mbeki presidency growth clung stubbornly to 3 per cent.[4] But, if economic growth meant a growth in the economic capacity of the private sector, and if it was to be this sector that provided in turn increased employ-ment, then 3 per cent meant that most of the poor – expecting new job opportunities – stayed exactly as they were. And it meant the state was constrained in devising any fall-back plan, since its own budgeting was already predicated on current account and balance of payment deficits which it needed to manage. Fall-offs in anticipated state revenue from taxation meant diminished state capacity to act where the corporations and businesses could not. Three per cent growth, against a target of keeping annual inflation below 10 per cent, also meant that the hugely ambitious gross domestic savings target of 21.5 per cent of GDP was unachievable. Everything went instead into the project of budgetary prudence, rather than increased budgetary provision for the poor – on the grounds that prudence and the scenario of a balanceable budget under protracted conditions of fiscal sobriety would increase foreign investor confidence and economic cooperation. As South Africa became more economically sober at home, it sought to implicate itself even more extensively in global capital. Without global confidence in the South African economy, and the consequent investment, nothing was felt to be possible.

Basically what happened during the Mbeki years was that the income of the poorest 40 per cent fell by 20 per cent. COSATU and the government engaged in an argument over whether employment had fallen or risen. Government figures suggested that the number of people seeking work had fallen from 23.3 to 22.5 per cent – although a reduction of less than 1 per cent was hardly the promised land of majority rule and equity – but COSATU figures were that actual unemployment had risen from 36.3 to 37.3 per cent. Either way, with such small percentage point differences, it confirmed that 3 per cent annual growth meant standing still or very close to still. There was also a lot of hustling and pleading at local level, a lot of running fast to stand still. The informal sector grew – hardly what had been anticipated in Africa's most modern economy. And the advent of mass numbers of Zimbabweans – up to three million – also hunting jobs and hustling, meant tensions now had a neighbourhood target. The Zimbabweans, alongside other foreigners, were not 'stealing' jobs that no South African wanted; South Africa was still in a position where almost every job was wanted. And, when no more jobs were available, wanted or not, the foreigners turned to crime. They also competed for accommodation and other services. All of this was in the context of grinding slowness or standstill in terms of amelioration of poor living conditions: the poor still had their homes flooded on the salt flats outside the modern splendour of central Cape Town; the poor could see the lights of the beautiful new stadia for the World Cup, while burning charcoal for light and heat.

But the outcome of GEAR meant that the more consultative state-led 'fireside chat' approach of Mandela would also have been, in the long run, doomed to failure. If the state was to be an active provider, in line with the promises made at liberation – with or without the private sector – it would have had to increase the money supply, accept larger recurrent deficits, race to increase employment faster than inflation, quite possibly engage in artificial job creation that returned no economic benefit except to the employees, and risk COSATU demanding higher wages on the political strength of its increased membership; and all this would have reduced international investor confidence. The Mandela strategy would have needed something like IMF balance-of-payments support. But this would have cast South Africa in exactly the mould of so many other African states, including those in the Southern African region, but also beyond, with the IMF dictating economic strategy in return. Mbeki, his African Renaissance in mind, wanted to avoid that. And, as I have said earlier, neo-liberalism was the international orthodoxy of the day. Liberal political figures like Clinton and Blair were neo-liberal in their economics. Clinton balanced the books. Blair and Brown launched themselves into public/private partnerships in which the private sector became a net beneficiary for its part in providing public goods. That was the way forward.

GEAR was meant to stand beside and help generate the wherewithal for two other programmes. These were RDP (the Reconstruction and Development Programme) and BEE (Black Economic Empowerment), more lately called BBBEE (Broad-Based Black Economic Empowerment).[5] The problem with bees is that they are aerodynamically impossible. They fly despite that. In many ways, getting BEE into GEAR was a contradiction, because it meant launching often immature young companies into major economic enterprises – without experience, training, guarantees or quality-assured results. This was particularly the case when new black-led companies successfully bid for housing contracts, to deliver the mass numbers of accommodation units promised by the RDP. The numbers were slow in being achieved and, certainly in the early days, the new houses could be of very poor quality. A mass of new, often small companies, working in both the formal and informal sectors, for example hiring very low paid Zimbabweans without legal papers to fulfil a government contract, did not always add to the macro-economic growth sought by GEAR. Inefficiencies led to losses as much as profits. And the new companies often provided poor results, resulting in social frustration for people like new home owners, and created social tensions if they employed illegal migrants rather than local people. Attempting to maximise profits while paying the lowest possible wages was not, in itself, the path to equity in the new rainbow land.

But together GEAR, RDP and BBBEE were unsustainable as a coherent combination of strategies.[6] GEAR was a macro-strategy, working at high capitalist levels; RDP was meant to benefit the poorest and was essentially a state-led strategy; and BBBEE was an intersection, whereby RDP could be served and whereby high capitalism could be expanded with new entrants to the business market. The key difference between the original BEE and its successor, BBBEE, was that BEE resulted in low-level entrants to the business market. Small firms and new businesses with low capacities or uncoordinated strategies proliferated. BBBEE continued this, but also began the creation of a black business elite that would integrate with the white business elite. Almost as if to force big business to incorporate aspects of BBBEE into their plans, quotas and targets were set: government would look favourably at those corporations that had achieved x number of black employees or had awarded y number of contracts to recognised Black Empowerment firms. Even if corporations could learn to play a numbers game, what this meant was that the vaunted ideals of a neo-liberal economy, without state-led direction or interference, were being eroded. The market set about incorporating government expectations into its policies and procedures, but in a way that expanded the capacity of neo-liberalism. Black members of senior boards were drawn from those with high ANC backgrounds. The 'pepper-potting' – sprinkling of black grains among white – took place most assiduously at executive level. People with senior ANC backgrounds took advantage of their credentials and pedigrees to secure the capital investment to begin firms, not at a grassroots level, but as direct entrants in the world of high business. The economic rise of former ANC luminaries such as Tokyo Sexwale and Cyril Ramaphosa, after Mbeki had truncated their political ambitions, was startling. They were much in demand in the business world and progressed their business interests with the connections they made – many while still in office. The response of academic commentators was to observe that a new elite class had been created, although it integrated seamlessly with the old.[7] Even those very close to the political process, by blood if not the holding of office, such as Moletsi Mbeki, Thabo Mbeki's brother, declared that the new policies were for 'the enrichment of a mere few'.[8] This was an arch comment, and one seen as slightly ironic – given that Moletsi Mbeki was a highly successful black businessman in his own right, one of a few, even though he did not seek to benefit from what was becoming an ANC gravy train. However, whether people entered the elite by virtue of their ANC connections, or whether they became successful in their own right, critics pointed out that the corporate sector, however enlarged, was concerned to protect its own rights and its own spheres of operation. Economic empowerment had been compromised by the creation of a group of black capitalists. And the new black elite, more tellingly according to one critic, was consumed by its own materialism and indifferent to the plight of the poor.[9] A subtext of this criticism was that white people who were skilled but not quite at the highest economic levels and who felt threatened by the new black elite – who had secured their economic entry, it was felt, by unfair advantage – often left the country, creating a skills and brain drain that the new black entrants to the business world could not fully replace, certainly not in the short term. This was not only an academic criticism but a political one from the ANC's opponents.[10]

As it was, GEAR and BBBEE were not successful enough by themselves to raise South Africa to the economic levels Mbeki had sought, nor did the new firms and enterprises absorb sufficient numbers of the unemployed to assuage political unrest, so the state had to assume in any case a greater responsibility for national development. But it didn't have a macro-strategy to do so. The macro-strategy was GEAR. Under Mbeki, much was done – there is no disputing that – but it was done by erratic increments and, at times, it seemed as if the car was getting into gear haphazardly. The car was stuttering forwards. There were still as many if not slightly more poor people than before, and their poverty was worse – in that escape from it seemed even more distant than before. Even so, the car could be seen to be on some sort of forward move. Foreign direct investment continued to see South Africa as an attractive destination – though not nearly as much as Mbeki and Manuel had hoped – and, in order to induce more, they were prepared to offer concessions to, for example, Chinese textile exporters to South Africa. The hope was that it would help engender other Chinese economic flows to South Africa, even though the gesture ruined a portion of the domestic textile industry. Increasingly, the path forward for South Africa was seen by Mbeki's government as being tied to the macro-international economic currents of the West – with a recognition of China's critical future role, and its current role as leverage which the South Africans could use against the West. What GEAR could not do by itself could perhaps be done by inducing a flow of liquidity from outside South Africa.[11]

That was a key reason for Mbeki's enthusiasm for NEPAD. That, and his ambition to demonstrate that an African Renaissance was possible in things political as well as economic. NEPAD, the 'New Partnership for Africa's Development', as an acronym gave rise to its own jokes. If the car couldn't get into GEAR, then the nation might have to rollerblade its way into the future and would therefore need NEPADs in case it fell over. In a more sombre but coruscating tone, many considered NEPAD to be closely associated with the era of Tony Blair in Britain, when many a problem was addressed by a cleverly calibrated form of gadgeteering that was then advertised as a visionary way forward.[12] Mbeki, however, was very serious about NEPAD – at least in its 'vision', if not always in its operation. And, in this, he was not alone. Mandela had committed himself to democracy and had even used the term 'African Renaissance': 'We know it is a matter of fact that we have it in ourselves as Africans to change all this. We must, in action, say there is no obstacle big enough to stop us bringing about a new African Renaissance.'[13] The Kenyan novelist, Ngugi wa Thiong'o had used the term too, and it derived as much from the Harlem streets of the early twentieth century as it did from Africa. But Mbeki made the term his own. NEPAD allowed him the close company of the Tony Blairs and the other great players of the world. One African president, at least, seemed the equal of the otherwise palpably white leaders of global politics.

NEPAD was simultaneously a complex and a simple concept. It was complex in that it was closely related to other policies such as GEAR. With GEAR most exchange controls were abolished and banks were subject to foreign competition. The idea was to create foreign confidence in the South African economy and to encourage the swift inflow of capital. NEPAD, launched in 2001, was meant to create foreign confidence in African governance – and reward good governance with foreign capital inflows. As interpreted and some would say commandeered by Tony Blair, NEPAD came to equate good governance with

democracy, and democracy was reduced to clean elections. Good electoral behaviour meant that a key box was ticked to qualify for development assistance and access to other financial instruments. No wonder
Robert Mugabe saw Blair as a self-righteous headmaster: hold nice
elections and nice teacher will give you a nice developmental handout.
In Blairite terms, NEPAD was reduced to the simplicity of aid from
the West in exchange for elections in Africa. That was the 'new partnership' – a barely reworked version of the old, in which approval and
benefaction flowed down to the natives as they became more 'civilised'.
The original Mbeki vision was more complex and involved not just
clean elections but peacekeeping and conflict mediation. One of
Mbeki's ministers, Sydney Mufamadi, played a key role in forging the
compromises required for elections to be held in war-torn Democratic
Republic of Congo, and was later deeply involved in the Zimbabwean
mediation. This involved advisory assistance far and wide – the intelligence minister, Ronnie Kasrils, travelled often to advise the
Palestinian Authority – and the formation of an international coalition
of like-minded countries from Africa, Europe and elsewhere that
could rival the United States and its formidable group of allies. It was
meant to be the clean alternative to the greatest power on earth: as
democratic and as peaceful as anything the West could field, and more
moral. South Africa would lead the new coalition. It was incredibly
ambitious. The ultimate aim was for the richer West to have no option
but to interact, above all economically, with a more moral Africa and
its allies. Mbeki trumpeted how South Africa was unique in dismantling the nuclear weapons developed under Apartheid, and even tried
to mediate in the US–Iranian standoff over Iran's nuclear programme.

But the sore point in all of this was the long gap between vision and
reality and, in between, the Blairs of the world in their typically well
meaning but opportunistic and reductionist ways made it into a critique
of Africa for being slow on democracy, and a critique of Thabo Mbeki for
going slow on Robert Mugabe. As for the meltdown in Zimbabwe, that
affected the Mbeki vision in more ways than one. Good governance was
definitely not there, but the economic disintegration of the country meant

that Mbeki's plans for an aggressive and economically performing SADC (Southern African Development Community) that would punch above the individual weights of its members, and negotiate on more equal terms with the EU and NAFTA (the North American Free Trade Agreement countries), was doomed to failure.[14] Mugabe ruined Mbeki's NEPAD in more ways than one. Poor governance and parlous economics meant there was nothing on which the country could stand when facing a judgemental West. And, before the economic meltdown began with the farm invasions of 2000, Zimbabwe was a key part of SADC which South Africa needed in order to portray the grouping as having more economic capacity than was found in South Africa alone. It was to be a renaissance involving a plurality of African countries – and SADC was meant to be the demonstration vehicle. While Mbeki saw Africa in expansive terms, Mugabe adopted the inward vision of a crabbed old man who could no longer look beyond the walls of his own house. But the Mbeki sense of vision also helps to explain why so many of his ministers stayed loyal to him in the dark days to come. They admired his idealism. It's easy to forget – looking at his stilted manners, his patrician almost Brahmin airs, his formal tailoring – that he was also a great idealist.

But he was an idealist with incredible blind spots. An excess of vision can mean a loss of sight. What lies beyond the horizon is imagined better than the dirt at one's feet. Mbeki didn't do much looking down. So that the grandeur of the African Renaissance, the hobnobbing with the global great and powerful, the sense of arrival for someone who was once an exile but now wanted to be a symbol for a continent, meant that the details of everyday poverty and despair never reached him. And, quite apart from the problems caused by BBBEE and the variable results of RDP, there was the problem of the administrative capacity and systems of the civil service inherited from the days of Apartheid.[15]

Even though the composition of the civil service changed, and its size enlarged, its practices and systems were derived from a time when public administration prioritised small groups of people – white people. Suddenly, it was meant to cater for huge new programmes for huge new swathes of population. It didn't reinvent itself, but tried to adapt its old modes of operation to the new requirements. It was never a Third World civil service. It was a civil service for sophisticated villages. And its systems of administration and approval were formula-driven. In the drive to disburse public funds faster and better, it relied on old formulas more and more. A particularly perverse example was the funding of schools.[16] The government couldn't fund schools in their entirety. The community was meant to meet part of the school budgets. But the size of the government contribution was determined by pre-set criteria. If a school was within x metres of a tarred road, it was a school in a 'developed' area, where the community could contribute more and, therefore, the government less. The same applied if the school had a perimeter wall. This was meant to be a luxury, a sign of discretionary capacity after meeting the core costs of education – so the government budgetary allocation went down. But it doesn't take long, even driving around South African cities in the most casual of manners, to find schools in desperately poor neighbourhoods that are situated directly under a motorway flyover – but that's within x metres of a tarred road; or to find schools in crime-infested neighbourhoods that have had to build a high wall to reduce theft – but that, according to the formulas, meant a well-off school. Some of the most deserving cases got least under rigid formulas, and the appeals of headmasters and communities would get lost in the processes of an overburdened civil service. In the Mandela years, spending on the part of public services was slow to grow. By the Mbeki years, prudence had become a hallmark to encourage foreign investment, so public spending did not grow as much as the poor required. But it was in the area of health, particularly HIV/AIDS, that Mbeki revealed his blindest spot. He will be judged a long time on this, and all the Renaissance idealism will be relegated for historians to ponder some decades from now.

Even though early estimates of HIV infection in South Africa – 12.91 per cent of the adult population in 1997, according to the UNAIDS Report – were overly pessimistic, the alarm bells were clear enough as Thabo Mbeki took up the presidential reins. The problem of

estimation has always been how to extrapolate projections from sometimes sketchy data and limited samples. Estimates of many African
countries are not only pessimistic but unreliable. In the SADC countries, where data is relatively robust, the estimate of HIV infection is
still conjectural to the extent that cultural barriers reduce the incidence
of testing for more accurate figures. Despite this, there is a very real
problem of HIV in Southern Africa, with Zimbabwean infection rates
consistently deemed to be the highest at up to 25.84 per cent of the
adult population.[17] The advent of almost three million Zimbabweans
on South African soil as a result of the Mugabe-led meltdown in the
2000s did nothing to reduce HIV transmission in South Africa.

Notwithstanding the Zimbabweans, there are peculiarities about the
situation in South Africa. The country with the world's most progressive constitution – guarantees of equality for people of different sexual
preferences – has an open and vibrant homosexual community. Much
early petitioning to government about HIV was situated in the framework used by gay communities in the West, and this meant that old
phobias about a 'gay plague', and government inaction being seen as a
deliberate pogrom against gays did not help recognition of a larger
heterosexual infection. Far from the relatively middle class urban gay
scene, the peri-urban and rural black populations that lived in poverty
were those who were infected most. Those who were politically most
inarticulate were those whose condition took time to be championed
by the urban centres of protest. The rainbow nation of races did slowly
become also a rainbow nation of sexual preferences asking government
to do something about HIV. But, when the protests came, Thabo
Mbeki was completely unready to respond.

Instead, he chose to focus on the problem of poverty, stressing that
HIV/AIDS was a by-product of poverty and not a specifically treat-
able viral disease. In fact, the Mbeki approach cannot be casually
dismissed. Poverty makes HIV deterioration rates worse. People with
less to eat have less resistance to the progress of the disease. The alle-
viation of poverty would slow the development of HIV into full-blown
AIDS – but it would not do away with HIV, the causes of HIV and

the eventual consequences of HIV, not to mention the spread of HIV through sexual and other forms of transmission. The Mbeki denial and hesitation was simply stupid. In the midst of budgetary pressures, however, and consumed by his African Renaissance – and calculating the figures generated by GEAR, RDP and BBBEE – the last thing Mbeki wanted to do was to increase the strain on an already over-stressed health budget. Rolling out a national programme of antiretrovirals would be expensive – and it would probably have to be rolled out to Lesotho as well, a separate state, though one enclosed by South Africa. This would take money away from the building of housing units and other programmes where there was a numerical 'result'. X number of houses built was more audit-friendly than a conjecture about a possible y number of lives saved – especially when there was often no *visible* evidence that the life was in danger and, in any case, the statistics were unreliable. There were budgetary and civil service procedural issues involved as well as Mbeki's own reluctance to recognise a growing problem. Having said that, Mbeki's ignorance of the disease was not only stupid but appalling in revealing his lack of leadership responsibility and, given his sense of himself, his lack of intellectual balance and rigour. Mbeki would say that he enquired assiduously into HIV, and it is well known that he spent some months in 1999 reading about the disease. But his reading was largely of literature and websites produced by an international 'AIDS-dissidence' community, a minority scientific community, which was opposed to what Mbeki himself later called a manufactured 'paradigm', invented by the West and of benefit to Western pharmaceutical corporations.[18] He did not read the findings of the majority medical community or encourage the import of generic antiretrovirals manufactured by non-Western companies. In fact when, in 2000, the journalist Mark Gevisser asked him whether, if he found himself HIV positive, he would take antiretrovirals, he said he wouldn't.[19] And when, in 2001, the television interviewer Debora Patta asked him whether he would take an HIV test, he said he wouldn't.[20] This was a leader with certain scientific prejudices therefore, and certain budgetary priorities, prepared all the same to be a strikingly visible example of denial and to be seen as an example of denial at the highest level when, all around him, others were trying to break down the culture of denial.

For Mbeki it was also about dignity. About having to take Western help for an epidemic which the West had already labelled most prevalent amidst the squalor of Africa. It seemed a kowtowing to an implied racism. The African was the poorest and the dirtiest. The African couldn't stop himself from being promiscuous. The African could do nothing to help himself. By the late 1990s, Mandela had already overcome his early sense of this dignity and had begun campaigning internationally on the HIV question. But the real example lay with the man whose assassination paved the way for Mbeki to become President. In the late 1980s, Chris Hani was already agitating for treatment and care of ANC fighters who had contracted HIV. The man who was meant to succeed Mandela had been, in fact, on this issue as wise as Mandela but earlier. The aloof and stiff Mbeki had been a long way removed from the condition of his fighters, and was uncomfortable with dirt and illness. When, in 1998, he had to stand in at the last minute for Mandela on a television broadcast on AIDS, and he was surrounded in the studio by a small crowd of HIV-positive children, he was nonplussed and so visibly ill at ease that even he admitted it was one of his most embarrassing public moments. He was not dignified. But the children probably died anyway.

In the end, Mbeki's own Cabinet was swayed by the growing example of ex-President Mandela and, slowly, though not without some spectacular instances of denial on the part of his health minister, Mbeki began to soften his stance. Antiretrovirals began to be rolled out – some would say too little too late – and the South African per capita expenditure on the disease is now the highest on the continent. Yet the curious wilful ignorance and misplaced sense of dignity and pride on this issue was not perverse individualism. On another issue to be sure, but perhaps even more perversely full of pride and the sense of the dignity of the black person and black ownership of a black continent, Robert Mugabe's long descent into Zimbabwe-as-nightmare was an enlarged replica of the Mbeki fiasco. Mbeki and Mugabe found a common set of intellectual bonds. The understanding and empathy between the two men was real, despite sometimes very real differences and quarrels. But at least Mbeki, for all his blind spots, did not destroy his country in order to own it. With all the talk of GEAR, RDP, BBBEE and NEPAD, there was a curious but very real desire to achieve something *modern* for Africa. Mugabe, whose melting-down of Zimbabwe began one year after Mbeki became President of South Africa, was prepared to go backwards. Mbeki wanted desperately to go forwards. And he did, on a raft of indicators, take his country forwards. But the car, once in gear, was meant to tow everyone in the country behind it. The problem of South Africa today – of Jacob Zuma as he began to be perceived as a challenger to Mbeki – is that those who were meant to be towed forward were left standing or being dragged in a cloud of dust.

CHAPTER 8

THE LONG ELECTORAL TREK[1]

The first three elections of the new millennium in Zimbabwe failed to dislodge Robert Mugabe and his ZANU-PF party. Violent 'conditioning' of voters before each election, and fraudulent counting of the ballots afterwards seemed uniform characteristics. However, each of the elections of 2000, 2002 and 2005 was different, and featured variations in both intimidation and rigging. Moreover, ZANU-PF was learning, election by election, how to rig both more persuasively and in an undetectable manner. The persuasiveness came from a rigging that was at pains to produce results that were not wildly divergent from previous voting patterns. The undetectability was borne out by the conclusion of both local and foreign observers that rigging occurred, but with no one being able to say exactly how it took place. Everyone knows when it occurs, but the forensics of how it is done remains to this day a mystery. The frustration embedded in Zimbabwean elections comes not only from their being 'stolen', and from the preceding intimidation, but from the often inept MDC performances in the lead-up to polling days. Ineptitude and courage have often gone hand in hand, but the latter does not excuse the former. The aim of ZANU-PF has never been to crush the MDC into oblivion. It has always wanted an MDC as tame opposition. A tame, or neutered, opposition party would be proof that Zimbabwe was a 'democratic', multi-party country. ZANU-PF took the Western agenda of democracy and sought to use it as a form of self-protection and validation. The MDC always thought the West would ride to its aid – but it never did. It took a hammering in election after election.

The elections of the early 2000s in Zimbabwe were set within complicated relationships between Zimbabwe and South Africa. The timelines in Southern Africa were congested. Often it seemed as if the South African and Zimbabwean leaderships, despite being in neighbouring countries with much in common, were determined to act as polar opposites. Thabo Mbeki launched GEAR in 1996. The war veterans made their appearance as a political force in Zimbabwe in 1997. Mbeki became President of South Africa in 1999 and, in the same year, the opposition MDC party was launched in Zimbabwe. The MDC defeated Robert Mugabe in a referendum in early 2000, but lost the parliamentary elections to his ZANU-PF party a few months afterwards. In between, the invasion of white farms began and, with it, a shrill international campaign against Mugabe. The Zimbabwean economy plummeted, but the Western response was built around a single tactic – it wasn't even a strategy – 'get rid of Mugabe'. Western leaders and civic action groups hoped the electoral process would do this so, in Zimbabwe, ZANU-PF worked hard to tarnish the MDC with the Western brush. Meanwhile, there was little help for the Zimbabwean people as their livelihoods and lifestyles crumbled. What they got was relief when starving. This was the least that could be done, but a song and dance was made of it. But it also meant the fortunes of Mbeki and Mugabe were bound together from the beginning of South Africa's renaissance and Mbeki's hope that Africa as a whole would grow anew. NEPAD was established as an emblem of good governance in 2001 and Mugabe and Tsvangirai went head to head in presidential elections in 2002. It was the first direct test of an Mbeki policy. However, there should first be a discussion about the polls of 2000. These conditioned what happened in 2002.

After defeat in the February 2000 referendum Mugabe was briefly despondent. Reports from his 'inside circle' suggest he was ready to retire, having never been rejected by his people before. The ZANU-PF hardliners, together with opportunists who depended on Mugabe, galvanised him and deployed a racial analysis of events. This was articulated most clearly by the ambitious Jonathan Moyo, sometime academic democrat,[2] in 2000 a Mugabe loyalist, later a plotter against Mugabe, then a dissident MP in the Zimbabwean Parliament, more lately a returnee to the ZANU-PF fold but situated within a faction that hopes to succeed Mugabe. In 2000 he was prepared to adopt any stratagem to retain Mugabe, then his political patron, in power. The turnout for the referendum was sketchy in the rural areas, but heavy in the cities. Fifty-five per cent, or 697,754 voters came out against Mugabe's constitutional proposals. 578,210 voted for them. The margin was only 120,000.[3] If ZANU-PF had mobilised its rural base properly, the margin would have been sharply reduced if not wiped out. But Moyo found a new analysis to account for at least 100,000 of the 120,000. Two days after the referendum, he said:

> Preliminary figures show there were 100,000 white people voting. We have never had anything like that in this country. They were all over town. Everybody who observed will tell you there were long queues of whites. The difference between the 'yes' and 'no' votes would not have been what it was had it not been for this vote.[4]

Mugabe decided to stay and fight the whites. The referendum had been held from 12 to 13 February. Moyo's comments were made on the 15th. A week passed without incident. In the last week of February, almost exactly 20 years after Robert Mugabe and ZANU-PF won the independence elections, the farm invasions began.[5] The land was to be seized back. It was to be seized back from the whites. Between the end of February and the parliamentary elections of 24–25 June the Zimbabwean landscape would be literally transformed. International condemnation poured in from Europe and the United States. The Commonwealth was in crisis, since Zimbabwe was a key member and had, for many years leading up to independence, been the organisation's *cause célèbre*. The issue of Zimbawe was what had kept the Commonwealth together.[6] It allowed everybody else to gang up on the British for their tardiness and ineffectualness in bringing down an illegal white government.[7] Now Mugabe would relaunch that critique of the British as Tony Blair stormed and protested against the treatment of the white farmers.

In Zimbabwe, the opposition MDC, buoyed by its referendum victory, thought it could win the June elections. But it had only a rudimentary party organisation, even in the cities; almost nothing in the rural areas. ZANU-PF was not going to be slack in its rural organisation again. There and in the cities the decision was made to wheel out the heavy battalions – to pummel the MDC physically as a prelude to defeating the upstart party politically. In effect, Mugabe was able to use Western concern over the seizure of white farms as a cover for persecuting the opposition. Dozens of black MDC activists were killed and many more attacked. But their faces did not fill the London newspapers or their names pass the lips of those in Westminster. By the end of the first week of June, 1,400 farms had been occupied and 29 MDC campaigners killed. The impressive thing about the MDC was that it never lost its composure. But, if the party kept its nerve in the face of pressure, many of the voting public could not – as ZANU-PF promises of reprisal swayed many to cast their votes 'safely'. And, at that time, the full economic cost of the invasions could not be appreciated. Many were persuaded by the promise of obtaining land of their own and, for those who owned some already, better land. To be a peasant in Zimbabwe was not always an Arcadian experience. It was not as if reasonably reliable pastoral subsistence meant pastoral happiness. The peasant too has aspirations – and those who left the land to find work in the cities have nostalgia. Those who have never worked the land have romanticism.[8] And then there was the sheer imbalance in terms of how few owned so much; and how so many of those few were reputed to have gruff and condescending manners and attitudes towards black people. It is amazing how few people came to the direct aid of the white farmers. Even those who opposed Mugabe did not physically resist the seizures. In a country of asymmetric ownership, the social and racial cleavages were also immense. Mugabe in some ways was a maestro: he played every string on the complex instrument called land. The 2000 elections were not rigged in terms of the count. There were certainly local irregularities and these were challenged in the courts. There was no nationally coordinated 'irregularity'. That would come later as the MDC challenge increased in its organisational capacity, as the true cost of the farm invasions became felt, and as physical intimation by ZANU-PF was no longer enough by itself.

In 2000, physical intimidation worked well enough. Even so, all 19 seats in Harare fell to the MDC. In the second city of Bulawayo in the east of the country, the MDC won all eight seats. In the two surrounding western Matabeleland provinces – where in the 1980s Mugabe had launched military reprisals against largely imaginary enemies – 13 of the 15 seats fell to the MDC. The strongholds of the opposition became clearly defined. Mugabe's ZANU-PF, utilising its long-time popular appeal and heavy-handed 'encouragement', swept most of the remaining countryside. On the night, it took Parliament with 62 seats. The MDC took 57, and one seat went to a dissident ZANU faction.[9] Electorally, it had been a close-run thing. Mugabe was able comfortably to pad out his majority with his constitutionally permitted quota of 30 presidentially appointed MPs. But the MDC had been blooded – literally – and it had arrived. The face of Zimbabwean land ownership had changed, and the face of the Zimbabwean political landscape had changed. Morgan Tsvangirai was always going to hold on to his Harare base. It was vitally important to him that he also hold on to his Bulawayo and Matabeleland base. From those he could launch out to challenge ZANU-PF in the countryside. For ZANU-PF the task was to retain the countryside, intimidate the MDC voting base in

Harare and, in the fullness of time, hope for a crack to appear between the MDC groups in Harare and Bulawayo. It was not going to appear before the next big test for the two parties. That next test was to be the first time Mugabe and Tsvangirai went head to head – the presidential elections of 2002.

In January 2002 Mugabe called the presidential elections for 9–10 March. By then, court challenges had reduced the ZANU-PF parliamentary majority to only the 30 presidentially appointed MPs. In electoral terms, Parliament was equally divided. Mugabe, however, was getting ready. On 13 February, Australian television screened the footage of Tsvangirai talking to Ben-Menashe about the need to get rid of Mugabe. This was an effort to smear Tsvangirai internationally, a week before the Brisbane Commonwealth summit and three weeks before the elections. In Zimbabwe itself, Tsvangirai was depicted as not only a stooge of the British but as the non-democratic half of the presidential clash – prepared to resort to assassination rather than election. But it was all cover as, behind the scenes, Mugabe's people had been recruiting and training youth brigades, young party militants organised along paramilitary lines. The war veterans were no longer enough. The new force for intimidation would be those who quickly came to be known as the 'Green Bombers'. This was a slang reaction to their appearance. Their uniforms were green. But 'bombers' were large flies who hung around shit. They became a much loathed electoral force, but a violently effective one. If the Bombers came for you as an opponent of the government, you were going to be beaten within an inch of your life. The Bombers developed their own slang. When they beat you, they were doling out 'forgiveness'. Mugabe also began disbursing farms to people – 1,000 in January alone – and introducing suppressive legislation in Parliament, where his personally appointed MPs would provide the required majority. Thus, smearing, violence, bribery and suppression of dissent became the key ZANU-PF instruments for fighting a 'democratic' election. They were taking Tsvangirai's challenge very seriously.

Although the beatings resulted in several deaths, that did not seem to be the primary aim. The methodology was beating and maiming just short of the point of death. The recovering victim would be the ripple effect, the warning, to all who came to wish his or her recovery well. Thousands were beaten and intimidated: the aim was to cause tens of thousands to fear being beaten. Attending an MDC rally, even in the MDC city strongholds, became a test of nerve and dedication. But, in the parks and stadia, at the rallies whenever Tsvangirai appeared the crowds would greet his arrival on stage with a thunderous '*chinga!*' The word meant 'change'. People wanted change. But Mugabe was also on the rally trail. Unlike Tsvangirai, who always wore a suit, Mugabe took to wearing a baseball cap and an open-necked shirt with his own portrait printed on it, and he would sometimes run across the stadium field to demonstrate that, in his late seventies, he was the man of vigour. And, to be fair, he was. He never was puffing at the end of those runs. He did look ridiculous, but that was the clothing. When he spoke, it was with a vocabulary from the past – about the struggle against colonialism and how it was, once again, the great struggle of the day. One man talked about the future. The other talked about the past. Violence and hope provided an atmosphere of extreme tension and expectation. But neither man's manifesto was anything but sound-bites. It came down to a question of style, and it came down to a question of who had the muscle. Would the violence led by the Bombers defeat the resolve of Tsvangirai's supporters? And, if not defeat that resolve, would the fear of intimidation sway sufficient undecideds, especially in the rural areas where support groups for dissidence were rare? And Mugabe had one last trick up his sleeve: on the days of the polls, especially in the MDC strongholds, casting a vote suddenly took a hugely long time. Every bureaucratic impediment possible was wheeled out by polling staff. The queues stretched for hundreds of metres. Hours could pass before it was your turn. It was a tactic to stifle the MDC vote by attrition. Many people could not wait and left the lines. But, by and large, the MDC support base toughed it out. Camaraderie developed. Strangers in the queue would keep your place if you had to take a toilet break or find a snack. On the second day of the polls, Tsvangirai cast his vote in his middle-class Avondale station. It was his 50th birthday. He looked presidential. Someone presented him with a cake shaped like State House, the presidential offices. Court challenges forced some extra hours of polling over a third day. This was in Harare only, but that was where the MDC strength was. The queues were still slow, but more votes were cast.

Tsvangirai lost. But the voting patterns were of great interest. The bald figures were 1,685,212 votes for Mugabe and 1,258,401 for Tsvangirai. Beneath those figures there were several tales to tell.

- In the second city of Bulawayo, Tsvangirai beat Mugabe 79 per cent to 17 per cent, but turnout was only 45 per cent of those registered.
- In the neighbouring provinces, historically the most offended by Mugabe because of his pogroms there in the 1980s, there was an interesting result. In Matabeleland North, where the bulk of the pogroms occurred, Tsvangirai defeated Mugabe by 61 per cent to 35 per cent, but turnout was only 53 per cent. In Matabeleland South, Tsvangirai's victory margin was narrower, 50 to 44 per cent, against a voter turnout of 54 per cent.
- In Harare, with voter turnout at only 47 per cent of those registered, possibly because of the deterrence of the long queues, Tsvangirai defeated Mugabe 75 to 24 per cent.
- The somewhat startling result was from Manicaland province near the Mozambique border where, in the 1970s, Mugabe's guerrillas would cross over to engage the white Rhodesian forces. This was an area regarded as the font of Zimbabwean liberation. With a turnout of 55 per cent, Tsvangirai defeated Mugabe 48 to 47 per cent. This should have been Mugabe's territory; it was almost his 'spiritual' homeland. It was where the liberation war had begun in earnest. It should have been what the Zimbabweans call Mugabe's 'totem'.

But Manicaland aside, the other results were predictable. Mugabe swept everywhere else, with majorities between 63 and 84 per cent.

Turnout averaged 65 per cent, much higher than in the areas where Tsvangirai scored his victories.[10]

ZANU-PF had learnt its tricks. It realised it couldn't stop Tsvangirai winning in certain areas, nor could it roll back the percentage margin of his victories. What it could do was to intimidate and deter voters so that, even if Tsvangirai won key areas, the mass of Mugabe's votes would still be more than Tsvangirai's. ZANU-PF, the war veterans and the Green Bombers worked the Tsvangirai strongholds with intimidation, basically to deter people from voting; and they worked the Mugabe hinterland with 'encouragement', a combination of inducements and threats, to turn out and vote for the President. But the Green Bomber threat was least in the two Matabeleland provinces. Somehow, Tsvangirai was not enthusing the voters in the west. There was an ethnic divide. The west was largely Ndebele, whereas Harare and the other great provinces were largely Shona. But it was more complex than ethnicities. After all, even though Tsvangirai was Shona, so was Mugabe. The Ndebele voted against Mugabe but did not turn out in full mass for Tsvangirai. Mugabe had slaughtered many of their people; Tsvangirai was the best bet to end the Mugabe era; but he was somehow not doing enough to convince nearly 50 per cent of the voters in the west – who simply stayed away from the polls.

For ZANU-PF, future strategy became clear: continue to roll back the numbers prepared to vote for Tsvangirai; continue to roll out those prepared to vote for Mugabe; bludgeon and induce accordingly; and somehow detach the west of Zimbabwe from Tsvangirai. In addition, ZANU-PF learnt what voting patterns could be sustained in future elections. The national rigging that was to come – largely absent in 2000 and 2002 – would be a rigging on a highly sophisticated basis. It would always be within the bounds of possibility, within the bounds established by past electoral behaviour. Particularly the pattern that, where Tsvangirai won, the size of victory could be made small – as in Manicaland and Matabeleland South – and, where Mugabe won, the size of victory could be made massive. In 2002 he took one province with an 84 per cent majority. ZANU-PF learnt much. Tsvangirai and the MDC learnt little. They had failed to dislodge Mugabe by full frontal electoral attack. Their strategy afterwards never deviated from full-frontal. They hurled demonstrations and crowds at Mugabe, and Mugabe's security forces beat them and tear-gassed them until people were afraid to demonstrate any more. And they pressed treason charges against Tsvangirai over the Ben-Menashe affair. They wanted to reduce the man to a psychological wreck.

The 2005 parliamentary elections were, in my judgement, the first in which nationally coordinated rigging was deployed.[11] This was not to sweep the electoral board as in Saddam Hussein's Iraq or other totalitarian jurisdictions, where the dictator would always be endorsed in the high 90 per cents. It was to look plausible and realistic and to reduce the opposition parliamentary strength enough so that it could not command a blocking third in Parliament. To change the constitution you needed a two-thirds vote in Parliament. If you can command two-thirds of the House, you can pass whatever laws you like, change the constitution, and say it was done democratically. If you want, you can rule like a dictator without being a dictator. But you realise dictatorships are out of fashion. You realise one-party states belong to the past. You join the surreptitious bandwagon that began in Singapore – and which the Singaporeans pulled off as sufficiently 'democratic' to pass muster – and install a dominant-party state. As with the ANC in South Africa, so with ZANU-PF in Zimbabwe, the creation of dominant-party states was simultaneously 'democratic' in its procedures, and a safeguarding of power. The ANC, however, won its elections openly. ZANU-PF was first going to 'condition' the election with intimidation and harassment and, secondly, when it was sure violence would bring victory, bespoke that victory until it was just the size it required. Mugabe's people almost took perverse delight in pointing out that there was an opposition party in Zimbabwe with many seats in Parliament. 'You see. We are democratic.' And, surely, without the farm invasions that alarmed the West, no American or European leader would have objected with the vigour and venom that characterised policy on Zimbabwe from 2000 onwards.

Having gone to Zimbabwe in 2004 to prepare the book of interviews with Tsvangirai, I went again for the 2005 elections. The book
was being distributed by the MDC to foreign press and observers. Its
use was to 'flesh out' the man, to show there was more thoughtful and
intellectual substance there than the Mugabes and Mbekis of the
world would credit. In the cities everything looked sleek. In addition
to the press packs, the MDC television advertisements looked immac-
ulate. At the airport, a long line of unaccredited 'informal' observers
and reporters were waiting at passport control, hoping to argue their
way in; or, with television cameras slung over their shoulders, convince
the passport officer they were simply tourists. Passport control didn't
care. Almost everyone who paid the temporary visitor visa fee got in.
The three weeks leading up to the polls were going to be orchestrated
in such a peaceful manner that no one would suspect the years of
violence beforehand; and the count 'adjusted' so plausibly that no one
would suspect rigging; and, if they did suspect, no one could prove it
was done or how it was done.

The Zimbabwean authorities didn't care much at any time about the
entry of foreign journalists. They might have been banned, but they didn't
find it hard to get in. ZANU-PF is inured to Western criticism, whether
in reports from Johannesburg or the streets of Harare. Whenever John
Simpson sneaked across the border and reported clandestinely from
Zimbabwe, and the hidden camera filmed him walking 'undetected' in
the streets, everybody had in fact recognised him. 'Oh look, there's John
Simpson walking down the street again. The camera must be in that
slow-moving car 25 metres ahead. Ignore the fat reporter. Let's wave to
the car! We might get on British television tonight.'

In 2005 the rat-pack of journalists and observers would have noted
that the ZANU-PF newspaper advertisements were excoriations of
Tony Blair. They claimed Tsvangirai was a stooge of Blair: as puppet-
master, Blair was the real evil, determined to restore colonial domination of Zimbabwe. However, the MDC television ads were so polished
and professionally produced they could have been used in a British
campaign. But it was hardly the urban television-owning and watching

population that needed this kind of effort. It was a three-week 'Harare Spring', designed by ZANU-PF as a showpiece, not least to other African states, that democracy was alive and well and that British condemnations were false. To an extent, the slick MDC ads helped convey that impression. The majority of reporters and observers wouldn't have the forensic 'back story' of election-by-election voting patterns even to try to demonstrate that 'adjustments' had taken place in the count. But this is what happened:

- The MDC lost one of its safest city seats, Harare South. Boundary changes were partly to blame, but more so the imposition of an unpopular MDC candidate and his failure to galvanise his voting base. The MDC had earlier failed to challenge meaningfully the boundary changes and was much at fault for insisting upon a candidate against the wishes of its local members.

- Otherwise, the MDC held on to its urban strongholds – and most, though not all, of its seats in the Matabeleland provinces. The overall level of support from the West was still there, but with perceptible small erosions.

- The MDC share of the total vote should have been higher, but many voters were turned away at the polling stations for not having proper voter-registration. The MDC had not earlier conducted a widespread voter education and registration programme.

- The majority of the rural areas went to ZANU-PF and Mugabe. Apart from 'conditioning' violence and 'encouragement', there were three other reasons for this. Firstly, ZANU-PF took great care to buy or coerce a majority of local chiefs and village headmen to 'deliver' their members to the party. The MDC never tried to 'work' those chiefs. Secondly, the mark of having voted was to have your thumb dipped in indelible ink. But this was regarded with suspicion by many rural voters in case their thumbprints strayed on to their ballot papers. Further, in accordance with African Union protocols, the ballot boxes were transparent. This was meant to discourage ballot-stuffing, but villagers feared their vote could be seen by outsiders.

Few dared to vote for the opposition in case they were detected by thumbprints or inspection of their ballots through the transparent box. The ZANU-PF militants encouraged such attitudes and the MDC did not counter them in any effective manner. Thirdly, many MDC party agents, who were permitted entry to the polling stations as witnesses to fair procedures, did not know what they were meant to do, having not been properly briefed by their own party.

- The above points enumerate some MDC mistakes. But, finally, there was the ZANU-PF use of rigging, and the pattern of how this occurred was as follows:

ZANU-PF's own internal political forecasting had got it wrong. Despite all the thuggish 'conditioning' prior to the elections, and a perceptible drop in MDC morale after all its street protests had been beaten down, the national mood for change had not disappeared. ZANU-PF, however, was convinced that enough had been done by the bullyboys for the election to be won without rigging. Rigging was waiting in the wings, but it was a Plan B. The decision to activate Plan B came just after 2 p.m. on polling day.

In an attempt to appear properly democratic to observers, particularly those from the African Union and Thabo Mbeki's NEPAD-conscious South Africa, reasonably objective political scientists were televised throughout the day offering analysis. One of them was Ibbo Mandaza. Many would say that Mandaza was hardly objective. He had, even then, the conviction that a 'third force' had to be created – some would say stirred into action, as it perhaps already existed – to challenge both ZANU-PF and the MDC. For Mandaza this would be a force comprising the younger technocratic wing of ZANU-PF and a very few of the best brains from the MDC. Many of these would be from the western base of the MDC in Bulawayo. He had been a senior civil servant who had fallen foul of Mugabe at an early stage, but had never stopped being a ZANU-PF fellow traveller. He was an immensely influential publisher and author of a neo-Marxist blend of political economy and African identity.[12] It was especially he whom

Tsvangirai had in mind when criticising intellectuals who spoke from their mansions. But, all the same, he was a good analyst and, at 2 p.m. on nationwide television, he made the prediction that, based on voting throughput figures in the morning, only a trickle could still be expected to vote in the afternoon. Driving around Harare all day I could say that he was, for that location at least, absolutely correct. The polling stations were almost deserted after lunch. Mindful of the long queues in 2002, everyone had got to the stations early. But, if that was the pattern in the countryside as well, as Mandaza seemed to suggest, it also meant that the ZANU-PF rural faithful were not voting in the same patterns as before, and the ZANU-PF rural vote – on which it depended – would be down.

When the results and partial results began to be announced on state television, all seemed to be regular and untoward. Suddenly, the announcement of results was suspended. When it resumed hours later the final figures in a number of constituencies, especially rural ones, showed large and unpredicted upswings in late votes cast. They were sometimes so large that not only was there no symmetry between the final results and earlier progress reports, but there was no symmetry between overall totals of votes and the number of votes accorded the candidates. These late announcements had almost all the new votes going to ZANU-PF. It was not a nationwide change in pattern. Sitting in front of the television screen, calculating percentages and variations on backs of envelopes, it was clear to me that the intention was to change just enough for ZANU-PF to have its two-thirds majority in Parliament with enough room to spare in case court challenges were at least partially successful. The problem is that everyone could work out *when* the rigging occurred – those few hours between one set of results being announced and then the rest – but no one has ever worked out *how*. Party agents were meant to have been present at the stations where the votes were counted. Nothing has *ever* leaked from any ZANU-PF source as to how it is done. And that's something, as this kind of operation can only be mounted with huge resources, much coordination and the involvement of hundreds of people. But the pattern of figures is something that forensic analysts depend upon, and because a Zimbabwean election has no special characteristics that would make it so different from those in other countries, or even earlier elections in Zimbabwe itself, the Mandaza projection was persuasive and the late figures aberrant.

Afterwards the MDC claimed it should have won 62 seats, enough for electoral victory – though not enough to command the House, where Mugabe could appoint a further 30 MPs and have a 24 seat majority in a House of 150. (Jonathan Moyo, standing as an independent dissident, won a seat, so the opposition total would have been 62 + 1, and the ZANU-PF total would have been 57 + 30.) Even so, such a figure would have been a huge moral victory.

The MDC claim is probably slightly inflated, however. The official result gave the MDC 41 seats, meaning the MDC claimed that 21 seats were stolen by the rigging process. My own calculations suggested a theft of 10 seats, meaning that the MDC should have been accorded 52 seats.[13] Even without Jonathan Moyo, that would have been the blocking third in Parliament. ZANU-PF didn't need to rig in order to win the election. The 30 appointed MPs would have meant, by anybody's count or claim, a parliamentary majority. ZANU-PF wanted to ensure a comfortable two-thirds majority. The opposition were to be a decorative emblem in the House to demonstrate that democracy was at work – but ineffectual as the ruling party did what it wanted. The democratic exercise as cynicism was probably not what Mbeki had in mind when he championed NEPAD as part of his African Renaissance. And an election where the opposition loses 19 seats from one election to the next, while the government leads the country into an economic meltdown, does not normally meet the rules of credibility. In its post-mortems, ZANU-PF wondered whether the attempt at nuance and believability could be sustained. Perhaps it had overdone the rigging in 2005 and should be more circumspect in the future. The hardliners replied that circumspection was unimportant. If we have to rig, we go for it hell for leather. Both sides of this party divide would appear very visibly in the next elections of 2008. But, well before then,

Thabo Mbeki was working behind the scenes, again trying to persuade ZANU-PF and the MDC to contemplate some form of coalition, with Tsvangirai as Vice-President. No one was biting yet but, as the 2008 elections drew closer and – with the announcement that parliamentary and presidential elections would be brought together to allow a single moment of choice for the electorate – the prize grew in size and meaning. And the temptations grew. The hardliners in both ZANU-PF and the MDC spurned the idea, but Tsvangirai wavered towards it. From the 2005 elections onwards, his behaviour, and his increasingly personal and arbitrary decision-making – often without consultation – were beginning to alarm his own lieutenants, including his powerful barons from the west. Incorporate Tsvangirai, encourage a division in the MDC, defeat Tsvangirai and the MDC in rigged elections, beat them to a pulp in between. It was the party barons of ZANU-PF, hard-liner or reformist, who held all the options. The ruling party was leading the country into ruin, but its top table was sure it was going to get away with it.

The bald drift of events seemed to bear this out. At the turn of 2005–6, the MDC split.[14] In the last quarter of 2007 with presidential and parlia-mentary elections looming in early 2008, representatives of Tsvangirai's part of the MDC and ZANU-PF met with Thabo Mbeki's emissaries on a houseboat anchored in Lake Kariba – the giant artificial lake between Zambia and Zimbabwe – and agreed a unity government with Tsvangirai as Vice-President. This was scuppered a little later by the hardliners in ZANU-PF. But ZANU-PF was itself heading for a split. The so-called 'third force' was plotting its breakaway from Mugabe. Suddenly, Mbeki's mediation in Zimbabwe had become more densely populated. But, over Mbeki's shoulder, back home in South Africa, storm clouds were looming. And he could not have known, as he scrutinised the reports of his people, mediating the Zimbabwean political standoff in Lake Kariba that, by the beginning of the next year, 2008, he would no longer be President of the ANC, and that his time left as President of South Africa was short. Over his shoulder lurked the lowering figure of Jacob Zuma.

CHAPTER 9

THE RETURN OF THE ZULU KING[1]

If elections in Zimbabwe were an arena where two large parties clashed, even if the results were fraudulent, elections in South Africa were dominated by the ANC. In the world of competitive democracy, it was monolithic. Within the ANC, however, the jostling for power was intense, and manoeuvres against rivals were far from transparent. At the same time, leading ANC members – who had spent their adult lives in the struggle, in prison and in exile, and who had never earned their own income or had to balance their household budget – were suddenly faced with the challenge of life in a new South Africa, where the concentration of power allowed patronage and created an opportunistic environment where people 'invested' in the possibility of obtaining future patronage. Jacob Zuma, the ebullient and larger-than-life 'enforcer' of the ANC when it was in exile, seemed to be beset by such problems on his return to South Africa. He made many mistakes, but these mistakes were used against him by political enemies in a deadly game of commanding power within the ANC. Whoever ruled the ANC ruled South Africa. The power games within the party were more decisive than the elections in the country. In these power games, the law of the country and its officers were put to the use of one ANC faction or another – or so it seemed, as

South Africa in the post-Mandela era unveiled a political world of deceit, treachery and high stakes. And even the most philosophical and well-read of ANC figures could move in this world with ruthlessness. In this era, the 'black idealism' of Thabo Mbeki was counterposed with the Machiavellian demands of a realpolitik which both he and Jacob Zuma practised. And Zuma had learnt how to move without sentiment or pity in his own exile years.

Those who were imprisoned with Jacob Zuma on Robben Island remember him as a joker. He was the one who kept their spirits up. There were long philosophical debates. 'There was no rush to finish these debates,' Mosiuoa Lekota, who went to Robben Island after Zuma, told me; 'we were there for years.' In the midst of such seriousness, Zuma was the one who lightened the mood. He was one of the least educated, and the legend is that his comrades taught him how to read in prison. This is not true, but they did help him to read more fluently. However, it meant he was not entrusted with senior responsibilities in the inmate society. It was a self-organised and self-regulating society. Educational and political-consciousness lectures were a regular feature, delivered by the inmates themselves. Zuma has claimed that, by the end of his incarceration, he was entrusted with delivering some of these lectures – but no one seems to remember them. In fact there is very little memory of him at all in his pre-ANC days. His history is as an ANC figure. Even as an ANC member, it was only after his release from Robben Island that he came to prominence. But his formation was not entirely ANC: his lack of learning and his traditional practices, including polygamy, define him simultaneously as a throwback to pre-modern times as well as the latest president of the most modern nation in sub-Saharan Africa. Jacob Zuma will always be something of an enigma. He can be brilliant as a politician, charismatic and sure of his popular touch. He can be crass and crude, and he and South Africa may learn the hard way that wily moves and stratagems are not enough to take a complex country forwards.[2]

Fast forward to election day in South Africa, 22 April 2009. This was to be Zuma's day, his apotheosis after years of persecution, his people said, at the hands of Thabo Mbeki. Zuma had served as Mbeki's Deputy President until his sacking on 14 June 2005. It wasn't an unceremonial sacking. Mbeki, speaking in Parliament, made it very ceremonial indeed. It was one of those sucking-in-breath moments as, with the coolest and most elegant language, recorded faithfully in the parliamentary record, Mbeki stuck a knife into Zuma and tore it across his guts. 'In the interest of the honourable Deputy President, the Government, our young democratic system and our country, it would be best to release the Honourable Jacob Zuma from his responsibilities as Deputy President of the Republic and member of the Cabinet.' It was deadpan – Mbeki didn't raise his voice or modulate his tone, barely looked up from his notes, and spoke slowly. Parliamentarians and the camera lingered on every word. It was a ceremonial evisceration. All who saw it were struck by the deadliness of it all. Whether Zuma was tainted with corruption or not, it was political execution as public theatre. But on election day in 2009, I was in Kliptown on the edge of Soweto and, in the long queues of people waiting to vote, every person was going to vote for the ANC – for Zuma.

Zuma had overcome what Mbeki did to him, and he was in the process of overcoming the challenge of COPE (the Congress of the People) led by Mosiuoa Lekota, the breakaway from the ANC after Zuma gained the presidency of the party. Neither Lekota, nor many others, ever got over the buffoon Zuma whom they met either in prison or in the early years afterwards. The South African rumours were that Mbeki's own mother was going to vote for COPE; that Mbeki's brother, Moletsi, was advising COPE; that Mbeki himself had close ties with the breakaway figures.[3] Everyone wondered where COPE's campaign funds came from. And it wasn't just that COPE broke away and challenged the ANC, but that it adopted a name that sought to capture from the ANC the foundations of liberation. It was in Kliptown that the original Congress of the People, in 1955, had adopted the Freedom Charter. All the groups opposed to Apartheid had sent delegates, including the ANC. It was far from an ANC event, and the ANC took a year to endorse the Freedom Charter – but it was the start of the fightback against Apartheid. In the photos, Mandela and the priest, Trevor Huddleston, are the tallest. Apart from Huddleston, there are few other white men. Some white women. I have always loved the photos of Huddleston, who was Louis Armstrong's emissary, delivering Satchmo's own trumpet as a gift to Hugh Masekela in South Africa. Not many people know of Satchmo's role in the fight against Apartheid. And too many have already forgotten Huddleston – the mad cricket-loving priest who came to the side of the first COPE. There is one hotel in Kliptown. It is new but people fear going there. I am the only guest. I blag the room above where people had sat to watch the speeches of the Congress of the People – before the police had waded in.

In the streets I met aged women who had thrown themselves forward as human shields to prevent the police, they said, from reaching Mandela. This story was probably apocryphal. By the time the police moved in, Mandela and other leading ANC figures had retired to a safe distance. But the women probably had thrown themselves at the police just to make life difficult for them. Tediously, the police took down the names of 3,000 people. One bent-over woman, woollen stockings no longer tight against her stick-thin legs, stormed at me that she would not vote. 'We have gained nothing. We expect nothing!' Indeed, the long queues were full of younger people who had time to await a future. Those who had played some minor role in history were stamping back to their hovels.

Kliptown is where the film *Tsotsi* was shot. They didn't need to grime it down. It really is like that. Shacks and improvised houses. The ANC has put in standpipes and, at irregular distances, in fact on any spare patch of ground, chemical toilets. It's like a rock festival gone to a shanty town in Mars. It's still full of tsotsis – street gangsters – or at least retired ones. I grin at the murkiness of it all. My observer and journalist friends are cascading around the country on election day, straining for glimpses of Thabo Mbeki voting before he flies off to Sudan that afternoon. He's going to mediate between the International Criminal Court and the African Union over the indictment of President Bashir for crimes in Darfur. But this also means Mbeki is not going to be around when Zuma starts celebrating. Meanwhile, I have been mistaken for Stephen Tang, the schoolmate of a bunch of retired tsotsis. Their old friend had left Kliptown decades ago and gone off to become prosperous elsewhere. They think I look like him. I'm not him but I'm welcomed anyway and spend part of election day in the company of multiple murderers. Seventeen knife killings, one boasted. And that's something else I learn: at the 1955 Congress of the People, Chinese grocers and a Jewish butcher had provided a lot of food for the delegates. Kliptown had a large Chinese population once.[4] I'm just delighted they did something to help the foundation of the struggle. But, if they were there, Jacob Zuma wasn't.

Zuma joined the ANC in 1959, four years after the Freedom Charter in Kliptown. The orphaned son of a Zulu policeman, he was educated to Grade 5 level and spent his childhood between the KwaZulu rural areas and the poor peri-urban fringes of Durban. He was 17 when he joined the ANC, 20 when he joined its armed wing, Umkhonto we Sizwe (Spear of the Nation), 21 when he joined the SACP (South African Communist Party), and the same age when – in 1963 – he was arrested and sentenced to Robben Island for 10 years. He had not yet fired a shot in anger and, in fact, did not know how to. It was Thabo Mbeki, in Swaziland in 1975, where Zuma first briefly took exile, who taught him. Whenever Zuma sings 'Bring me my machine gun', his favourite among the fighting songs of the ANC, and dances jubilantly to its music at his great public rallies, the irony is that the elegant and aloof man whom he eventually overcame ruthlessly to snatch the ANC presidency from him, Thabo Mbeki, was the man who first helped Zuma curl his fingers around the trigger of an AK47.

Zuma went on to Mozambique from Swaziland, and there was responsible for receiving the thousands of volunteers who flocked to the ANC banner in the wake of the 1976 Soweto uprising. This would have been his first exposure to the wild young men of Kliptown. As a result of his work he was welcomed into the ANC National Executive Committee in 1977. Zuma's visibility as an important ANC personage dates only from 1977, when he was made ANC Deputy Representative in Mozambique, being promoted to Chief Representative in 1984. He moved to Lusaka in 1987 and was made Head of Underground Structures and Chief of Intelligence. Many ANC exile fighters – some estimate hundreds – were purged during Zuma's time in Intelligence. Executions, torture and maltreatment were commonplace, and many were wrongly accused of dissidence. It was the first great witch-hunt in the ANC. How much was Zuma's responsibility is widely debated. 'Speculated' might be a better word. There is no evidence linking him directly to torture on the ground. But he was the man in charge. He certainly secured his place in the ANC hierarchy, and in the SACP as well – being elected to its politburo in 1989.

But in early 1990, after the release of Nelson Mandela, Zuma went back to South Africa. The joker in the prison pack was now a serious player. But what sort of serious player? It is worthwhile meditating a little on the torture of ANC personnel under Zuma's portfolio. Very shortly after his release from prison, Nelson Mandela admitted that dissident guerrillas had been tortured by the ANC. His statement came on 14 April 1990, and he added that those who were responsible had already been punished. It was almost as if he was clearing the way for Zuma's return. The issue, however, refused to go away and Mandela felt constrained to establish an independent commission of inquiry into the abuses. The release of its findings in 1993 stunned the South African public with its candour.[5] Simultaneously it served two Mandela objectives: to gain plaudits for honesty and soul-searching – the ANC was presented as a reflective party capable of admitting mistakes; and to draw a line under the abuses as soon as possible. It was as much a bold political move on Mandela's part as it was an ethical statement. The bringer of moral rainbows was always a highly astute political player.

Most victims of the ANC torture had been detained in an Angolan camp formally called the Morris Seabelo Rehabilitation Centre, but more infamously known as 'Quatro'. It was run by a warden who used the name 'Mbokodo': the Stone that Crushes. The jailers under his command also had their nicknames: Stalin, Fury, Commissar Hammer. And that's what they did – crushing and hammering were part of it.

The two favoured positions – by the jailers, hardly by the victims – consisted in being suspended naked on a spit, like a pig about to be roasted; and being made to lie face down and naked and, in both cases, beaten and flogged. Many died. The commission, composed of three polite people – a South African businessman, a Zimbabwean barrister and a Massachusetts judge – was plainly shocked. Unused to such revelations, they misnamed the naked on a spit position the 'helicopter'. This is not the 'helicopter'. The 'helicopter', as I have found – while defending deserters from the Eritrean army in British courts who have been charged with fleeing their country and entering Britain on false passports – is somewhat worse and still used by repressive regimes today.

The commission named Jacob Zuma as one of those who should be held accountable for these abuses. To be fair, these and other abuses saw other senior ANC figures implicated, and even those who are still regarded internationally as having the most impeccable moral credentials, people like Albie Sachs, were in 1990 pleading lack of training, inexperience and youthfulness on behalf of the jailers and torturers.[6] But the release of the commission's report in 1993 made such pleas seem ingenuous. Even so, nothing was done. The entire tone of 'confess, forgive and move on' seemed necessary in those early days, and carried over into the basic tenor of Archbishop Desmond Tutu's Truth and Reconciliation Commission. Although its report, released in 1998, included detailed testimony of ANC torture, and castigated the ANC for 'gross violations of human rights', it also concluded that such torture was not part of regular ANC policy. Again, no individuals were punished after the report's release. But the published testimony to the Truth and Reconciliation Commission paints a sorry picture.[7] One testifier spent four years in Quatro and described electrocution, suffocation, beatings, forced climbing of trees infested with wasps, naked staking out on the ground infested with ants, and starvation. He described himself as 'one of the Soweto generation', one of those who had joined Jacob Zuma in 1976.[8] Perhaps it is no wonder that Mosiuoa Lekota, a student leader of the 'Soweto generation', instantly left the ANC when Jacob Zuma overcame Thabo Mbeki and forced his recall as President of South Africa. The man who sings of asking for his machine gun to be brought to him – though never found guilty in a court of law or given the chance by any commission to defend himself – is still in some minds the one who turned that gun on comrades who, guilty of dissidence or not, were unable to defend themselves.

Finally, there is the question of what qualified Jacob Zuma for the posts, Head of Underground Structures and Chief of Intelligence. A veil is drawn over this. Unlike Thabo Mbeki, he never made the trek – via Paris – to Moscow for military or security training. But, given the operational procedures employed by Zuma and his people, it would not be far off the target to surmise that he was trained by East German intelligence operatives in Angola, just before the end of the Cold War. These people were involved in a great deal of such training and mentoring throughout Southern Africa. Both Zimbabwean and Zambian intelligence forces received training from the East Germans – including in interrogation techniques. These were not gentle, but they did not rule out refinements added by their students who, in such matters, were regrettably swift learners. And it also helps explain the use of Camp Quatro in Angola – whose government was grateful to the Eastern bloc for its military help in defeating South African Apartheid forces at the great battle of Cuito Cuanavale.

But there is another side of Jacob Zuma, and that is the settler of conflicts, the reconciler, the bridge-builder and peacemaker. After the release of Mandela and the unbanning of the ANC, there was much competition to command the black polity. In KwaZulu, the Inkatha Freedom Party, led by Chief Mangosuthu Buthelezi, refused to defer to the ANC. It is hard to say how much of an ethnic component went into this refusal, and how much it was a bloody-minded contest for political dominance in the province. Many Zulu people, however, died in the pogroms that involved many members of Inkatha. I was a visiting lecturer at the University of Natal for part of this period, and it wasn't hard to uncover evidence of how the rural pogroms were conducted. It was Shaka's method: the military stratagem of the famous Zulu king.

Called the 'bull horn' because it was curved, it was a pincer movement, whereby Inkatha militants would sweep upon an ANC village in an enveloping movement. Those able to flee had to escape a gauntlet closing in on them. Following behind, as the cradle of the horn, the Zulu women would sweep in to loot all that the living villagers had left. Many were unable to flee and died. This happened in the hills of KwaZulu while it was perfectly possible to lead an oblivious life by the sunny beaches of Durban – just as many people never seemed to see the sufferings of Apartheid. The vast land of South Africa has always been a string of insularities. But it was into the maelstrom of these killings and violence that Jacob Zuma was sent by the ANC.

Zuma was successful in reducing the level of violence. He himself was Zulu, and he slowly persuaded Inkatha that the quarrel with the ANC should be seen entirely in political rather than ethnic terms. It was probably his work that allowed Mandela successfully to invite Buthelezi into his Cabinet. But there is more to Zuma's mediation skills than a Zulu-to-Zulu encounter. In the 1990s he was also used internationally, and he facilitated the Burundi peace process where – as in neighbouring Rwanda – Hutus and Tutsis had gone to war against each other.[9] Insofar as anyone can be successful in such a complex conflict, Zuma was at least temporarily successful.

So the Jacob Zuma who has become President of South Africa has a reputation, deserved or not, as the ANC's bloody enforcer – but also as a conciliator and peacemaker. He also has a reputation as someone born into rural poverty and who, as a successful politician, was accused of deriving financial benefits from shady dealings with shadowy figures over important national issues.

Just as it was not Thabo Mbeki, but first Chris Hani and then Cyril Ramaphosa who were meant to succeed Mandela as President, so it was not meant to be Jacob Zuma as Mbeki's Deputy President. Probably most of the ANC seniority preferred Mathews Phosa – a learned and lawyerly man – but it was Mbeki himself who insisted that it should be Zuma. Perhaps it was because Phosa had himself briefly contemplated the presidency. In years to come Mbeki probably rued his insistence. At the time Mbeki began his first term in 1999, Zuma had just entered Parliament. He had been elected Deputy President of the ANC in 1997 and, in that sense, had some claim to be Deputy President of the country. He had also held by this time a variety of other senior positions, particularly the national chairpersonship of the ANC from 1994 – so that he was a shadow of sorts to Mandela during his years as President. But his real claim to the position was that he was owed. When Mandela became President, Zuma stood aside to allow Mbeki a clear run at the deputy presidency.[10] Now it was his turn. And perhaps Mbeki remembered the gauche young man who had come as an exile to Swaziland. The South Africans were most upset that the Swazis should harbour him, so the move to Mozambique had to be swift. But, in that brief time, it seems Mbeki and Zuma formed a bond. An unusual one for a learned and fastidious man on the one hand, and a shepherd boy of poor education and rough manners on the other. Perhaps Mbeki remembered tutoring Zuma in how to control the kickback of an AK47, how to keep his aim lower, and came to a lingering thought that Zuma could be no threat. Certainly, as Deputy President of South Africa, Zuma carved out no distinguished record whatsoever. And despite Zuma's record in settling conflict in KwaZulu and Burundi, as Mbeki began his vexed mediation in Zimbabwe, he made absolutely no use of Zuma in the complex talks with the steely and intellectually accomplished Robert Mugabe. Mbeki may not have wanted an intellectual equal as his Number 2; like Mugabe, he may have wanted or needed intellectual courtiers; and to walk into a room and be the man of learning. In which case, Zuma seemed a perfect choice. For Mbeki, perhaps. For South Africa? Questions of judgement began to be lodged against Zuma at an early stage of his time as Deputy President. From 2004, legal fingers have been pointing at Zuma. A rape charge followed in 2005 – suggesting male violence, male insatiability (in a man with multiple wives and a history of lovers) and, as a twist in the tale, ignorance of HIV and its prevention. A man couldn't conspire to be so clumsy and maladroit; he really must be so clumsy and maladroit. And this is what his supporters and defenders were at times reduced to claiming. He would not *knowingly* set out to be corrupt. His finances have always been a mess. He has no interest or knowledge in his finances – while, at the same time, never losing sight of a power struggle to come in which he would claim sufficient competence and self-control to be President of South Africa.

The timeline of Zuma's legal woes is like the instalments of a soap opera. It has certainly gripped South Africans in the same way.[11] In June 2005, Zuma's close associate, Schabir Shaik was found guilty of fraud, with suspicion cast on Zuma as a possible recipient of its bene- fits. As a result, later that month, Mbeki 'released' Zuma from both the deputy presidency and the Cabinet.

By October 2005, Zuma was himself charged with corruption. Shortly afterwards, he was accused of rape by the daughter of a family friend, and in December he was formally charged with rape. The trial began in February 2006, with Zuma denying the charge.

In April 2006, Zuma was acquitted of rape and, in May 2006, the ANC voted to reinstate him in his party duties. The respite seemed as if it might endure as in September 2006 the prosecution in Zuma's corruption trial requested more time to prepare its case and gather evidence, but the delay resulted in the trial being struck from the court list. It was a false respite, however, as in November 2007 the Supreme Court of Appeal allowed charges to be brought again, after much controversy over the seizure by police of documents from Zuma's home.

Zuma fought back by going on the political offensive. In December 2007, after a bitter contest, in which Zuma both strategically and tacti- cally outmanoeuvred Mbeki, Zuma won the ANC presidency at the party congress in Polokwane. There was no avoiding the legal battles, however. Only ten days later, prosecutors filed new corruption, racket- eering and tax charges against Zuma. In June 2008, Zuma filed a court petition to have his prosecution declared unconstitutional and invalid and, in September that year, he seemed vindicated when Judge Chris Nicholson declared the prosecution invalid on technical grounds. He also said that there was evidence of political interference in the legal proceedings, that Mbeki had colluded with the prosecutors against Zuma.

Although five days later, on 17 September, the National Prosecuting Authority announced it would appeal Nicholson's ruling, there was fury within the ANC, with Zuma's supporters pointing to Nicholson's judgment that Mbeki had interfered with the legal process. As a result of this fury, Mbeki was recalled by the party and stepped down as President of South Africa.

Despite Zuma's huge political victory over Mbeki, in October 2008, the prosecutors were granted leave to appeal Nicholson's dismissal of charges against Zuma.

In November 2008 Mbeki lost an attempt to quash the ruling that said he meddled in the prosecution of Zuma. But in January 2009 Nicholson's ruling was overturned by the Appeals Court. The charges against Zuma could stand. But, in the swings and roundabouts that politics and law had become over this issue, the Chief Prosecutor dropped charges against Zuma on 6 April 2009, just weeks before the elections, citing again the question of political interference.

On 22 April, South Africa voted decisively for the ANC – though not as heavily in percentage terms as before – clearing the way for an ANC-dominated Parliament to elect Zuma as President. Mbeki phoned Zuma from Sudan to congratulate him. The phone call was apparently cordial, unforced and unstilted. In early May, Mbeki returned from his mediation mission in Sudan to attend the inauguration – where Zuma spoke warmly of Mbeki, referring to him by the endearment name which he probably once used in Swaziland. On the podium, Mbeki was inscrutable, but it seemed that a public peace had broken out between the two men.

But there are key aspects of this saga that need closer examination. The key moment of Polokwane, the ANC party congress where Zuma became ANC President, revealed much about South African politics – some of which will haunt the country for years to come. The die was cast at Polokwane. That was the decisive battle between Mbeki and Zuma. Simultaneously, while the great struggle was going on between the two men, another titanic struggle was occurring in Zimbabwe.

Zuma's tribulations began because of his association with Schabir Shaik. All the commentary on the Zuma–Shaik saga has concentrated on Schabir Shaik, and he is depicted as a Durban businessman with a dubious academic record. (He had cheated in his engineering exams.) But the Shaik family is the real matter of interest. Schabir had brothers and at least two of them were involved in the anti-Apartheid struggle and were arrested, though later released. One brother, Mo, had introduced Schabir to Zuma in London. Schabir himself was used by the ANC to carry funds raised for the struggle from London to South Africa – so he took his own share of risks in the days before Mandela was released. He and Zuma became close.[12] Even so, it was another brother, Shamin or 'Chippy', who was to feature in the episode that directly led to Zuma's downfall. Chippy was in charge of arms acquisition in the Ministry of Defence. First, however, Schabir wove a financial net around Zuma that procured Zuma's gratitude and, to a large extent, dependence. When that eventually faded, there was still the sense of obligation felt by Zuma because of all the help Schabir had given him.

In early 1990, Zuma returned to South Africa from exile. He was penniless. When, in 1994, Zuma commenced his work in KwaZulu, Schabir began making him significant loans – of the size Zuma could never repay – but Schabir would periodically write off these loans. It was at this stage that Zuma developed his taste in fine tailoring – but even then his financial affairs were in a constant state of chaos. His defenders are right: he had no idea of how to handle money and his bank records were a long litany of overdrafts, loans and threats of sequestration. He began life as a country bumpkin, went to prison, went into exile, no doubt passed judgements on other people's lives while in exile, but never learnt finances. Money raised abroad for the struggle, and smuggled into Africa by people like Schabir Shaik, paid for his upkeep. He was simply hopeless in a world where income and expenditure had to be judicious and balanced. Four different banks seemed to have been involved in advancing money for Zuma's retail therapy. Schabir Shaik repaid all these loans and gave Zuma more money from his own fortune. It may have been friendship. If so, it was an exceedingly generous friendship. It was also buying influence.

A very large French arms company, Thomson-CSF, had enjoyed close and profitable links with the Apartheid government. Frozen out of its preferred tendering status by the new ANC government, it wanted back in. It set about achieving this in two ways. The first was legitimate and careful. Thomson-CSF began tendering for non-defence contracts in airport construction, transport, telecommunications and identity card production. It sought to establish an image of itself as a reformed and constructive player – wanting to help rebuild South Africa and not profit from the arms industry alone. Secondly, it began buying shares in South African defence companies, and also sold its own shares to local players – including Schabir Shaik's Nkobi Holdings. It seemed a strategy of integrating itself in the local 'scene'.

But the strategy also involved ingratiation and the possibility of dirty deals. Chippy Shaik told Thomson that, in return for an acceptable 'position' towards himself and his friends, he could finesse the tendering process for Thomson to get back into the mainstream South African arms industry. In 1996, when tenders were being invited for the electronic systems in a new fleet of naval corvettes, Schabir Shaik was desperate that Nkobi should have a prime role in the tendering process and there followed a complicated series of manoeuvres and share deals between Nkobi and Thomson, with Schabir assuring Thomson that – both through Chippy's pivotal position in the Ministry of Defence, and Schabir's own friendship with Zuma – the bid would be successful, and that Thomson would be back in the arms frame, albeit with Nkobi as a key beneficiary.

They pretty much got away with it – at first. But two things intervened. Firstly, in early 1997, there was an opportunistic burglary at Chippy's house and, along with valuables, the thief made off with a briefcase of incriminating documents. These were later found. Secondly,

Zuma had now acquired the funds to begin accomplishing one of his dreams: to develop a traditional residential village estate, at staggering cost, in rural northern KwaZulu. It was a huge strain on both his and his friends' resources. Schabir Shaik called in Thomson at the end of September 1999. By this time, an investigation into the corrupt nature of the arms deal had been launched. Shaik offered Zuma's protection to Thomson, in exchange for a payment which would have been enough to cover most of Zuma's debt from his village project. But Thomson prevaricated. Zuma's need for the money was urgent. He wrote a cheque to pay off his developers – but Shaik refused to cover the cheque.[13] There was now a rupture between the two men. It is impossible to say in what manner the relationship between Shaik and Zuma waxed and waned in this period. Certainly, when the investigators caught up with Shaik, it became necessary for Zuma to distance himself as much as possible from him and there was no protection forthcoming. Zuma himself found that he too was under investigation.

The image Shaik has always tried to project – in much the same way as Zuma was consistently projected as a man out of his depth in financial management – was that of a man who had only tried to help Zuma. Shaik had also tried to help the ANC and would have felt aggrieved that the entire party apparatus now stood aloof from his predicament. For instance, in 1994, Shaik had tried – unsuccessfully – to persuade Malaysian interests to pay off the huge 40-million-rand debt the ANC had incurred in becoming an organised political party and running an election campaign. Shaik had a genuine interest in the Malaysian model as a vehicle for Black Economic Empowerment. Shaik had named his company, without the Nkobi family's permission, after the late Thomas Nkobi who had been ANC Treasurer-General. He had tried his best to associate himself with the ANC and had in fact been of great value to it. He was on speaking terms with Thabo Mbeki and a large number of the ANC seniority. He was 'one of them'. He had put a lot on the line to help 'them', not just Zuma, and he was 'owed'. In many ways, Shaik's attempt to make the system work commercially for him, and to imagine it proper to do so – as a just return for assistance to the party and personnel of liberation – was only a reflection of what the ANC itself came to believe and practise. Shaik tried to do too much with a man who could return too little and who exposed himself too clumsily. Otherwise, Shaik is as much a symbol of the new South Africa as Zuma. Perhaps as much as many fat cats with political histories – who have not been and will not be caught. But, to catch Zuma, it was first necessary to catch Shaik. Whether or not Mbeki and Zuma had by this stage fallen out, and Zuma was chosen for public humiliation – whereas many other corrupt ANC persons were left unmolested – or whether the visibility of the corvettes deal was so large that it could not be ignored, all roads eventually led to Shaik and the investigators produced incontrovertible evidence of his dealings. On 2 June 2005, Durban High Court Judge Hilary Squires sentenced Shaik on two counts of corruption and one of fraud. One of the corruption charges was that Shaik had attempted to solicit a bribe from Thomson for Zuma. In his judgment, Squires said there was 'overwhelming' evidence of a corrupt relationship between Shaik and Zuma. There was evidence of 'a mutually beneficial symbiosis' between the two and that the monetary gifts and advances Shaik had made to Zuma could 'only have generated a sense of obligation in the recipient'.[14] The judgment created a public outcry and, on 14 June 2005, Mbeki sacked Zuma. The investigators now turned their full attention to Zuma and, in October 2005, he was charged with corruption.

Thereafter for a time, it seemed Zuma could do nothing right. Everything he touched turned to dust. In December 2005 he was charged with rape, and the extraordinary trial that resulted led to his being made a laughing stock – as well as a feminist symbol of everything that was sexist in South Africa. The person bringing the charge was a 31-year-old HIV-positive family friend. Despite being much married, simultaneously, Zuma agreed he had sex with her. It was, however, consensual – and he knew she wanted sex, he said, because she was wearing a short traditional wrap around her hips and offered no resistance. It was, he said, contrary to Zulu culture to refuse the offer of sex from a woman. He did not wear a condom but took a shower afterwards to 'cut the risk' of HIV infection.[15] (He was head of the South African National AIDS Council at that time.) The trial was, like so many rape trials, not noted for its delicacy. Zuma's lawyers painted a picture of the young woman as someone with a sexual history and reputation. The prosecution accused Zuma of exploiting and corrupting a relationship that had been like that of father and daughter.[16] Although Zuma was acquitted in April 2006, with the judge castigating him for his recklessness, the various remarks made in court caused a furore.

But then, two things began going very well for Zuma. The first was that his lawyers kept fighting a technically superb battle to delay the corruption proceedings. In this they were greatly aided by a prosecution that seemed to be having genuine difficulties mustering its case. Some of these were related to obtaining documents in Zuma's possession, but the applications for postponement of the trial did not suggest a prosecution in full control of the charges that had been laid. The second was that, almost organically, a huge section of the ANC began to look upon Zuma not just as Zuma, the man of the people as he had always claimed to be, but as Zuma-Who-Was-Not-Mbeki. In May 2006 Zuma was reinstated to his former ANC party duties. What the amazing resurgence of Zuma demonstrated was the huge unpopularity of Mbeki within key sections of his own party. The distance that his aloofness and austere intellectualism had created was now going to destroy him. So the real questions of this case are not to do with whether Zuma was corrupt or not, but whether Mbeki used the case to seek to destroy Zuma, and whether Zuma's eventual overthrow of Mbeki was revenge – or whether he was simply carried along as the beneficiary of many others who used him to overthrow Mbeki. This is a case about corruption but, in more ways than one, it is a case about what sort of party the ANC is. If it is a party that 'rewards' its supporters and those who struggled for liberation, and it has been selective in how it identifies these people, can it also be a party of the masses if those who successfully identify themselves with the masses feel left out of the rewards – and want in? Mbeki was never prescient enough, or had his ear close enough to the ground, to understand or hear the grumblings of dissatisfaction.

It took until as late as 8 November 2007 for the National Prosecuting Authority finally to receive Supreme Court permission to seize documents from Zuma – including the personal diary of a senior Thomson executive. Even so, it was not until 28 December 2007 that Zuma was served with an indictment to stand trial in the High Court on charges of racketeering, money-laundering, corruption and fraud. But this was 10 days after Zuma had been elected President of the ANC at the party conference in the city of Polokwane, crushing Mbeki's bid for another term by 2,329 delegate votes to 1,505. Mbeki, who remained President of South Africa, was furiously accused by Zuma loyalists of manipulating judicial procedures to ensure that Zuma, if he were convicted of such crimes, could never become his successor. Conviction accompanied by a prison sentence of more than one year would have debarred him from high office. It was, therefore, at the turn of the year, as 2007 flowed into 2008, that the campaign began to remove Mbeki as national President, just as he had already been deprived of the party presidency. And, just as at Polokwane, so also in the ANC hierarchy, Mbeki learnt to his cost that it wasn't just the supporters of Zuma who were arrayed against him: he simply no longer had the votes in the high levels of the ANC as a whole. However, in the context of South Africa's place in the region, it all seemed like a giant introspection – old arguments with new twists involving old people still fighting for their slice of the new South Africa. Zimbabwean migration into South Africa had become a major problem. In the month before Polokwane, the Mbeki mediation in the Zimbabwean crisis had almost produced a breakthrough – negotiated in, of all places, a houseboat on Lake Kariba, between Zambia and Zimbabwe. And early 2008 would see what became the vexed rounds of Zimbabwean elections where, first, Robert Mugabe lost – and then didn't. Uncertainty in South Africa was accompanied by chaos, turmoil and strong-armed clinging to power in a bankrupt Zimbabwe.

Meanwhile South Africa was beset by chronic rolling power shortages. No one had planned increased capacity for hugely increased demand. There were problems at home and abroad – but Mbeki and Zuma had a feud to fight through and there was to be a casualty at the highest level.

Polokwane is a small city in the north of the country. Here a new stadium was built for the 2010 Football World Cup to feature first-round matches from which qualifiers emerge for the more important stages of the competition. The first round is an elimination.

In the middle of December 2007, the ANC gathered for its party conference.[17] Consensus was that Zuma would capture the party presidency. Almost all the media pundits agreed. Yet Mbeki was determined to stand again and thought he could win. If he did, he could continue to influence, even determine, ANC policy long after he relinquished the national presidency at the end of his second and constitutionally last term.[18] Either Mbeki and his people were hopelessly out of touch with delegate feeling, or they calculated that the much-rumoured candidacy of Tokyo Sexwale would divide the opposition vote and allow Mbeki to come through between Sexwale and Zuma. But even this calculation was naïve.

Tokyo Sexwale – the nickname 'Tokyo' derives from his boyhood fascination with all things Japanese – had been an ANC heavyweight, Premier of Gauteng province, and a highly successful businessman with interests in many ventures. These included the South African corporate penetration of China. The new-generation Chinese links with Africa are not entirely one-way. The darling of the formerly white-dominated business community, Sexwale demonstrated great corporate skills and manoeuvrability. That community is still white-dominated, but players like Sexwale give it the patina of accessibility and plurality. Now a black fat cat, he hardly seemed likely to steal votes from the populist Zuma, whose natural constituency was the mass of deprived Africans who had not, unlike Sexwale, benefited from a rainbow nation that left them still poor. But Sexwale gave every impression of canvassing support and building alliances. The South African Communist Party had been uneasy about Zuma during his rape trial and some senior members worried about a future consumed by personalities rather than issues.[19] Real alliances were possible, even if not probable.[20] But Mbeki's people bought the line Sexwale was purveying – standing without formally declaring himself but, to all intents and purposes, behaving like a candidate.[21]

When Thabo Mbeki became heir to Nelson Mandela he overcame all other claimants to the throne. Cyril Ramaphosa had been the front-runner. It was said Mandela himself had preferred Ramaphosa. Another rumoured claimant had been Sexwale. Mbeki moved against both. There are two versions of Sexwale's candidacy back in 1998–9. One was that he seriously eyed the succession; the other that he was misconstrued by Mbeki as doing so. According to this second version, put forward by Mbeki's critical biographer, William Gumede, as soon as Sexwale discerned that he had inadvertently offended Mbeki and his ambitions, he ensured he would not be a candidate and, indeed, removed himself from the centre of the ANC and went into busi-ness.[22] However, it is very much the case that Sexwale was ambitious, both then and now. Zuma has made him a cabinet minister and, once again, the stories have circulated that Sexwale has his eyes on the presidency – this time in 2014, at the end of Zuma's first term. As do others – Mathews Phosa and Kgalema Motlanthe being at time of writing foremost amongst them. This would be dependent on whether Zuma stands for a second term. He has waxed and waned about this, now being a one-term president, and then wishing to go on.

But what happened at Polokwane was that Sexwale sold the Mbeki camp a blind. At the last minute, he threw all his weight – including those delegates he had on his side – behind Zuma. Ramaphosa also supported Zuma and used his influence to persuade delegates that Zuma held the future. Sexwale and Ramaphosa, possibly the two richest men in the senior history of the ANC, played a decisive role in ensuring that Mbeki never received the number of votes he had counted on.[23] With Zuma's triumph at a noisy and rumbustious conference, revenge was sweet for Ramaphosa and probably Sexwale. Was it sweet for Zuma? The defeated Mbeki had a trump card up his sleeve.

After Zuma's acquittal on rape charges, and with the difficulties the prosecutors faced in bringing their case against him to court, Zuma's followers concluded that they had sufficient space for unstoppable momentum. Their triumph at Polokwane delighted them. At that stage, however, they had no ambition further to humiliate Mbeki. They were content to see him reach the end of his term: there was little over one year to go. Mbeki's apparent next moves, however, infuriated them. Mbeki has always denied he was the person responsible for the prosecutors bringing fresh charges of corruption against Zuma a mere ten days after his victory at Polokwane. It was, he has said, the prosecutor's decision and he did not interfere with the legal processes.

However, if a conviction and a sentence of more than one year could be secured against Zuma before the national elections, then Zuma could not be President of South Africa. There was just enough time to do this. And, frankly, the suspicion that Mbeki was prepared to intervene in legal and prosecutorial processes was already widely held. When, in the previous months, the National Director of Public Prosecutions, Vusi Pikoli, was closing in on the National Police Commissioner with charges of corruption, Mbeki abruptly suspended Pikoli and replaced him with Mokotedi Mpshe.[24] The day after Zuma won the ANC presidency, the same Mpshe announced that it was highly probable that charges would be reinstigated against Zuma and, shortly afterwards, they were. In the month before Polokwane, with court authority, the investigators had seized documents from Zuma's home. They were getting ready to move just before Zuma's elevation, and were ready to move immediately afterwards.[25] Some people saw the seizure as insurance against a Zuma victory, and the charges as the activation of that insurance. To be fair, however, the investigators had been attempting to secure these documents for some time and the coincidence of the party conference was perhaps just that – a coincidence. But many saw the prosecution of Zuma as selective. If the

National Police Commissioner did not have to face charges, why should Zuma? If many people were corrupt, why should there not be many prosecutions? If many were corrupt, and only Zuma was chosen, on what grounds was Zuma chosen? Were they political and what was the nature of such politics within the ANC? The atmosphere in South Africa at this time was febrile.

The episode cast a huge cloud over Mbeki's final year and, in his mediation of the Zimbabwean crisis, he became progressively more and more a lame duck. But the struggle between Zuma and Mbeki had more chapters to play out, and the interweaving of court rulings, appeals and their political consequences would change South Africa as much as any election. In neighbouring Zimbabwe, Robert Mugabe was determined that the elections in his country would change nothing. South Africa may have been febrile. Zimbabwe was in political chaos and economic catastrophe. The consequences of that were going to impact on South Africa – on its own soil. Mbeki never could move fast enough, except to secure his own political advantage – and he often got it wrong. Even when he got it right, overcoming Ramaphosa and Sexwale for the presidency, he didn't see their revenge lurking in the wings of Polokwane. He moved within a narrow frame. And surely, he thought, he could exclude Zuma from that frame. Zuma, in his shambolic way, simply widened the frame.

And, despite the struggle to come in 2009, the astute members of Mbeki's own Cabinet – moderates as well as so-called radicals – saw that power had seeped from Mbeki. Immediately after Zuma's triumph at Polokwane, Finance Minister Trevor Manuel, the celebrated epitome of fiscal prudence and the architect of so much that Mbeki could claim to have accomplished – despite its flaws and shortcomings – spoke out in favour of Zuma. It wasn't a full endorsement. Well-judged and measured as always, it was a signal that the wind had changed and that Manuel, like many others, was tacking hard and changing the colour of his sails.

CHAPTER 10

THE ELECTIONS OF NO ELECTION: THE PRELUDE TO VEXED COMPROMISE IN ZIMBABWE[1]

Jacob Zuma defeated Thabo Mbeki for the presidency of the ANC at the end of 2007 but, in the early part of 2008, Morgan Tsvangirai hoped to defeat Robert Mugabe in the elections in Zimbabwe. A weakened Thabo Mbeki who, in any case, had philosophical affinities with Mugabe, did not intervene to halt the rigging that ended the first electoral round, and Africa as a whole watched as increasing violence preceded the second round. Mugabe was determined to contest and win the elections – by any means possible. Even he, however, wanted a figleaf of legitimacy – so the rigging was protracted and painstaking. It was a lot of tailoring for one figleaf. Mugabe faced a challenge, not only from Tsvangirai, but from within his own party ranks. The disgruntled technocrats, led by Simba Makoni, finally broke ranks with the rest of ZANU-PF. But Tsvangirai was facing splits of his own. His leadership style had alienated many within the MDC and, after one misjudgement too many, the opposition split and the breakaway wing rallied around Arthur Mutambara. Suddenly, the two-horse race that had characterised Zimbabwean electoral politics since 2000 was more complicated. It made the mobilisation of support more difficult. It made rigging more difficult as a judicious choice had to be made in terms of whose votes should be 'miscounted' or counted down, or appropriated, in which constituencies. It would also make mediation in the huge dispute that followed more difficult. But, before then, a vicious political conflict was curiously punctuated by some plangent biblical allusions from Robert Mugabe – about Robert Mugabe. Deep inside himself, the old man still believed in his destiny and his cause.

Alexandra is on the way to the richer part of Sandton in Johannesburg. It's only a 20-minute fast walk or slow jog from Alex, as it is commonly and almost affectionately known, to Sandton City and Nelson Mandela Square. The latter are temples to elite consumerism. One merges into another, and they both become an air-conditioned shopping mall like Knightsbridge under cover. The finest Swiss watches can be purchased there more cheaply than in Knightsbridge. There is a rich local market, but the idea is also partly that foreigners will fly in, buy the watches at a lower price than elsewhere, even including the costs of the trip, yet still bring a huge profit to the retailers. The mall is almost a perfect representation of how, in the new South Africa, the local elite and the global neo-liberal order meet. But a person from Alex, looking at the display cases, will simultaneously know envy, avarice, covetousness and disgust at the contrast only 20 minutes away.

I first went to Alex in 1991. I had just come up from Cape Town where I had spent a short time helping to monitor the truce in a taxi war on the Cape flats outside the city and close to the airport. A taxi war involved a form of organised gangsterism that uses minibuses and the control of minibus routes as a legitimate front; when routes were pirated by other operators, or fares were 'unfairly' discounted by rival operators, a 'war' broke out. This involved much public bloodshed. Economic life came to a standstill or slowdown, as people in the poorer suburbs depended on the minibuses for transport into work. It was one of those intersections where criminal life and formal economic life collided in South Africa. And they could be politicised wars as well: ostensibly ANC-supporting taxi operators against those who purported to support others. But what struck me in those early days after Nelson

Mandela's release was the grinding poverty of the shanty towns on the Cape flats. It was the rainy season and much of the area was under water. For hundreds of metres in every direction, people were walking knee-deep in flood waters and entering and leaving homes that were also knee-deep in water. But when I came to Alex, it seemed a picture of development – even if derelict development – compared to Crossroads and Khayelitsha outside Cape Town. There wasn't Table Mountain brooding in the far distance – seeming to impose a very different impression to the one received by tourists in the centre of Cape Town. It was not as distant from the main parts of the city and was a relatively small settlement built on two sides of a narrow valley. The streets were unpaved, and much of the electricity was clearly hot-wired. The hostels used by miners looked like mental asylum dormitories, but there was running water. A small cluster of new, almost middle-class houses sat on the high end of one slope and, by and large, the rest of Alex was a slum rather than a shanty. But, in the small buildings in the valley, as many as 15 people could crowd into each house. In Alex, accommodation was at a premium. And yet, as in so many such locations, there was a community spirit and sense of belonging. People wanted Alex to get better, but they didn't necessarily want to leave.

In Alex in April 2009, there were none of the outdoor chemical toilets I later found in Kliptown. Every road had been paved. And, on the higher slopes, there were many new buildings that, all the same, seemed of low construction standard. The plaster on the outside walls would crack in five years. But they were two storeys high, painted in a burnt orange, had a view of all those below – who had a view only of the area as it had always been, but now with paved roads cutting through what still seemed to be hot-wired dereliction. The new buildings were social housing, built by Black Economic Empowerment as part of Reconstruction and Development, and they should have been for those on a transparently constructed list of long-term Alex residents. Their allocation was in the hands of not well paid administrators. On this visit I learnt in the streets of Alex that the going bribe to get you up the list was 1,000 rand. Not much in international terms, pocket money to the children of those who shopped for Swiss watches in Sandton City – but a very great deal to those who lived in Alex. In 2008, those who had been actively bribing the officials were recently arrived Zimbabweans.

Not all Zimbabweans who fled to South Africa, for the most part without employment papers, were destitute. They fled because of economic meltdown at home, but the television clips of ragged men scrambling under barbed wire at the border told a partial story. Many, with passports, just got on the bus with their savings and, at the other end, began finding ways of making their little pots of capital work for them. They found places like Alex unproblematic. A little could go a long way. A little could bribe an official with ease. The trick was not just to obtain one house, but as many as possible. Live in one, rent out the others, secure a guaranteed regular income, and send assured sums home each month to the extended family. As Thabo Mbeki's slow-motion diplomacy dragged on and on, the inert pace of progress over Zimbabwe created dynamic problems in his own country. It wasn't just Zimbabweans competing for jobs, or Zimbabweans without jobs turning to crime. It was also Zimbabweans with a little money securing housing – when, all around them, decent housing was at a premium.

Housing has always been a key ANC electoral commitment. The promised numbers have never come. The lag is a serious issue and heightens both expectation and frustration. The use of Black Empowerment firms has, in many locations, resulted in substandard building standards. Not everywhere: in some parts of Western Cape the new housing units come with solar-heating panels and other refinements. In Alex, they seemed very quickly put up indeed. But, in May and June 2008, starting in Alex and spreading throughout South Africa, huge riots broke out against Zimbabweans and other foreigners. It was quickly labelled 'xenophonic violence', and several died.[2] The timing was not just a product of accumulated frustration, nor was it merely xenophobic. It was also a recognition of political reality. They followed on the heels of the troubled elections in Zimbabwe. If Robert Mugabe was determined to stay put, then the Zimbabweans on South African soil were also going to stay put. If they were going to stay put, they would take away houses, jobs, whatever, for ever. It was certainly frustration at the slow pace of the ANC programmes and the corruption of officials, and this frustration resulted in more violence just three months after the election of Jacob Zuma, but it was also a venting of anger at international relations that made their hopes for their own national and local progress futile.

But if their hopes seemed futile, so did those of a huge number of Zimbabweans. From the farm invasions of 2000, but particularly as the economic consequences of having lost a national productive base began to be felt, from 2002 onwards, up to three million of them had decamped, with or without funds, to South Africa. Up to one million had made it to the United Kingdom, clogging up the asylum system and swiftly making their mark in the shadowy world of illegal employment – doing the work no one else would do. The Zimbabwean writer Brian Chikwava, in his acclaimed novel *Harare North*, called them BBCs – British Bum Cleaners – who worked with the incontinent in old people's homes.[3] But, if Brixton was Harare North, Luton would be a strong contender for northern Chitungwiza. The majority of the exile Zimbabweans in the UK were MDC supporters – but not all. A strong ZANU-PF element not only lived among them but was often feared for real or imagined reportage of their activities to the authorities back home. All of them were fixated on the 2008 Zimbabwean elections. Because, for the first time, it would be not only ZANU-PF and the MDC – Mugabe and Tsvangirai – going head to head, but a split ZANU-PF and a split MDC. For once it would not be just two monolithic actors playing a zero-sum game. With many people in the game, the spread of possibilities, even of coalitions and sharing of power, of some prospect of Mugabe and ZANU-PF not maintaining absolute power, was on. Most, in and out of Zimbabwe, thought the MDC by itself had no chance of taking over from ZANU-PF. It was no longer strong enough and had split with rancour. The reasons for the split were attributed to Morgan Tsvangirai – even by people who had been his closest friends and allies.

Even his worst enemies within ZANU-PF attributed decency and courage to Morgan Tsvangirai. Mugabe hated him, but this was as much to do with condescension as political antagonism. As if he thought, 'who are you, a person without education who did not fight in the liberation war, to challenge me, I who am the epitome of both?' Mbeki and his ministers involved in the Zimbabwean mediation quite liked Tsvangirai – but did not think he could ever be a good president. Among other things, he changed his mind too much and, quite often, he changed his mind and made pronouncements without consulting his own people. In the West, Tsvangirai was lionised for his courage and his integrity on the big political issues. No one had a clue about his capacity to manage his own people: it was assumed he could do it and was doing it. In a world where hero worship has its place in the clear demarcation of who and what is right or wrong, with demonisation of others as the necessary foil to this, Tsvangirai was a hero. In many ways, he was. In some other ways, key figures in the MDC found him a nightmare. And, after the Ben-Menashe affair, when death on treason charges had seemed a real possibility, the embattled Tsvangirai increasingly seemed unable to formulate a way forward. Everything the MDC threw at Robert Mugabe and ZANU-PF – particularly mass rallies – not only failed to work but rebounded, as the MDC had begun losing by-elections for seats it had held. People beaten up in the rallies asked what other tactics and strategies the MDC had. Mugabe would laugh at the Tsvangirai challenge in his own speeches. Under these pressures Tsvangirai became not only erratic but pre-emptory. He began ignoring his own executive, in terms of consultation, but also with respect to decisions the executive – with him present – had taken. This aroused great frustration and resentment. Where was the transparency and democracy in the party of transparency and democracy? ZANU-PF was ecstatic. Without even trying as hard as they had first thought necessary, they saw that the MDC was going to split before their very eyes.

In fact Tsvangirai had been putting into place what amounted to a parallel party structure as early as 2002, in the aftermath of the lost presidential elections. Ostensibly, in the face of the often violent ZANU-PF threat, this was to facilitate speedy top-down responses to the orders of the MDC leadership. It bypassed local organisers who were often slow or inept, and sometimes corrupt. What it also did, however, was to raise suspicion and resentment in the official structures and, because it was first designed to counter the violence of ZANU-PF, the parallel structures had the capacity to be violent in turn. In 2004, this violence was turned against senior officials within the headquarters of the MDC itself. Even the MDC's official Director of Security was subjected to violence.[4]

During Morgan Tsvangirai's treason trial in 2004, the parallel structure of militants was convinced that he would be found guilty and hanged. The succession became a major issue with them and, above all, they were determined that the MDC Secretary-General, Professor Welshman Ncube, should not become Party President. Some of this was a residual antipathy on the part of Shona militants to the idea of an Ndebele person becoming their leader. Some thought Ncube would be prepared to enter a compromise with Mugabe. Some simply hated intellectuals – many of the youthful militants having come from unemployed and uneducated slum backgrounds – and Tsvangirai's early anti-intellectualism appealed to them. Ncube, by contrast, a distinguished professor of law, was the intellectual's intellectual.

In May 2005, inner-party violence broke out again at the MDC headquarters, in the provincial office in Bulawayo and in the town of Gwanda. The laboured inquiry afterwards expelled some of the militant youths, but left untouched the small number of Tsvangirai's closest associates who many felt were the directors both of the parallel structure and its violence.[5]

All political leaders have a 'kitchen cabinet' of those they trust most. These are not always people elected or trusted by others. But leaders need those in whom they can confide and with whom they can rehearse policy options. In the West, both the White House and 10 Downing Street have populations of aides and advisers whom no one elected, and they become very powerful. One thinks of Alastair Campbell under Tony Blair, Karl Rove under George W. Bush. In Paris, each minister has his own official Cabinet of personally chosen advisers. Tsvangirai insisted to his internal critics that his own 'kitchen cabinet' was no danger to the official party and its structures. Yet many of the party seniors who bearded him about the power his aides were assuming were also those who would later leave him, having had enough of being – as they felt it – undemocratically undermined. But there was more at stake than party democracy. The MDC was well funded by overseas sources. The Scandinavians put a lot of money into the party as part of a commitment to international democracy. Position within the MDC, or leverage against those who had position, could become the pathway to resources. Financially the MDC was sometimes as murky as its internal democracy. And money just kept coming in. As with Jacob Zuma in South Africa, accountability never became an assiduously refined art.

But, quite apart from questions of parallel structures, very real questions arose around Tsvangirai's personal impositions of policy or departures from previously agreed policies. This would come to a head in the latter part of 2005. It was at this time that Robert Mugabe, precisely to create new positions of patronage – whereby ZANU-PF loyalists could be rewarded with access to funds – recreated the Senate. The Upper House had been disbanded under majority rule. Now the MDC, having taken a rigged electoral beating at the hands of Mugabe and ZANU-PF earlier that year, was divided over whether to contest the Senate elections. All this was in the wake not only of lost elections a few months earlier, but of the dreadful Operation Murambatsvina of May 2005, in which – under orders from Mugabe's government – bulldozers and wrecking crews, in the middle of the Zimbabwean winter, tore down and razed to the ground huge sections of Mbare, an MDC inner-city stronghold, and made tens of thousands of people homeless. This was ostensibly in the name of civic improvement.[6] Tsvangirai's mood was no longer to play ball with any election organised by such a government. But the MDC National Council voted 33 to 31 that it should contest the Senate. Tsvangirai refused to accept the decision. And, since there were two spoilt ballots, he announced to the press that the National Council had been deadlocked at 33 and 33 and that he had used his casting vote against participation in the Senate elections. This was false.

Welshman Ncube publicly asked in what ways could the MDC challenge Mugabe except through elections? 'Even if ZANU-PF says there is an election for a toilet caretaker we will participate.'[7] The party split. But Ncube knew he could not be the leader of an alternative MDC. Even on the eve of 2006, the majority Shona would not vote for an eastern Ndebele leader. The long absence of ethnic violence did not mean that ethnic accommodation and ethnic cooperation had reached the stage of an ethnic minority president being acceptable. It was the end of 2008 before the USA accepted a black president. There has never been a black, brown, yellow or mixed-race president or prime minister in any European democracy. There is not going to be an Ndebele president in any democratic Zimbabwe in the near future. Those who split from Morgan Tsvangirai faced their first problem. They had split on principle. But they had split without a leader. There was pig-headedness on both sides – on Tsvangirai's for going against the narrow will of his own National Council, and without an alternative strategy to elections; and on the side of his dissidents, who felt a repulsion towards unilateralism and its manifestations in violence, but had no alternative leader. The celebrated spokesman for Zimbabwean civil society, Professor Brian Raftopoulos, who was brought in to mediate the two factions – unsuccessfully – found it hard not to cry during the fruitless negotiations between the sides.[8] If, during Operation Murambatsvina, Mugabe acted like Saturn devouring his own children, then the MDC, at the close of 2005, was like a man without ideas for food cannibalising himself. Everyone wanted control of the mouth.

It was the breakaway faction that moved swiftly to create a new body for itself. Almost all internal political figures were in some way compromised by association with ZANU-PF or one or other of the bickering MDC factions. There was a need to present an uncontaminated figure, a youthful figure – Shona but not mired in the ethnic divisions of the liberation era with its two competing armies drawn from opposite ends of the country – and one who was technocratic. Arthur Mutambara was plucked from years of obscurity in the United Kingdom, the United States and South Africa. He had not always

been obscure. He had been born in 1966 and so was only 14 when
majority rule was won. As a student leader in the late 1980s he had cut
a dashing, firebrand image.[9] He had called the African Union a club of
dictators and, like all student leaders of his era, he had talked much and
was excellent on a public platform. Time would tell if he had moder-
ated his inability to accept compromises around a committee table.
Certainly age had emphasised his already protuberant forehead and
the appearance of bulging eyeballs when he raised his voice. But he was
tall, wore good suits and was as bright as Robert Mugabe. He had won
a Rhodes Scholarship to Merton, Oxford, and had taken a doctorate
there in robotics. He had held visiting professorships at both Caltech
and MIT, and was a successful consultant in South Africa. His election
by the breakaway group in February 2006 electrified all those who
had become disenchanted with Morgan Tsvangirai, and his acceptance
speech apportioned blame for the country's ills – not in the dyadic
way of the simplified opposition politics that had arisen around
ZANU-PF/Mugabe and MDC/Tsvangirai. Mutambara criticised the
government, the opposition, the British, the international community
and the region. Then he presented himself as the man with the range
of vision and ability to pull all these complex and vexatious strands
together. His experience both internationally and regionally was a
strength that his new people emphasised. But, if the tired but still
vigorous warhorses of ZANU-PF thought that here was a young
pretender, a lightweight in terms of recent political experience inside
Zimbabwe, someone who could be picked off – or encouraged in order
to deepen the rift in the MDC's electoral base – someone, in short,
who could be manipulated, handled, they were just as concerned over
how to handle dissent in their own house.

The first serious moves against Robert Mugabe's rulership of
ZANU-PF had not come from young pretenders, but from the
strongest of strong men and women in the old guard – the Praetorians
of liberation – those upon whom Mugabe had depended in
Mozambique in the second part of the 1970s to ensure he won control

of all ZANU-PF and its guerrilla army. The move came from a husband and wife team. It was a problematic team, simultaneously together and competitive within itself: Solomon and Joice Mujuru. Joice was Mugabe's Vice-President, and Solomon had become seriously rich in the first decade of liberated Zimbabwe. Their names had changed from the war days. Then, he was General Rex Nhongo, feared commander of ZANU-PF's guerrilla army. She was Teurai Ropa, a celebrated fighter of conspicuous heroism. As the 2000s progressed, they had realised that the Mugabe path was leading nowhere but to rack and ruin. Simultaneously, both having benefited from the Mugabe years, they were anxious that any change should be on their terms. No one knew which of them wanted more to be president. But, despite teasing Joice with vague promises of an eventual succession falling to her, Mugabe was going nowhere. In 2006, the Mujurus began planning a palace coup. What they wanted was what Jacob Zuma later accomplished, when the ANC recalled Mbeki from the South African presidency. The coup was to be for control of ZANU-PF and then the party's recall and replacement of Robert Mugabe. The fight in the first instance was for control of the party, and only after that for the country. The rumours in Harare were that an internal party putsch was timed for September 2007.[10]

This never happened. Mugabe mobilised his serving generals and strongmen. They had interests in a Mugabe future because they had become as rich as the Mujurus via a web of local corruption and mining concessions in Democratic Republic of Congo, where they had been sent by Mugabe to fight and stayed with his blessing to exploit – with the help of many Western accountants, bankers and lawyers. These had already pledged their loyalty to Mugabe in the face of Tsvangirai's original MDC challenge. Curiously, their strengthening of resolve and solidarity with Mugabe came with the plots of the Mujurus. Solomon Mujuru seemed the prime plotter at this stage and, when it became clear the big battalions would not shift to him, the strangest of alliances began to form for the second stage of his challenge. Mujuru made soundings towards Simba Makoni,[11] promising him support for a bid of his own. In Makoni, a dashing former finance and planning minister, regarded by the West in the days when it had time for ZANU-PF as the technocrat's technocrat, the party would have a direct equivalent of Arthur Mutambara. Suddenly, generational shifts seemed the agenda in Zimbabwean politics. But, just as Mutambara fronted for Welshman Ncube and those of the first MDC generation who had become disenchanted with Morgan Tsvangirai, Makoni was meant to be the front for those of the first ZANU-PF generation who had become disenchanted with Robert Mugabe. But both men would seek to impose a more modern, technocratic agenda upon the old players. They too had their price. Multiple symbioses grew up in the Zimbabwe of 2006 and 2007.

Makoni is older than Mutambara, having been born in 1950; and two years older than Morgan Tsvangirai; but young in ZANU-PF terms. This meant he was only 30 at independence, and became a junior minister that year, rising to the Cabinet in 1981. He had spent the years of war as a student abroad, taking a BSc. in Chemistry at Leeds University and a PhD at what is now called De Montfort University in Leicester. Unlike Mutambara, and rarely in the region, he has never used the academic title. In 1983, however, he left government to become Executive Secretary for the SADCC (Southern African Development Coordination Conference) the forerunner of the Southern African Development Community. It was an honour for him, and a recognition that Zimbabwe had now joined the SADCC club which, for years, had been united against white minority rule in Rhodesia. Makoni resigned from SADCC in 1993, after a financial scandal in which he was not involved but for which, as Executive Secretary, he took responsibility. But that meant he had accumulated a decade of regional experience on top of his years in the United Kingdom. In 1997, he entered top management in the Zimbabwean newspaper world and would have, at that time, forged links with another ambitious publisher, Dr Ibbo Mandaza;[12] the pairing of these two would return to influence Zimbabwean politics a decade later. Mugabe recalled Makoni to the Cabinet as Minister of Finance and Economic Development in 2000. By 2002, with financial meltdown well under way, Makoni clashed with Mugabe and left the Cabinet when his plans for a devaluation of the currency were refused. But he remained a member of the politburo of ZANU-PF, so on top of his credentials as a relatively youthful technocrat were the credentials of someone who had – even if unsuccessfully – stood up to Mugabe but who still retained senior links within the party. The West had always liked him. He was a staunch ZANU-PF man, but represented a form of modernising ZANU-PF-lite. Ibbo Mandaza would call this the 'third force'– neither MDC nor old ZANU-PF, but the seeds of a revitalised and modern party that took the old ZANU-PF ideals into a modern future, rather than insisting that they be mired in the symbols and goals of the past.[13] But, if all of this complicated Zimbabwean politics, it also complicated Thabo Mbeki's mediation. That had been based, right up to September 2007 – the very moment when Solomon Mujuru had timetabled his internal putsch – on a power-sharing deal between Morgan Tsvangirai's MDC and Robert Mugabe's ZANU-PF. In that month, led by one of Mbeki's ministers, senior members from both mainstream parties, sequestered on a houseboat on Lake Kariba and fortified by a large stock of alcohol, agreed just such a deal – with Tsvangirai as Vice-President. But it was exactly the powerful Generals whom Mugabe had gathered to resist Mujuru who vetoed the idea of any such arrangement. But, as early as September 2007, well before the 2008 elections which he thought he could not win, Morgan Tsvangirai was ready to share power with his arch-enemy. But the two additions to the national scene, Mutambara and Makoni, thought that in the first instance they would rather share power between themselves.

Both, however, made some effort to be true to their sources. As 2008 dawned, and with it the prospect of an election for both the presidency and Parliament, Mutambara made overtures to Tsvangirai for a joint-ticket. At first the two men found it difficult to agree on which of them should be the presidential candidate. When Mutambara ceded that to Tsvangirai, asking instead for a guarantee that the two factions would not put up candidates in the same parliamentary constituencies, but that his faction would have a guaranteed number of candidates unopposed by Tsvangirai's people – particularly in Welshman Ncube's western strongholds – Tsvangirai first agreed; then reneged; and the joint-ticket was lost.

Meanwhile, throughout January 2008, Simba Makoni had been denying to Mugabe's face that he planned a breakaway bid of his own. Ibbo Mandaza was pressing him to make his move. From the United Kingdom, Dr Nkosana Moyo, another former Mugabe minister and now a senior financial executive in London, was preparing complex plans by which a Makoni candidacy could be made to work; and both Mandaza and Moyo were planning how to finance such a candidacy. But Makoni wanted to be sure Mujuru would be there, in his corner, when the moment came. Mujuru promised. Other ZANU-PF heavyweights promised. On 5 February 2008, the day after Mutambara and Tsvangirai had failed to agree a joint-ticket, Makoni declared.[14] On 15 February, Mutambara announced he would not stand for the presidency himself, and threw his weight behind Makoni.

Mujuru never declared for Makoni, and most of those who had pledged their support for him also held back. The machinations and arm-twistings within ZANU-PF at that time were immense. There followed a period of indeterminacy. Would Makoni be expelled from ZANU-PF? Would he resign as a public point of principle? It was like a phoney war as, behind the scenes, both sides fought for support from key ZANU-PF figures. Finally, Makoni resigned, but his campaign was left without much front-bench support, and Mandaza and Moyo had not raised enough money for a lavish challenge. He launched himself as an independent presidential candidate, standing as a new, clean face when compared to Mugabe and Tsvangirai. Several senior female figures from ZANU-PF history came to him. This is often overlooked. But his senatorial candidates for the Harare constituencies were remarkable: Fay Chung, previously a Mugabe minister and with UN experience;[15] Margaret Dongo, one of the first ZANU-PF dissidents;[16] and Rudo Gaidzanwa, the country's ranking Professor of Sociology and a staunch feminist.[17] It was a rare assemblage of female intellectual and dissident talent – all with insider ZANU-PF knowledge but all, like Makoni, breaking away. They illustrated his effort to secure female and feminist support, and the sense that even former ZANU-PF ministers had lost faith in the party. And, in his broadsheet, distributed like a free newspaper on the streets, Makoni pointedly said that, in contrast to Tsvangirai, Mugabe could never accuse him of lacking education. Makoni never had solid policies. All the parties promised improvement in the dire situation faced by Zimbabweans, but Makoni's message was that this could only come from someone who was not Mugabe, and someone who was not Tsvangirai; it had to come from someone who, unlike Tsvangirai, knew what government was like and who could attract the cooperation of at least parts of ZANU-PF. Later, analysts would ponder how many votes Mugabe's people pilfered from Tsvangirai in the rigged counting. But they also pilfered much from Makoni's total. Makoni's symbol was a sun rising over a green land. It was not destined to rise much.

The 2008 elections were called 'harmonised elections', where presidential, parliamentary and senatorial contests were held simultaneously. This ended the expense of separate contests and, one imagines, the need for separate exercises in intimidation and rigging. It was a concentration of minds and a concentration of resources. But it was also the occasion for some lowering of expectation on the part of both factions of the MDC. After the failure of talks for a united front, Welshman Ncube was content to speculate that perhaps there could be a stronger and more united opposition after the election. Both MDC wings had no expectations of winning. They thought the electorate had been sufficiently bullied in advance even to think of endangering Mugabe and ZANU-PF. The ruling party, for its own part, was so confident that it hardly bothered to design slick posters or other campaign materials; and it did not initiate a programme of intimidation immediately before the election. It too thought the results were sewn up. In mid-March, the atmosphere was extraordinarily calm – even calmer than in both 2005 and 2002.[18]

And there was a rerun from 2005 of very similar media advertising. Morgan Tsvangirai's media onslaught was built around the slogan, 'Morgan is More', meaning more things to more people – although it was as easily read as all things to all people. The campaign was professionally designed by a South African agency and would have done credit to an American or British politician. The ZANU-PF response was very interesting. Looking only at newspaper advertisements by way of example, there were a total of 21 different ZANU-PF advertisements, starting from the beginning of March. Of these, nine were directed against Tsvangirai, three against Makoni, three against international sanctions; there was one on the land issue, four on other electoral issues – of which one dealt with education – and only one, at the end of March on the eve of elections, that declared a list of ZANU-PF qualities and principles. The advertisements against Tsvangirai were vituperative and the entire campaign was negative.

Almost all the ZANU-PF advertisements were tacky. Not much thought had been put into their design. Almost as if to compensate, in the last week glossy billboards appeared portraying a beautifully suited Mugabe with clenched fist. He is declaring that Zimbabwe will never be owned by foreigners. He is clenching his fist with Victoria Falls in the background. The green vegetation and blue water look beautiful. It is a beautiful hoarding. I wondered why no one seemed to notice, but it showed the Zambian side of the Falls. It seemed Mugabe was laying claim to the neighbouring country. In the next round of the elections, the Falls were pixilated to make them look less obviously Zambian.

There were six Makoni newspaper advertisements. Almost all extolled his qualities as a unifier and perfect president. There were four Mutambara advertisements on behalf of his faction's parliamentary candidates and all of them were on policy issues: gender equality, HIV/AIDS, land and agriculture, and the economy. There were ten Tsvangirai advertisements, all slick, colourful and professional. Tsvangirai's wonderful smile radiated from them. He photographs very well and, in many key ways, is the advertiser's dream. They listed the sorts of improvements Tsvangirai would make to people's daily lives, but they were also about the qualities and character of Morgan Tsvangirai – including his scriptural animation. Robert Mugabe, who did not use a scriptural theme in the first round, sought to hijack scriptural allusions in the second. But, in the first round, all the running was made by Tsvangirai and his last advertisement showed a runner crossing the finishing line, calling for a 'victory vote'. In the last days of the campaign, the excitement and gossip in Harare, as people traded voting intentions in conversation, suddenly seemed to engender a critical mass of determination to vote for the MDC. The sense was that an upset might just be on the cards.

ZANU-PF didn't think so. In the last days of March, the *Herald*, largely a party mouthpiece, ran a front-page headline that an academic survey indicated a Mugabe victory by 57 per cent, with just 27 per cent for Tsvangirai and 14 per cent for Makoni.[19] This seemed to confirm the sense pundits and the political parties themselves had at the beginning of March. Only, unpublished by the *Herald*, and not made known to ZANU-PF, the authors of the survey had substantial reservations about their final figures.

One of the key contradictions of Zimbabwe in economic meltdown is the proliferation of cellphones. The MDC used them in its early days to circumvent the landlines that were either denied it by government agencies, or tapped. But, as in most parts of Africa, a leap in technology has been accomplished. For this, much thanks to a pirate operation in a Hong Kong tenement where, behind the façade of a backpackers' hostel, an entire multi-storey complex is devoted to cannibalising old phones, upgrading the components and cloning the new models under established brand names – then exporting them to the streets of Africa. Sometimes China comes with blessings. So the trick for a solo election observer is to hang out at taxi ranks, use the taxis liberally – paying liberally – and assemble from these and other places a 'sample' group with relatives in all key parts of Zimbabwe. The 'key' parts are selected from endless maps of past electoral results. It is crude but highly suggestive. Amazingly, no observer team fielded a more sophisticated operation. People in the villages have cellphones.

Get the 'sample' group right and there is instant nationwide coverage in all the sensitive electoral areas. If there is enough shift in such areas, it is clear something is happening – and something was happening.

However, there was a major disadvantage to the cellphones. Precisely because they were often imperfectly cloned, their camera functions could not be guaranteed and, even if working, would not be capable of clear detail. This became vitally important in the verification of the election results. Zimbabwe had agreed to conduct the elections under African Union and Southern African Development Community protocols designed to ensure transparency. Literally so, in that the ballot boxes were transparent as a deterrent to clumsy ballot-stuffing. But counting was also meant to be conducted at each and every polling station, in the presence of party agents and registered observers. Those inside the station, once counting began, could not leave until counting finished. Local observers who had received training from interested NGOs were warned not to drink water before counting started, and to ensure they had a tight bladder. Most importantly, the completed results had to be posted on the outside wall of the polling station. Nationwide rigging would require the coordinated manipulation of a huge number of separate results. Civic action groups and both MDC factions had their supporters take photographs of the posted results and send them to their Harare headquarters. In this way, there was meant to be evidence of what had happened in every polling station so that, when the previously counted votes were taken to Harare to be centrally 'verified', the electoral commission could not 'verify' embarrassing results downwards. But many of the photographs electronically sent in were not clear. The cellphone cameras couldn't achieve the resolution required for the often tiny rows of numbers. And a consignment of fully functional cellphones with hi-res camera capacities, organised under the aegis of Ed Davey, the UK Liberal Democrats' Foreign Affairs spokesman, never made it in time.[20] South African customs kept them waiting on the docks.

The elections were held on Saturday, 29 March 2008. Everything was orderly and queues moved swiftly compared to the deliberately crafted slowness of earlier polls. By mid-morning I was outside Mugabe's palace in the elite outer suburb of Borrowdale Brooke. Gideon Gono, the Governor of the Reserve Bank, has a palatial mansion nearby – some say several such mansions – as do other senior ZANU-PF figures, including senior military commanders. The bling makes Hollywood look primitive. I am told by favoured visitors that there are marble staircases, fountains, dining-room tables with glass tops that reveal aquariums built into the length and breadth of the tables, and bathrooms with jacuzzis with built-in waterproofed plasma television screens. There are very few bookcases. It's all vulgar ostentation. Hollywood stars at least pretend to have reading habits. Grace Mugabe, the President's staunch but long-suffering wife – Amazing Grace, as she is nicknamed by the public, for her immense retail therapy needs – also has her own mansions in the area. This is in case, the Harare rumours go, she needs shelter from Robert – whose taste in wife-beating, according to the same rumours, is one where the beating is delegated to his bodyguards. But the President's residence is a palace. Set in a huge forested estate, it is surrounded by tall white walls surmounted by beautiful blue Chinese ceramic tiles. The gates to the palace grounds are like a scene from a Chinese kung fu movie – the Temple of the Pavilion of Dawn – tall and white and, again, surmounted by a pagoda-shaped crenellation of blue ceramic tiles. It is extravagant, and the tiles could only have been imported from China. I breathed deeply. The man has the taste of a potentate. Ordinary people were no longer sure of running water, certainly not treated water, and certainly not – as the rumours suggested of Mugabe's palace – water that came from gold taps. Suddenly, the gates burst open and Mugabe's outriders charged forth, driving my car off the road. A cavalcade followed. Mugabe and his daughter were in the dark smoke-glassed Mercedes. At this time, there was a website election organised by Zimbabwe wits: which of the two daughters, Mugabe's or Tsvangirai's, is the more beautiful? In the national election, however, the first vote was to be cast by the President's young daughter. By past practice, the presidential Mercedes should have been followed by an open-topped Land Rover carrying a detachment of soldiers with AK47s. The Land Rover came and it carried soldiers. Only now they were all carrying rocket-propelled grenade launchers. This lot could have carved a way through quite formidable opposition. The motorcade drove to Highfields, the industrial district. There were six working factories left there, but Mugabe wanted to vote at Highfields. It was a rallying point in the very early days of struggle against white minority rule. He entered the polling station in the derelict area, wearing an impeccably cut suit. It wasn't even merely tailored. It was bespoke. That had to be a floating canvas beneath the exquisite material. No suiting rode up as he lifted his arm to acknowledge the crowds. Half a kilometre away he would find sewage leaking into the street, but he was not taken to see that. Then he said to the television camera: 'Anyone who loses this election should retire from politics.'

Sunday, 30 March, the tallies were posted outside each polling station. It was clear that the ground had shifted beneath Mugabe's feet. Morgan Tsvangirai's MDC claimed it had won 60 per cent of the vote. Later it would have to retreat from this claim as its 'evidence', the photographs taken on cellphones, was unclear. Even then, it still claimed 50.3 per cent. If one presidential candidate took a majority of more than 50 per cent, he would have won outright. Otherwise, it would have to go to a run-off between the two highest-placed candidates. On the night of the polls closing, South African Broadcasting analysts estimated the MDC had won 52 per cent. I was certain it had won 56 per cent. Factoring in a huge raft of variables, dependent on ethnic mix, population density and past electoral behaviour, the pattern was clear nationwide. ZANU-PF, at the very least, must have lost. Not only that, Mugabe would not, by my estimates, have received as much as 40 per cent. The rest was Makoni's.

There followed much coming and going. The Central Intelligence Organisation (CIO) went into an all-day crisis session on Sunday, 30 March. They had not been expecting this. But Mugabe, in a sense, was psychologically ready for it. On the campaign trail, even in normally loyal rural strongholds, village leaders had bearded him, sometimes with great rudeness, with their immense dissatisfaction – especially about malnutrition, lack of agricultural support, and party thuggery. That same Sunday he gathered his family around him in Borrowdale Brooke and told them he would step down. Grace agreed with this. She, for all the outrageous rumours about her and them, wanted him to be spared further burdens, and for their children to be spared further agonies. At school, their son – even though it was an exclusive school – was being taunted by fellow pupils. 'Your father has ruined the country!'

Mugabe told his confidants and the high men in ZANU-PF – but the Generals baulked. They contemplated two lines of action. The first was a coup. But they were divided in their enthusiasm for a full-scale coup. In the end, some of the Generals decided upon a sort of 'coup by stealth', in which Mugabe remained the front man, but with themselves as the decisive background figures directing a fightback based on national intimidation.[21] However, there were differences between the overall armed forces commander and the army commander. And the head of the CIO was ready to respect the national vote. The organisation had recently, however, been shored up by the appointment of a Mugabe-loyalist as the deputy to the head of the CIO. Not that the CIO chief, Happyton Bonyongwe was delighted by Tsvangirai. He had hoped for Makoni. The South Africans sent word up that they would be strongly against a coup.[22] They would like Mugabe to make a gracious concession speech. The second line of action was, therefore, to force a run-off by counting down Tsvangirai's vote until it was under the 50 per cent required for outright victory.

Meanwhile, the Zimbabwe Electoral Commission, after its early announcements that it was verifying Tsvangirai ahead of Mugabe two-to-one in the urban areas, had suddenly slowed down the announcements to a snail's pace. Behind the scenes, the CIO was going to work. In this, according to the rumour mill in Harare, it was aided by Mossad personnel who flew in from Israel on Monday, 31 March. In the afternoon of the 31st the rumour was that the Generals, the CIO and the Mossad agents had agreed that they could 'credibly' fine down the results to force a run-off – although the Generals had first requested a result showing 52 per cent for Mugabe and 48 per cent for Tsvangirai and Makoni combined.

As a genuflection to democracy, they would allow Parliament to be won by the combined MDC factions – with Mutambara holding the equivalent of a casting vote between Tsvangirai's MDC and ZANU-PF – provided key ZANU-PF figures such as Joice Mujuru did not lose their seats. Any results of that sort would also need 'refining'. The coup plans were finally called off on 2 April. But the final decision on how to go ahead was to be made at a full ZANU-PF politburo meeting called for 4 April.

The politburo meeting was scheduled to last two hours. It took five and a half. For the first two hours, the doves seemed to be in the ascendant. As early as election night itself, several doves had met with MDC leaders and begun bargaining for a soft landing with full ZANU-PF parliamentary rights, some cooperative decision-making protocols, perhaps even some ZANU-PF ministers in the Cabinet as a gesture towards national unity and healing, and unmolested space and time in which to regroup – probably under a technocratic banner that would reincorporate Simba Makoni. They also wanted immunity from prosecution for every senior ZANU-PF figure. Very late on election night, the South Africans ferried to ZANU-PF an undertaking from the US State Department that such immunity could be arranged in return for 'going quietly'.[23] Tsvangirai should have seized the chance that very night and agreed to the doves' proposal – but key members of his own National Executive were against accommodation. Now, on 4 April, the ZANU-PF doves argued that the package should be pursued, that the US and South Africans would help them press their case for some kind of inclusion, and that ZANU-PF could be resurgent in the future. If Thabo Mbeki had put the boot in at that point – and he had full intelligence on what was happening in the politburo – Mugabe would have gone. He had already been emotionally prepared to go since Sunday, 30 March. But Mbeki didn't.

The hawks rallied in the politburo and, at the end of the marathon meeting, they emerged with the decision that ZANU-PF would contest a run-off. Mugabe, a staunch party man, girded his loins and prepared himself for a bitter new fight. But it took the Electoral

Commission until 2 May to 'refine' the presidential results in a 'credible' manner and declare the official need for a run-off. Those areas where the photographic evidence was irrefutable had to remain much as declared. Areas where the evidence was less trustworthy had to have any Tsvangirai lead fined down, but in keeping with national patterns. It was a most scientific rig, and many votes were pilfered from Makoni to make it work. In the end, Tsvangirai was declared as coming modestly under the required 50 per cent. Meanwhile, the delay also allowed the Generals time to prepare and begin a nationwide campaign of violent intimidation. There wouldn't be any need to rig the run-off. The electorate, who had voted against Mugabe out of sheer protest at the degeneration of living conditions, would have a knife held to its throat. And a highly specific strategy of intimidation was designed and aimed at Morgan Tsvangirai himself. It wasn't just turning loose the troops – the Green Bombers in particular and any gang of party militants that could be mobilised in time – but a carefully planned strategy. And the party's newspaper advertisements would be a lot better this time. These were strange and it seems that Mugabe himself had a hand in their wording. Using scriptural allusions they indicated a man who had been hurt by rejection.

The trick in voter intimidation is not necessarily to kill people. In some respects that is contraindicated. A dead person has less 'multiplier effect' than a living one with tales of terror. A dead person creates enemies in the form of vengeful relatives and friends. A person still alive can spread tales of terror and excite fear rather than revenge. An indication here, and this happened to one of my own students: two weeks before the run-off, as the circle of violence closed in from the rural areas and into the outer 'high density' suburbs of Harare, ZANU-PF militants came and force-marched my student and many others from Epworth, where they lived, to a remote location; for three days they were kept seated and silent; but, all the while, their captors berated them with threats – 'we could kill you and no one would even know where to find your bodies' – over and over again, making false moves all the while to begin executions; after three sleepless and foodless threat-filled days, the captives were physically weak and psychologically distraught. There was one more phase, where they were allowed to break silence, but only by being required to sing endless ZANU-PF songs. When they were broken, they were finally released, with warnings to vote for Robert Mugabe. 'If you vote for Tsvangirai, we will know, and will return to kill you for real next time. And we know where your families are. We will kill them too.'[24] With roughly 30 members of an extended family and some 50 friends and acquaintances for each person, the ripple effect was immense.

To Tsvangirai, the threats were delivered more subtly. They were filtered through his own security people. Always they seemed to have a credible source – a sympathetic insider from the CIO, or a friendly relative who served tea to a high general. Always there were specific details, not of death to come, but of precisely how it was to come. The man was to be made wary of his own shadow in every situation that remotely resembled the setting for death. The intimidation before the presidential run-off was physical as well as psychological but, for the first time, it was the psychological that took precedence. It was not meant to destroy the opposition, but to make the opposition self-destruct. It was ruthlessly brilliant. And, in Tsvangirai's case, the threats came with details of collateral damage. If members of the family were standing close by, they would also be in the line of fire. Tsvangirai sent his family outside Zimbabwe to separate locations. There would be no smoked-glass limousine ride for his beautiful daughter to the polling station. When that happened, ZANU-PF knew their man was biting, and piled on the psychological pressure even more.

The result was that Tsvangirai, with his deputy Tendai Biti, spent more time in the build-up to the run-off out of Zimbabwe than inside it. Ostensibly, this was to campaign regionally and internationally for support. There was very little regional support, except from Botswana and, to an extent, Zambia. But this was known well before Tsvangirai and Biti toured the region at this time. It left his supporters inside Zimbabwe to take a hammering without leadership. The run-off was set for 27 June. Tsvangirai returned to Zimbabwe for the final weeks of the campaign, but he was obviously uncertain about direction. He relied increasingly on Biti – a hard-nosed civil liberties lawyer – and it was clear that, without him, Tsvangirai would suffer. So, two weeks before the run-off, ZANU-PF had Biti arrested on treason charges.

With Biti in custody, ZANU-PF just waited for Tsvangirai to crumble. He began to make bizarre manoeuvres. Claiming assassination threats, he began sheltering in the Dutch Embassy. This was in fact a carefully planned backup provision for him. The US Embassy had set it up and the Dutch were agreeable. Embassies don't have such unilateral powers. It wasn't Dutch Embassy acquiescence: it was sanctioned by the Dutch government. Unlike the impression Tsvangirai tried to give, it was anything but spontaneous and driven by sudden new threats. He was afraid from the start. But the reliance on the Americans was to take even more dependent turns. About this time, two young female Americans began to be seen advising Tsvangirai. They seem to have been operatives of Washington think tanks. One was reputed to have been employed by the Heritage Foundation. Their presence alarmed some of Tsvangirai's normal aides, but the women were probably a clumsy front, being used as a 'deniable' conduit of regular advice from official US sources. It gave ZANU-PF material which it used among the high political classes of all parties and factions – that Tsvangirai really was in the hands of foreigners; Tsvangirai was having an affair with one of them; MDC secrets were being revealed in the pillow talk – and the objective was to have his closest supporters no longer trust him.[25]

The US was convinced the run-off was to be stolen, like the March elections before. In the face of this conviction, Tsvangirai could not win. Even if people survived the intimidation, which kept winding up until ten days before the run-off, and voted for him, his vote would again be wound down in the counting. But the US had not counted on African pressure actually having an effect. Alarmed at the increasingly naked repression, a succession of African leaders had called emphatically for the violence and intimidation to stop. Public expressions had come from people like Kenya's Odinga but, behind the scenes, other

leaders as well as senior figures in the African Union made clear their
disquiet. Just before the last week of the campaign, there was a notable
decrease in the violence. There was also huge behind-the-scenes pressure on Mugabe's government, again from other African leaders, to
count both more swiftly and transparently.

Everyone I talked to on my June visit to Zimbabwe seemed determined to vote – and vote for Tsvangirai – no matter what the consequences. In some quarters the repression had exactly the opposite effect
sought by ZANU-PF. It would have been a close-run thing but, having
come this far, many were determined to continue to the end – and the end
was only a few days away. So that, having survived until five days before
the run-off, Tsvangirai's announcement on 22 June that he was pulling
out of the race, citing violence and the advice of his party members,
took many by surprise. It probably took even ZANU-PF by surprise.
Some senior ZANU-PF figures were worried that they had not done
enough to win the run-off, but felt they had done all they could.
Tsvangirai cited advice from his own people that they were taking a
beating for no winnable result. In fact, his consultations with his party
activists were brief and sketchy. His decision seemed to be in response to
American advice to pull out and fight the battle for Zimbabwe on the
diplomatic front. But, as long as Thabo Mbeki was at the forefront of
diplomacy, the Americans didn't have a game plan except either to influence Mbeki or marginalise him. Mbeki, however, could be remarkably
stubborn. He was in no mood to be influenced beyond a certain point and
certainly not willing to be marginalised.

Without Tsvangirai in the contest, Mugabe won an indecent victory.
This time the counting took two days, not a month. He was reinaugu-
rated with haste and immediately flew off to an African leaders' summit
in Egypt.[26] He arrived to criticisms from Zambia and Botswana in the
Southern African region, Kenya, Nigeria and Senegal. It seemed, on his
arrival, that Mugabe would have a rough reception. Some of the
comments were emphatic and harsh. Then Mugabe took the floor and
delivered himself of an impassioned speech on how, in the long cycle of

history, he would be vindicated. Mbeki reminded his peers – although he did not know he would be their junior very soon – that his mediation could be the only way forward. But the entire episode had left a bitter taste in the mouths of many who were not themselves highly democratic, but who saw the need for convincing camouflage when faced with international pressures for pluralism. Many applauded Mugabe's speech, all declared the need for an African solution to African problems – meaning that the Americans should desist from their interventions, and that they supported Mbeki – but several wondered why Mbeki had been so patient for so long with a man who had been so obdurate in the midst of such self-destruction.

But it was almost as if Mugabe craved not only the validation of his own people, even if he had to steal it from them and then bludgeon it out of them, but also the validation of other African leaders. He saw himself in the long line of the Nkrumahs and Cabrals of the world. His youthful supporters put these iconic figures alongside Fanon, Malcolm X, Bob Marley and Ben Bella. It was a claim to idiosyncratic geneaology. Marley, like any of the others if they had been alive, might have dissented from his inclusion – as the rebel musical greats of Zimbabwe, Thomas Mapfumo and Oliver Mtukudzi, dissented from the rule of Mugabe. But, if Mugabe stole and bludgeoned his way to victory in Zimbabwe, his Egyptian speech came from the heart – even if it also came from his immense sense of insecurity and hurt. He sees himself as the selfless father of the nation rejected by his own children. The advertisements for the run-off are almost poignant expressions of this.

These advertisements, covering entire newspaper pages, were fascinating. Mugabe was likened to Moses and King David: the deliverer of Israel, and the first great King of Israel, God's chosen nation. Then Morgan Tsvangirai was likened to Absalom, the son whom David loved, but who rebelled against David and was killed, against David's own orders, by a general who knew that the King would never have any rest as long as his rebellious son lived.

But Moses, although he delivered the children of Israel from slavery, was not permitted by God to enter the promised land. He was permitted to glimpse it on the banks of the Jordan. Then he died. Was Mugabe reflecting on his own mortality and unfinished work? The legends and Jewish folk tales surrounding the Bible have Moses forbidden to enter the promised land because he had too often sinned against God. Was Mugabe sending a coded message that he knew he had got things wrong, but still deserved the respect of his children? For the example of Absalom is striking. Did Mugabe read the biblical story carefully enough? Absalom was the chosen one who could not wait. He was a decisive character. He had avenged his sister who had been raped. Strikingly handsome, he had long luxuriant hair into which he daily combed oils and perfumes. Once a year, he would cut the heavy mass off and it would be weighed in public. Then he would donate its weight in gold to charity. This made him highly popular and when King David had reached a forgetful old age and people no longer thought he could bring justice to their grievances, Absalom set himself up in a chariot at the city gates and advised petitioners on how to frame their cases before the King. When he raised his banner in rebellion the people rose to it. It was the Generals, led by Joab, who saved David. Did Mugabe know the full import of the story when he likened himself to David and Tsvangirai to Absalom? How does Mugabe confess himself in the Catholic Church at which he worships? Is it a self-validation as in Egypt? Is it like Moses, begging forgiveness and longer life to see the fruition of his works and his final validation when the world understands him at last? Is it like David determined to crush Absalom but unable to control his own unsentimental Generals?

Both Arthur Mutambara and Simba Makoni vowed to fight another day. Mutambara would find it easier to forge some sort of alliance with Tsvangirai than Makoni would with Mugabe again. If Mugabe went, Makoni could parachute back into a reformulated ZANU-PF – but Mugabe had not gone. In some ways, given Mugabe's lack of capacity for easy forgiveness, and given how Makoni had denied to Mugabe's face that he would desert him, it would be easier for Mutambara to gain Mugabe's trust than for Makoni. If Mugabe stayed in power, Makoni would have to form a new political grouping – perhaps with educated urban women as its foundation, and some technocrats like Ibbo Mandaza and Nkosana Moyo. Such a party, largely of urban intellectuals, could form at least working relationships with the MDC faction of Arthur Mutambara and Welshman Ncube.

As for Tsvangirai, it has been easy to be highly critical of him. But he was subjected to huge pressures. In a way, a very real way, it is amazing he clung in there as hard as he did. He had very little real support. Everyone around him was fighting their own corner for survival and watching over their shoulder in case the ZANU-PF machine came for them too. When ZANU-PF took Tendai Biti from him, it took one of his remaining pillars of support. Then it spread the story that Biti had received ZANU-PF emissaries in prison, and that they had discussed Biti's displacing Tsvangirai as leader of the MDC – with promises of cooperation and power-sharing with ZANU-PF. If the strategy had been to isolate Tsvangirai so much that he could no longer sustain his direction, to make him resort to his renowned prevarications and changes of mind, then it worked. A huge machine came for Tsvangirai and he tried to stand up to it. In fact, and here the ZANU-PF advertisements were misplaced, it was he who was like the shepherd boy alone in the Valley of Elah, and casting a nine-foot shadow over him was the hugely armoured Goliath. Tsvangirai tried to hide sometimes in the course of the run-off campaign, and finally he stood down. But he did not break and run.

CHAPTER 11

THE LEGACY OF MIXED LEGACY: MBEKI BREAKS THROUGH ON ZIMBABWE, ZUMA BREAKS THROUGH ON MBEKI[1]

In the wake of the rigged and violent Zimbabwean elections, Thabo Mbeki plunged into mediation of the crisis. From the outset, he worked for a power-sharing government. The principle seemed to be that, to overcome division there had to be inclusiveness. This was well and good, but was not necessarily derived from the democratic will of the electorate. Inclusiveness thus became a higher principle than choice. However, Mbeki and his team did not invent a power-sharing formula for Zimbabwe. They had already field-tested the formula in their mediation in Democratic Republic of Congo in 2006. Kofi Annan applied a variation of the formula in settling the conflict that followed the Kenyan elections held at the end of 2007. Zimbabwe in 2008 simply followed a pattern – even though it featured a particularly vexed and protracted set of negotiations, characterised by extreme ill will and vacillation. Back home in South Africa, however, Mbeki's quarrel with Zuma would not go away. Having been defeated by Zuma for the ANC presidency, Mbeki now hoped to forestall Zuma's candidature for the presidency of South Africa. The accusation was that Mbeki was seeking to use the courts and the organs associated with the independent judiciary to ensure that Zuma, if tried and found guilty of corruption, could

not contest the national presidency as a convicted criminal. But it all back-
fired. Little more than a week after Mbeki's much-heralded, and controver-
sial, breakthrough in Zimbabwe – the announcement of a power-sharing
government – the ANC rallied around Zuma and recalled Mbeki from the
presidency of the country. This also was not national democracy at work, so
there is some irony in that the man who 'settled' Zimbabwe with a govern-
ment not derived from proper electoral processes was unseated by a party
decision that seemed to take precedence over the fact that Mbeki had been
nationally elected. It was not done by a no-confidence vote on the part of the
people's parliamentary representatives. It was done as part of a power play.

The least anyone can say about Thabo Mbeki is that he never had
pause to rest. Abroad he was struggling with the intransigence of
Robert Mugabe and the battered vacillations of Morgan Tsvangirai. At
home he was struggling against the new President of the ANC, Jacob
Zuma. He clung even more tightly to his band of loyalists. But it was
these very same loyalists who had not seen the momentum Zuma
had gathered to depose him at Polokwane. Now, figures in the ANC,
such as Blade Nzimande, General Secretary of the South African
Communist Party, were plotting the recall of Mbeki. It had to be a
recall by the ANC, the party to which Mbeki – by belief, choice, exile,
struggle and genealogy – was faithful. It could not be by constitutional
means – a vote of no confidence in Parliament – for such a move would
fail. The opposition would rally to the Mbeki loyalists if the alternative
was Zuma. So the plot was to assert what many had already started
to feel: that the ANC as a party had primacy over the ANC as government. And Nzimande's complaint against Mbeki was not simply
because of the fact that he loved Zuma more, but that Mbeki and
Trevor Manuel's economic policies such as GEAR, never mind whatever amelioration or otherwise BBBEE might have brought, were
prioritising the fiscal health and balance of the country, and not the
redistribution of wealth to the poor. So a curious set of factors began
to coalesce: genuine populist and ideological desires to help those at
the bottom; leadership by an elite political class, epitomised by Zuma

but hardly confined to him, which saw its own privileges and riches as just repayment for earlier sacrifice and suffering; and the inexorable transition of the ANC towards the behaviour of earlier African one-party states, but settling into a comfortable mid-point niche as a dominant-party state – with considerably smaller opposition parties as necessary window dressing and advertisements for 'democracy' – in which dominant-party choices and party needs, not to mention internal party struggles, determined the shape of government, the leadership of government and, in the desires of many like Blade Nzimande, the policies of government. The autonomy of government, including the executive autonomy of the presidency, was subservient to the primacy of the party. This is well and good if politics is unidirectional. But what about subservience to the will of the electorate? Perhaps, even in September 2008, the month of Mbeki's recall by the ANC, the electorate would have preferred Jacob Zuma to Thabo Mbeki. But no one bothered to ask the electorate. This was a palace coup, a party putsch. It was the accomplishment that had eluded Solomon Mujuru in Zimbabwe. But, as the South Africans are fond of saying, they can do anything better than their neighbours anyway.

This notwithstanding, events in the two countries began moving in a curious tandem. In June 2008, Zuma's lawyers filed papers to have his prosecution declared invalid and unconstitutional. That was the same month as the vexed presidential rerun in Zimbabwe. And the breakthroughs, if they may be called that, in both countries came in September. Mbeki was to have his last triumph that month, in Zimbabwe, and then fall from grace and power in South Africa the week after.

It was almost as if, throughout the intrigues within the ANC, Mbeki was oblivious to them. It was almost as if he were certain that the ANC would not recall him, sanction his impeachment or a parliamentary motion of no confidence. He bolstered no old alliances and built no new ones. It is just as well he was oblivious, since this meant his body language betrayed no sign that he was in political jeopardy as he mustered a compromise breakthrough in Zimbabwe. It was clear to the Zimbabwean parties that Mbeki was weakened, but neither Mugabe nor Tsvangirai thought Mbeki would fall, despite Judge Nicholson's bombshell judgment just three days before the signing of their agreement to form a unity government. The dignified Mbeki who superintended the signing was manifestly more at ease than either the somewhat surly Mugabe or the anxiously over-enthusiastic Tsvangirai.

It was as if, even on the eve of his departure from power, Mbeki had not learnt the lesson of Polokwane. After the party conference his advisers and he had conducted their own post-mortem and concluded that Zuma had attained the ANC presidency because of his strength in delegates from the municipal levels of the ANC – not the provincial and national levels. And their take was that these municipal delegates represented precisely that layer of ANC functionaries most anxious to retain their vested interests, patronage rights and pilfering rights under the local trickle-down from BBBEE and other forms of tendering and petty corruption. Zuma was their man because Zuma understood the idea of the spoils of office being 'owed' – if not to those who fought Apartheid, those who had in one way or another become activists within the ANC. Victors by struggle, or victors by association – all had entitlements. The lofty Mbeki despised such people, but thought that those at the higher provincial and national levels would stand by him. But there were those at higher levels who, although disgusted by the perceived corruption of Zuma, saw him as being singled out when other ANC personnel had not. And there was the question of Mbeki's own association and, if not direct association, implicit permission to associate with other arms deals and the 'benefits' from them.[2] Thomson, Schabir Shaik and naval corvettes aside, what about earlier air defence contracts with providers such as British Aerospace and Saab?

It is Andrew Feinstein, a former Member of Parliament who worked closely with Tokyo Sexwale, who has written and spoken most cogently about the BAe/Saab deal.[3] Despite his association with Sexwale, who had himself been bruised by Mbeki, Feinstein was a senior member of the Public Accounts Committee and so had direct investigative knowledge of this deal. The defence contracts concerned derived from the time of Mbeki's deputy presidency, when he was also head of the parliamentary subcommittee that awarded such contracts. There was wide public questioning of the need for so many new weapons during what was meant to be the Mandela era of peace. The justification was that the weapons contracts would create jobs – which they didn't. Even if they did, the skills base required for such jobs would not have been there. But the real problem was that the weapons procured were not even what the defence chiefs wanted. The BAe/Saab deal, costing £1.5 billion, was for jets that the air force had not sought. Those it had in fact sought would have cost just over a third as much. The meeting that decided, nevertheless, to go for BAe/Saab involved Mbeki and the Minister of Defence, the late Joe Modise. The most senior civil servant in the Ministry of Defence resigned in protest, and the Auditor-General's criticisms were never published. Feinstein was sacked and subsequently left the ANC.[4] But it would appear from the unpublished findings of the Public Accounts Committee and the Auditor-General that Modise received millions of rand in bribes from BAe. There is no suggestion Mbeki himself benefited from the deal – but Feinstein argues that he covered it up. The question Feinstein and others who stayed in the ANC asked was a simple one: if one corruption scandal is covered up, why not another? What are the criteria used to cover up Modise and expose Zuma? The critique of Mbeki – quite apart from the issue of HIV/AIDS, quite apart from his protracted and indulgent relationship with Mugabe, quite apart from his aloof intellectualism, quite apart from his political ruthlessness against rivals – is that he inaugurated the era of deceit, selfish gain, and the selective use of state institutions to facilitate his sense of the party agenda, and not for the benefit of the nation. From the Mandela era onwards, something was rotten in the heart of South Africa.

But, if this critique is correct, why does the ANC still seem to believe its own rhetoric? Why is it, in its own self-belief, and the belief of a huge majority of South Africans, the party of equity, of redistribution, of clear justice, and of opportunity? Just as Thabo Mbeki cannot be explained only by his faults, Jacob Zuma cannot be explained only by his deficits – financial and otherwise. After the fall of Mbeki, however, Zuma set about winning the South African presidency for himself. He had first to overcome his legal problems.

In June 2008, Zuma's legal team filed papers to have his prosecution declared invalid and unconstitutional. It was a direct challenge to Mbeki in the sense that the petition was built around the implicit assertion that the President had abused his powers. The judge agreed. On 12 September 2008, Judge Christopher Nicholson gave what can only be considered a technical legal victory to Zuma – but a crushing political rebuke to Mbeki. There were two key parts to his judgment. The first was that proper process had not been followed. Zuma had not been allowed, as was his right according to Nicholson's reading of the law, to make representations on his own behalf before being charged by the National Directorate of Public Prosecutions. The charges had therefore to be dropped. They could be brought again, provided proper process and representations were observed. It was the second part of his judgment that shook the South African political firmament. Not that anyone in Pretoria or in the nationwide chattering class was naïve about the matter, but that a judge should be so explicit in an on-the-record judgment that was being extensively covered in the media was simultaneously a victory for the independence of the judiciary, and a strike by the judiciary against the executive. Nicholson might have been *too* explicit – but his wording was obviously carefully crafted and purposeful. He was clearly offended by the use of high office to apply law against political enemies. It was a ruling that commenced the overthrow of Thabo Mbeki.

Firstly, Nicholson commented on the events surrounding Polokwane. He mentioned the timing of events and referred specifically to Mbeki's replacement of one Director of Public Prosecutions by another.

The timing of the indictment [of Zuma] by Mr Mpshe on 28 December 2007, after the President suffered a political defeat at Polokwane was most unfortunate. This factor, together with the suspension of Mr Pikoli, who was supposed to be independent and

immune from executive interference, persuade me that the most plausible inference is that the baleful political influence was continuing.[5]

Nicholson was consciously making a stand in defence of the independence of all aspects of the judicial and associated apparatus. Pikoli, as we
have seen in Chapter 9, was replaced because of a case of corruption and
prosecution involving a person quite apart from Zuma. But Mpshe,
Nicholson inferred, was appointed as his replacement because he was the
President's man. More widely than either the Pikoli/Mpshe case or the
Zuma charges, Nicholson saw these as simply two examples of a wider
trend of abuse. 'It is a matter of grave concern that this process has taken
place in the new South Africa given the ravages it caused under the
Apartheid order.'[6]

One phrase stood out in all the media coverage. It was not to do with
the wider points of judicial independence and political abuse. It was to do
specifically with what Nicholson called the 'titanic political struggle'
within the ANC. Whether Nicholson had remained within his limits of
authority as a judge, or whether he had himself transgressed the dividing
line between judicial authority and political judgement, was a matter that
would be played out in the appeals to come. He certainly acted as a
concerned citizen, and his assertion – judiciously or injudiciously made –
of the powers of the judiciary and the separation of functions should have
sent a message northwards to Zimbabwe, where Mbeki, Mugabe and
Tsvangirai were locked in a bitter debate on how the spoils of the state
and the disposition of the offices of state could be divided – far away from
courts, electorates, polling booths and democratic ballots – in an African
version of a smoke-filled room. Mbeki concentrated on Zimbabwe and
did not consider the Nicholson judgment in any sustained fashion.
When, after the 'breakthrough' in Zimbabwe, he did turn his mind to
Zuma and Nicholson, he misjudged the mood of his party's most senior
people.

The 'breakthrough' in Zimbabwe was not extemporaneous. Mbeki had
always sought a senior position for Tsvangirai, but one that was not

more senior than Mugabe's. That position had been rehearsed often enough in the months and years gone by. But this time there was a clear electoral will for change in Zimbabwe. To what extent would this influence Mbeki's approach? To be fair to him, he contemplated the relative merits of democracy on the one hand, and the militarised and civil violence from ZANU-PF if he tried to push Mugabe out on the other; he contemplated the possibility of a semblance of stability and a possible platform for recovery if all the key players in the Zimbabwean saga were gerrymandered into a working relationship.

There were two further aspects to his thinking. The first derived from his pan-Africanist intellectual excursions. Surely there was an 'African' way to deliver democracy. The 'winner takes all' formula, as advocated by the West, meant perpetual cycles of exclusion, resistance and sabotage. It meant exclusion on a by-turns basis not only from power but from access to economic benefits. If both power and patronage could be more inclusive, more widely distributed, then there was more chance for a communitarian outcome in African political contests. This is well and good and, in some ways as I shall discuss later, Mbeki had stumbled upon a model of democracy that merited further discussion and debate. He tried to apply it deficiently in Zimbabwe: Tsvangirai the victor should have, by Mbeki's inclusive model, offered Mugabe a senior post that was, all the same, junior to his own. But, in the case of the 2008 Zimbabwean elections, the rules by which the contest was fought had nothing to do with inclusiveness. If those had been the rules at the start, there would have been a foundation for the premise of inclusiveness from which Mbeki fought – while, in his own home, seeking to exclude Jacob Zuma from power. But they were not the rules from the start. The rules were to do with a Western-style election with a clear victor who would form a government from his own party. The clear loser would form an opposition from his own party. Any coalition would be at the behest of the victor and on his terms. So Mbeki had a principle in mind that he immediately corrupted in the name of pragmatism. Mugabe and ZANU-PF held all the major cards of violence and coercion and non-cooperation.

There was, Mbeki felt, a need for pragmatism. Whether that meant the inversion of a principle in which he philosophically believed is another question. But it should have been Tsvangirai, as victor, who offered inclusiveness, not Mugabe the rigged 'victor' who had to be persuaded to be inclusive. Secondly, philosophy or not, the model for the Zimbabwean settlement had already been established – once by Mbeki and his mediators in the Democratic Republic of Congo civil war;[7] and once, independently of Mbeki, by Kofi Annan in the tumultuous Kenyan elections at the end of 2007. Mbeki thought in terms of principle, structured his strategy in terms of pragmatism, and moved in terms of precedent.

Democratic Republic of Congo is the most vexed part of Africa. I say that without fear of challenge. Its colonial history and post-colonial rulership have been epochs of plunder and barbarity.[8] It is a huge country, with a huge population, and huge mineral deposits. The wealth from these deposits is so unevenly spread – with an international oligarchy enjoying its benefits – that the majority of the Congolese have had to invent self-governance by ingenuity, opportunism and localised solidarities. They are prepared to be petty-criminalised in a land of grand criminals who are the ruling elite. Local acts of resistance are magnificent in their splendour and anarchy. The sight of streets full of dandies called *sapeurs* – dressed in a cross between the latest Milanese and Parisian fashions, only in flamingo bright colours, with fedoras, spats and cigars – the peacocks of the slums; together with the music and art of protest are symbols of defiance.[9] But these acts and symbols contest no government. That contest is between what are essentially warlords, each with his own international support base, and each international supporter has economic interests in the country; and some change sides depending on the prevailing winds of war, international alliance needs and greatest opportunity for plunder. Out of this came the model for Zimbabwe's coalition government.

After the 1997 fall of Mobutu, whose family-based kleptomania was endorsed by his alliance with the United States, the country hoped it had emerged from a vicious civil war – from which Laurent Kabila was the victor. Kabila had been an opposition leader in exile for years. In the 1960s, Che Guevara had left Cuba to fight at his side.[10] But Kabila was never at his side. He was in the bars and clubs of Dar es Salaam in Tanzania while Che sweated it out in the jungles. Disgusted, Che went back to Cuba after a year and prepared for his even more unsuccessful, and fatal, expedition to Bolivia. As for the playboy Kabila, he tried to be a good president for 100 days – before the forces who had brought him to power demanded their payoffs. Despite the weariness of the people of the country, a second civil war began in 1998 and became even more international than the first. Robert Mugabe sent the Zimbabwean army into the fray on Laurent Kabila's side. The cost of this intervention, at some US$1 million per day, was a major plank in the newly formed MDC's opposition platform even before the farm invasions began in 2000. But Mugabe secured from Kabila an immense array of rights to mineral extraction in the country and, by distributing these rights, purchased the loyalty of his top Generals. This second civil war involved rival armies from southern, western and eastern African states, and its lingering aftermath, cost 5.4 million civilian lives. Unlike the Balkan conflict and the public mobilisation around terribly simplified views of the horrific Darfur conflict, these deaths – almost as many as those in the Holocaust – have caused not a ripple in the world's concern and compassion.

In 1999, President Frederick Chiluba of Zambia, himself no stranger to corrupt practices, secured a Peace Accord among the combatants. It was largely disregarded at first, although it did set benchmarks as to what the stages of disengagement should look like. Such as it was, it was Chiluba's only diplomatic triumph. In the same year, a largely ineffectual United Nations peacekeeping force was sent to the country. To be fair to the UN, the country was so vast, and the armies of the warlords and their external supporters so huge, that the peacekeepers were doomed to be overstretched, overexposed and outgunned. Their mandate was insufficient and their officers too cautious. The pristine white vehicles were the *sapeurs* of the conflict zones. A 2000 peace conference in Harare led to agreement for some pullback from front lines, but was never implemented.

Things changed somewhat in 2001, after Laurent Kabila was assassinated and succeeded by his son, Joseph. Everyone expected him to be weak enough to be manipulated. But he was young and just idealistic enough to want an end to the conflict. This didn't mean he was consumed by notions of wealth distribution, equity, justice and transparency. But for Democratic Republic of Congo, a peace, any sort of halfway reliable or even protracted peace, was something.[11] A high-level mediation of the conflict began under former Botswanan President Masire. But it was the mediation of the South Africans that saw constitutional foundations put in place, upon which all contesting internal parties were prepared at least to pretend to stand. Complex constitutional compromises and peace: these became the key to unlock several African conflicts to come. It is not Mbeki's African Renaissance. It is, problematically, imperfectly, but perhaps inescapably, his greatest legacy in the continent. Nobel Prizes have been won for less. With distance and hindsight there may be redemption of Mbeki in the years to come.

At the very end of 2005, 25 million Congolese voted in a referendum on a draft constitution. Eighty-four per cent approved it. In July 2006 elections were held with the prospect of enacting the constitution. They went to a run-off in October that year and Joseph Kabila, who had campaigned nationwide as the 'man of peace', became the elected President of the country.

Kabila is now President within a complex governmental structure. It is not as complex as the transitional or interim structures the South Africans brokered en route to the Congolese constitution. In those, the allocation of ministries seemed almost like a redistribution programme in itself. Ministries seemed to subdivide and multiply until there was something for every serious fighting faction. The emphasis was on peace and inclusivesness, and not on effectiveness and efficiency. A place in government meant peace, but it did not mean that government would work.

Under the new constitution, DRC is basically a decentralised semi-presidential system – although, in reality, the centre retains huge and decisive powers. It is at the centre that competition can jeopardise governmental progress of any sort. But there is enough decentralisation – to 25 semi-autonomous provinces – to ensure tensions in every stage of government. So that governance, if that is what it can be called, is built around 25 centres of patronage; and one centralised epicentre of patronage which has a constitutional check and balance not just among executive, legislature and judiciary, but between president and prime minister.

The President is elected and he appoints the Prime Minister, who must come from the largest elected parliamentary party. Cabinet ministers are proposed by the Prime Minister but appointed by the President. The two operate in a constant dialectical relationship – which is to use a philosophical label to indicate a constant state of tension, manoeuvring and exchange. The stuff of Congolese politics is the transaction of power and privilege by a constitutional bartering system. Power is bartered between the President and Prime Minister – although, at this moment in time, Kabila as president is by far the more accomplished in the accumulation of day-to-day power.

But it means that, if the President and Prime Minister come from different parties, both parties have leverage over how power is transacted. Power is transacted rather than simply owned. In that, it is a clear progression from the dictatorial and unidimensional corruption of Mobutu in the Cold War years. To be fair to both the Congolese – and to the South Africans who saw this complex package through the protracted and complex stages of negotiation among warring parties, right up to its implementation, including an election which, given the circumstances, could rightly be described as fair – there was an already existing model of how cohabitation can work. This was of course the French model. There has been, under the Fifth Republic, more than one *cohabitation* between president and prime minister from different parties. But there is a clear difference as well. The powers of the French President are immense. To an extent, and certainly within Western governmental frameworks, the French President is as close to a totemic quasi-dictatorial figure as possible. It takes an immensely skilful prime minister to compete. But the President is fairly elected. Kabila was also fairly elected. What happens when a complex constitutional package is negotiated, with this kind of power-share, where the President has *not* been elected? This question should be posed in the Zimbabwean case, but was first posed in Kenya.[12]

There were, however, three crucial differences between Kenya and Zimbabwe. Firstly, in Kenya the two antagonists, Mwai Kibaki and Raila Odinga, had been colleagues in the previous government and knew how to work with each other. Secondly, it was Odinga who had inherited the pedigree of fighter for the nation, given the nationalist work of his father, Odinga Odinga. Thirdly, there was far more ethnic mobilisation in Kenyan politics than in Zimbabwe. This was calculated on both sides. It meant that both men could field force and answering force – and call those forces off – while, all the time, being aware of each other's personal strengths and weaknesses, and knowing throughout that each could finally work with the other. Both were consummate politicians and, even though it looked an assiduously heroic mediation by Kofi Annan, in the face of primordial violence and national emergency, Annan knew exactly in what language to speak to two deeply cynical creatures. His mediation was different to that attempted by Mbeki in Zimbabwe, with the asymmetry between what Mugabe and Tsvangirai could each muster in terms of leverage, and Mbeki's was a much harder feat than that managed in a very short space of time by Annan. Even so, there was a key parallel in the cases of Odinga and Tsvangirai: each had won his country's election; each should have been president. In Democratic Republic of Congo, Joseph Kabila had won the election and was legitimately sworn in as president. The outcome in Congo is, insofar as it is capable of stability – even if it is not especially capable of good government or the impersonation of governance – the epitome of Mbeki's African mission. The settlement in Zimbabwe is considerably more imperfect than that; even though, curiously, a battered form of governance tried to struggle forward. Zimbabwe was a grand, complex and clumsy compromise which prioritised inclusion over democratic processes. It may be that Mbeki saw contrary virtues in a situation of impossible meltdown, and simply chose a virtue that would work. It was not as cynical as the outcome in Kenya. But those who criticise or condemn Mbeki must ask the 'there but for the grace of God' question. What would any of us in Mbeki's stead have done, or been able to do? There is a little of Henry Kissinger in Mbeki's work: the grand goal, the trumpeting of virtue, the elision of other virtue without a moment's pause.

In Kenya, Odinga was seen in the final months of the presidential campaign as a clear favourite. The aggregate of opinion polls in September and October showed him ahead of Kibaki. In weekly polls throughout November and December, except for one week in November, he remained ahead of Kibaki. The election was held in December 2007. The early counting had Odinga ahead and it is thought by many that rigging began to occur in the later stages of the count until, finally, the electoral commission declared for Kibaki by 4,578,034 to 4,352,993. It certainly seemed disproved by a US Government exit poll in July 2008, in which Odinga came out ahead of Kibaki 46 to 40 per cent. And, even though the concurrent parliamentary vote was complicated by the presence of many parties, Odinga's party won 99 seats and Kibaki's only 43. Odinga's people cried foul, and huge violence erupted, widely described as being perpetrated along ethnic lines. It is almost certain that the 'ethnic militias' who rallied to Odinga had been put into place before the elections for exactly such a contingency. One side cheated and the other side had prepared to fight. The aim seemed to be to 'ethnically cleanse' certain voting districts so that, in the event a rerun was forced, greater votes would come to Odinga. Kibaki, having been hurriedly sworn in on 30 December, now mobilised his supporters to fight back and the situation seemed likely to degenerate into ethnic war. It stopped, as if on command, as soon as Kofi Annan began his mediation in late January 2008. It had been a month of orchestration of violence, not simply along ethnic lines, but consciously along electoral lines. Whether it should be called 'cleansing' or violent securing of electoral bases is an unanswered question. By the time Annan arrived, Nairobi was awash with conflict mediators, invited or not, of every stripe. Conflict mediation is big business. The mediators, who often have a bag of techniques but no knowledge of particular situations – but who fly from zone of violence to zone of violence hawking their services – can be used by conflicting sides as cover, 'Look, we are trying to find a way to talk; we are using all these mediators', while they continue to fight. The industry sometimes does peace more harm than good.[13] The more noble-minded will, in a case like Kenya, seek some agreement on ways of restarting the democratic process. All the while, militias cleanse so that the process is preconditioned by the time it starts again. 'Keep talking. The boys haven't finished clearing out such and such a constituency yet.' Annan didn't try to restart the democratic process. He was going to broker a deal.

The deal was for power-sharing. Kibaki remained as President. Odinga became Prime Minister. The Cabinet was to be shared. In the end, to accommodate the ambitions of both main parties, and to keep the distribution of Cabinet places 50:50, there was the glorious spectacle, with allocation of portfolios finally agreed only on 13 April 2008, of a Cabinet with 40 ministers. There were, in addition, 50 assistant ministers. However, Kibaki's people secured the key portfolios of Foreign Affairs, Finance, Internal Security, and Defence.

Annan announced the outline of his deal on 28 February 2008. One month later, at the end of March, Zimbabwe went to the polls. By that time, a model had been established that reinforced the one that emerged from Democratic Republic of Congo. In the vexed Zimbabwean negotiations that followed, brokered by Mbeki, Odinga was constantly advising Tsvangirai and supporting him in African fora and summits. In Kenya, despite the imbalance in important ministries, Odinga was then deftly outmanoeuvring Kibaki in the day-to-day cut and thrust of politics and the accretion of advantages. But Tsvangirai didn't have Odinga's skills. And Mbeki was far more patient than Annan. Annan had driven hard for a deal in the swiftest possible time. Mbeki allowed the Zimbabwean negotiations to be drawn out and, all the while, ZANU-PF kept hammering home its violent authority on the ground, bullying and beating local MDC chapters, and seeking to drive Tsvangirai into tighter and tighter negotiating corners. Tsvangirai was running out of options and, in his heart, against the advice of many of his senior people, he was prepared to accept the position of Prime Minister.

The path forward was protracted. As well as Odinga, Tsvangirai had support and advice from the young President of Botswana, Ian Khama, the son of the independence leader of Botswana, Seretse Khama. He was the offspring of the era's most celebrated – and, in Southern Africa groundbreaking – mixed marriage. Khama was easily vilified by Mugabe's henchmen for being young, inexperienced and half white. But his apprenticeship had been as commander of the Botswana armed forces. His army had never fought, but had participated in peacekeeping missions. Even so, it contained sufficient threat for ZANU-PF constantly to wonder whether MDC activists were not crossing the border to undertake military training. At one stage, Tsvangirai's lieutenants even fantasised aloud about abandoning talks and establishing a government-in-exile in Botswana. The problem with Khama, however, was precisely his military background. He took a long time to decipher why politics did not work to logic and order. He was never much use to Tsvangirai as an adviser, but he provided a retreat of last resort. What Odinga and Khama meant was that Tsvangirai gathered strength from his finally having heads of government on his side. And the feeling that he had advice was better than the sense of being bereft. Tsvangirai didn't make a good existential hero; he needed people around him; he was becoming more careful about listening to them. But his own MDC activists were becoming hotheaded with the knowledge that their electoral victory had been stolen and many were in no mood to compromise.

After the fiasco of the presidential run-off in Zimbabwe, Mbeki continued his mediation. There was an added impetus in that, despite Mugabe's impassioned self-defence in Egypt, many African leaders were deeply disturbed that the crisis was continuing and that it had such a debilitating effect on the image of Africa. If Mbeki wanted to have an African Renaissance as his legacy, he had to break through. But, to Tsvangirai and the MDC, he seemed constantly to be advancing compromise positions that favoured Mugabe and ZANU-PF. Tsvangirai called for alternative mediators, and got Mbeki augmented by other African dignatories. The new faces agreed immediately that compromise was the only way forward, and also had difficulty adjusting to the by now truculent Tsvangirai. Meanwhile, Mugabe saw an opportunity to divide the MDC's support base by initiating private discussions with Arthur Mutambara. The idea was that, if he could detach Mutambara from even superficial support of the larger MDC faction, he would begin to eat into MDC morale and create doubt among Tsvangirai's people. Having said that, a real chemistry developed between Mugabe and the Oxford-educated Mutambara. It was almost like a rerun of what occurred between Mugabe and Afonso Dhlakama, the Mozambican rebel leader in 1992. In both cases, Mugabe saw a younger version of himself. Mutambara, moreover, observed the traditional etiquette of at least appearing to defer to the older man. And it was clear he was educated and cultivated. Mugabe almost seemed to view him as a son, in which case some form of succession was possible. Even Mutambara's own people grew alarmed at the closeness that was developing between their leader and Mugabe, and they had to work hard to pull him back from a unilateral decision to cooperate with Mugabe. From Mugabe's perspective, the exercise of detaching Mutambara from the opposition may have begun cynically, but the warmth he developed for the younger man was real and surprised even himself. No such warmth developed with Tsvangirai. As for Mbeki, was he really favouring Mugabe in the negotiations? He certainly seemed to like Mugabe. Here too, there was some evident warmth – notwithstanding times in their history when Mbeki had stormed and raged at Mugabe's reneging on carefully eked out ways forward.

There were five clear reasons for Mbeki's closeness to Mugabe. Firstly, Mbeki knew he was not dealing with Mugabe alone – but also with his hardline military commanders. Some even detected signs that Mugabe was as much their captive as their leader. That overstated matters considerably. Even so, the Generals would not go away on Mbeki's say-so and, in a sense, he needed to reinforce Mugabe precisely so that the Generals would not seek to overwhelm him. Mbeki had to be sure that each of the principals at the talks really commanded their forces. A deal with puppet leaders or leaders with dissident followers would not hold.

Secondly, precisely for that reason, Mbeki continued to distrust Tsvangirai's capacity – not just to be leader of Zimbabwe, but even as leader of the MDC. Constantly in the talks, Tsvangirai maintained he could not agree to certain positions because he doubted he could sell them to his followers. The very rare occasions of mutual understanding between Mugabe and Tsvangirai arose when each confided to the other exactly how difficult they found it to control their own parties. Despite this, even now, Tsvangirai was not looking presidential enough for Mbeki. Negotiations could degenerate into statements of position and their repeated defence, and it was almost always Tsvangirai who became shrill and hectoring first.

Thirdly, as I have suggested before, Mbeki and Mugabe simply got on intellectually. Mugabe was the only Southern African president – in fact he was probably the only African president – able to understand the literary and quasi-philosophical essays that Mbeki wrote as a means of 'communicating' with the ANC. Some of the francophonic presidents would have appreciated the sense and gravitas of the essays, but would not have been familiar with the anglophonic writers Mbeki was always quoting.

Fourthly – and this was noted even by the entourages of other presidents at Egypt and those who witnessed some of the talks in Zimbabwe – Mbeki seemed almost to defer to Mugabe: like Arthur Mutambara, in the manner of a younger man towards an older. Whether this was simply traditional politesse, or indicated a reluctance to press beyond certain points, is uncertain. One of Mugabe's former ministers Nkosana Moyo, citing his colleague Simba Makoni, said that Mugabe would always hear Mbeki out, and then utter the words, 'I have heard you'. This form of words was both politesse and an injunction that no more should be said. The older man would go away and think about it and if, after thought, he rejected what had been proposed, the younger man had no grounds for feeling slighted. The courtesy of listening to the younger man had already been accorded.[14] Moyo has his own clear bias for Simba Makoni of course, and there is something reductionist in his account. But it is suggestive and hints at an Mbeki whose African Renaissance is not only a modern vision but a curatorial and inhibiting one as well.

Finally, Mbeki – as in the case of HIV – simply has blind spots. After he has thought about something, he doesn't change his mind.

But there had to be a breakthrough. No one involved imagined things could go on for much longer as they were. The pressures on all sides to settle – somehow – were immense. And the pressures on Mbeki, from his colleague presidents, to get some sort of agreement were also immense. The breakthrough agreement on 15 September 2008 was extraordinarily clumsy – where every gain by one party was balanced with an equal gain by another.[15] ZANU-PF retained the presidency and two vice-presidencies simply by *force majeure*. It lost the first round of the elections. It won the second round because Tsvangirai had abandoned the contest at the last. The second round would not have been democratically needed if the results of the first round had been fairly counted. But ZANU-PF had the guns. Tsvangirai became Prime Minister. Arthur Mutambara became one of two deputy prime ministers, the other being from Tsvangirai's wing of the MDC. So the big players had their places set out. Fitting in all the other players was an exercise in stagecraft.

And an exercise almost in the futility of making room for all – in this case not so much by the multiplication of ministerial positions as in Kenya, but by the careful balancing of the entire organigram of government. Tsvangirai as prime minister chaired a Council of Ministers, but was only deputy chair of the Cabinet. This was chaired by Mugabe as president. However, the Council of Ministers included all members of the Cabinet. More importantly, Mugabe chaired the State Security Council which included all the powerful Generals – the hard men of the Zimbabwean story – but also now had to include Morgan Tsvangirai. The Cabinet itself contained 31 ministers, of whom 15 were drawn from ZANU-PF and 16 from the two factions of the MDC (13 Tsvangirai and three Mutambara), reflecting the ostensible results of the parliamentary elections. What it all represented was an elaborate exercise in checks and balances.

It was not the checks and balances of established constitutional democracies – with the emphasis on clear lines between executive, legislature and judiciary. Those were still nominally there. Rather, it was checks and balances among the three major political forces: the Council of Ministers and the Cabinet overlapped, yet each was a balance to the other, at least in the sense that they had separate and, to an extent, competing chairmen. The President and Prime Minister were those chairmen, those competitors, and the uneasy power-sharing heads of the country. The disposition of Cabinet places gave something to Mugabe's people, Tsvangirai's people and Mutambara's people. If Mutambara cooperated with Tsvangirai, then the combined MDCs had a majority both in Parliament and Cabinet. If Mutambara cooperated with Mugabe, then ZANU-PF had a majority in Parliament and Cabinet. Everything was an inducement towards cooperation – in case the house of cards lost balance and fell down – or to a contest of tactical manoeuvres as each tried to outflank the other within a complex system that was still capacious enough for such manoeuvres. ZANU-PF was delighted with the package, in the sense that it was confident it knew how to manoeuvre. It was astonished when Tsvangirai accepted it.[16] That he did was against strong last-ditch resistance from his own party: because he considered it was the best he could get; because it had worked for Odinga, and Odinga told him to accept it; because he was ready, even excited, to become Prime Minister; because it would at least take the struggle to a different and higher field; and because he thought he would win the struggle to hammer out the last check and balance in the system. If Mugabe chaired the National Security Council, and thus retained direct reporting lines and control over his military and security chiefs, then what Tsvangirai wanted was ministerial control of at least some of the departments from which these chiefs operated. He was prepared to give up Defence. He worked on the basis that 70 per cent of rank-and-file soldiers had voted for the MDC. If push came to shove, soldiers might not obey their commanders. He wanted control over the police.

Although the Mbeki plan did not authoritatively allocate portfolios, leaving that to a second stage of more detailed negotiations, Tsvangirai thought – or at least he told his followers that he thought – he had an implicit promise that Home Affairs, which controlled the police, would go to an MDC minister. Others in the negotiating chamber have told me that this was not the case. But Tsvangirai had to sell the package to his people and so either he was mistaken in his understanding of what was implicit and what was not, or he glossed what all his supporters would have viewed as a loss at the negotiating table. This would return to haunt him for months to come, as disputes over the disposition of portfolios raged until the end of January 2009, and Tsvangirai did not become Prime Minister till then.

By then, inflation had reached the staggering level of 6.5 quindecillion novemdecillion per cent.[17] It meant almost nothing in that the figures had long been surreal – and even graduate mathematicians would have to think before saying how many zeros that meant. Zimbabweans just saw their living conditions getting worse and worse. The sewage that ran in many poorer suburban streets now began to spread cholera and the Ministry of Health had no medical supplies to treat it. Nurses, doctors and teachers were all, in any case, refusing to work – as their salaries now meant nothing and transport to work cost more than their total income. Barter increased as currency became notional and almost abstract. Even the corrupt elite around Mugabe was finding it harder to operate its separately enclosed economy in that it could not function as its own enclave without economic interaction with the impoverished state and the mass of its citizens. ZANU-PF realised it needed Tsvangirai as an acceptable face for the international beggary to come.

Before then, with the broad outlines of the deal agreed, Mbeki mustered Mugabe, Tsvangirai and Mutambara for a grand televised ceremony of signature on 15 September 2008. The elections had been at the end of March. The presidential run-off had been at the end of June. The negotiations had dragged on for two and a half months. Mbeki looked older but at ease and triumphant. He needed this. Internationally, Zimbabwe had seen his reputation take a hammering. At home, the vultures were circling – but he had no idea how close to mortal danger he really was. Above all, his African Renaissance needed the breakthrough. Philosophy was well and good. The operationalisation of the guts of Renaissance was what was at stake in Zimbabwe. And, in that sense – the politics of Zimbabwe to one side – there is something to be said for a form of government in which all parties competing for power are delicately given a place. It was Mbeki's inclusiveness, as pioneered in Democratic Republic of Congo. But the delicacy of the balance in Zimbabwe was something that could be easily upset. If Africa needs robust machinery, then this was a series of filigrees and not a construction of girders. Having exhibited his skill as a master craftsman, though not necessarily as an engineer, Mbeki left for home, and Zuma. Before then, he milked the photo opportunity the Zimbabwean signing ceremony afforded. It dominated every news broadcast by every major international channel. Mutambara tried to appear positive, futuristic, energised. Tsvangirai sought to appear eager to grasp an opportunity for reconciliation and progress. Mbeki beamed all the while. Then Mugabe, sometimes capable of great speeches of the sort he had most recently given at Egypt, gave a sneering, truculent, snide and whimsically contemptuous speech of almost bitter acceptance. It didn't ruin Mbeki's party. He, at least, was delighted with his success.

Now he turned his attention to events back home. Three days before the Zimbabwean deal was signed, on 12 September, Judge Nicholson had delivered his bombshell judgment. Zuma's supporters had danced in the streets. Now Mbeki flew home and, on 17 September, just one full working day after his return, the national prosecutor said that Nicholson's judgment would be appealed. The mood of euphoria on Zuma's behalf was, at a stroke, transformed into vengeful rage. ANC rank and file, the grassroots supporters of Zuma, saw Mbeki's hand behind the prosecutor.

Whether Mbeki did influence Mokotedi Mpshe, the prosecutor, or not is open to question. But Mpshe had been appointed by Mbeki to replace someone who, many thought, was getting too close to practices of corruption by people other than Zuma. He was Mbeki's man. It seemed a deliberate persecution of Zuma, and it seemed selective. Why Zuma? Why not everyone else in what was rumoured to be an all-star cast of possible defendants? It seemed as if Mbeki was determined to prevent any possibility of Zuma succeeding him as president, while simultaneously seeming unaware of how attractive an alternative Zuma now posed to his style of government. The earthy, clumsy, accident-prone, straight-talking – even if he tailored his talk to whatever audience he confronted – heavily married and ramshackle Zuma was everything that the buttoned-down Mbeki was not. And his populism appealed directly to those who had yet to benefit from the end of Apartheid. And, despite what Mbeki considered a momentous breakthrough in Zimbabwe, he had again misjudged just how it would be seen back home. There was amazing scepticism about the bona fides of Robert Mugabe and ZANU-PF. There was not a great deal of being overwhelmed by Morgan Tsvangirai either – but it was widely believed that he had won the election in March and should be given his chance. And the so-called 'xenophobic' riots in poor urban areas were still fresh in the popular memory. The Zimbabweans on South African soil – refugees from Mugabe's meltdown of his own economy – were a problem to poor South Africans. They were seen as getting in the way of their own struggles and their own survival. Now, the man who had created this huge diaspora, Robert Mugabe, had been enshrined as President in a power-sharing deal engineered by their own President. It seemed a case of 'all the top toys for the top boys', and for Tsvangirai there were breadcrumbs. In South Africa, those who were sick of breadcrumbs piled huge pressure on the ANC National Executive. And there were those like Blade Nzimande, the South African Communist Party leader, who had real hopes for a new start, not just under anyone who was not Mbeki, but under someone who would break from Mbeki's neo-liberal economic line that seemed to Nzimande to have denied the poor.

Before the last week of September began, the ANC had placed notice of recall before Mbeki, and he resigned. He had few friends left in high places to defend him. His cool despatch of rivals had become a legend and part of the Zuma call to arms was that it should not happen again – to him.

Mbeki resigned as a good party man. The party had recalled him. He accepted the recall and went.[18] In a wide sense, the party was more authoritative than the electorate. In the narrow sense, the elected party in turn elects the President – but this would normally be interpreted as the party in Parliament. Mbeki's recall came from the party's seniority, not its parliamentary representatives. That seniority had been transformed by the party's own elections in Polokwane. Once Mbeki lost at Polokwane he had effectively lost any real leverage over Zuma. He didn't want to accept that. Even with Nicholson's judgment ringing over South Africa, the ANC would not have recalled Mbeki. His antagonists would have been happy to have him rendered a lame duck by the judgment.

Zuma was not at that time a Member of Parliament, so could not have been elected by parliamentarians as president. He was content to wait for the 2009 elections. It was Mpshe's announcement that he could appeal Nicholson's judgment that was the straw that broke the camel's back. In a way, Mbeki was seen as traducing the separation of powers by intruding the executive upon an organ of the judiciary – by applying presidential pressure upon the prosecutor. But the constitutionality of the ANC's own action of recall will long be debated. Can a party recall a president when he might still command parliamentary support and never put it to the test of Parliament? Mbeki, however, like Mugabe in Zimbabwe, was a good party man. It was just that his party was now dominated by Zuma and Mugabe's party was dominated by his Generals.[19]

After his resignation, Mbeki made a plaintive appeal against Nicholson's judgment. He called the judgment improper, far-reaching, vexatious, scandalous and prejudicial. On 12 January 2009, the Supreme

Court of Appeal agreed with him. It said that Nicholson's court had 'overstepped the limits of its authority'.[20] If this was a vindication of Mbeki[21] – in that Nicholson's court should not have suggested that a titanic struggle for power lay behind Zuma's prosecution – the Supreme Court had a sting in its tail for Zuma. It also said that Nicholson's interpretation of law – that Zuma should not have been prosecuted because the National Prosecuting Authority had not given him a chance to make representations before charges were laid – was wrong. The technicality which Nicholson used to have charges against Zuma dropped was not such a technicality after all. The charges could be brought again. If this was a year of turmoil in South African politics, it was not over yet. Now, all eyes were on the countdown to the 2009 elections. Even without Mbeki, could Zuma be stopped by legal means? If not, could he be stopped by electoral challenge? If there was no existing party that could defeat the ANC in the elections, why should senior people within the ANC not create such a party? Kgalema Motlanthe, the Deputy President of the ANC and a parliamentarian, was declared caretaker President until the elections. Mbeki-loyalists and other ANC figures antipathetic to the prospect of a Zuma presidency prepared to split from the parent party. Led by Lekota, the new party would have a smattering of senior names behind it and a huge amount of organisational legwork before it. Many who would not follow Lekota, feeling wedded by struggle, genealogy or sentiment to the ANC, nevertheless secretly advised him. He had significant closet support. His new party was called COPE – the Congress of the People. It harked back to 1955, the original Congress of the People and its foundation principles of the struggle for equality agreed in Kliptown. Those principles are inscribed in a tall hollow monument in the centre of the only part of Kliptown that has been renovated. The use of the name in 2008 was a call for renewal. But the Kliptown monument is in some ways a take on the one that stands outside Pretoria, commemorating the deeds of Andries Pretorius, the dashing commando leader of the *Voortrek* of white Boer settlers into lands owned by black communities.[22] It was Pretorius who was the victor of the great Battle of Blood River in 1838. He was revered as a hero of the 'white resistance' to black rule and the *Voortrek* monument is a tall hollow column with a narrow open top. Once a year, at an exact time, light pours down in a narrow stream upon the engraven memory of Pretorius and the trek. One monument seems to imitate another. One COPE sought to emulate an earlier COPE. Impersonations, real movements and calls for renewal sprang up all over South Africa. But the existing opposition was also mobilising. And now, the last name to be added to the cast of this book, Helen Zille, began to make her presence felt. A white woman, leader of the Democratic Alliance (DA), defeater of the ANC in Cape Town, fluent Xhosa speaker, a rare environmentalist in South African politics who drove a Toyota Prius, and tough as nails, prepared for the campaign trail.

In March 2009, just weeks before the election, with Zuma leading in the polls – despite the efforts of Lekota and Zille – Schabir Shaik was released from prison after serving only 28 months of his 15 year sentence. The reason given was grounds of health. Zuma denied he had interfered with the course of justice. But justice was to offer yet another shock just before the elections, with Mpshe featuring once again. All the while, in Zimbabwe, the power-sharing formula that Thabo Mbeki had brokered remained broken until the end of the first month of 2009.

CHAPTER 12

A DIVORCE, A FORCED MARRIAGE, AND AN HISTORIC ELECTION[1]

As soon as Mbeki was recalled from office, the ANC – like both ZANU-PF and the MDC in Zimbabwe – split. Mosiuoa Lekota broke away to form COPE as an alternative, non-corrupt and non-oligarchic version of what the ANC should have been. Its problems in self-organisation soon led to its early promise fading – so that the South African elections of 2009 pitted the ANC against a field of small parties, and the strongest of these proved to be Helen Zille's Democratic Alliance. There is some irony here, in that the ANC, as party of the black majority who had sought freedom, democracy and the uplifting of living standards, found its main challenge coming from a white woman who, as Mayor of Cape Town, had uplifted the living standards of her constituents more swiftly and efficiently than the ANC had in other areas. The opposition parties, Lekota's and Zille's foremost among them, urged the electorate not to give Zuma's ANC a two-thirds majority. This was to safeguard the country's constitution, they argued – by far the world's most progressive and liberal constitution – from being watered down by an all-powerful ANC that had shown, on both sides of its divide, a seeming willingness to transgress the constitutional separation of govern-mental and judicial powers. Meanwhile, the coalition government in

Zimbabwe stuttered into its early phases, and the ill will of the negotiations continued into the running of the country. It took the tragic death of Susan Tsvangirai, Morgan Tsvangirai's wife, to breathe at least a temporary sense of possible unity into the fractured world of Zimbabwean politics. Back in South Africa, more than 77 per cent of the electorate turned out to vote. Of the votes cast, the ANC received 65.9 per cent – not quite enough to change the constitution of its own volition. On paper at least, South Africa was set to remain a constitutional democracy – albeit one with what was still a huge dominant party in control, and one in which, right down to the eve of the elections, political games were being enacted within the 'independent' legal system. But the voting itself was free and fair. President Zuma took office with a mandate from his people. As they had when Mandela walked free 19 years earlier, they wanted to live in a better South Africa.

After the recall of Mbeki by the ANC, several ministers refused to serve in Kgalema Motlanthe's Cabinet. They had nothing against Motlanthe. In many ways he was the best possible person to bridge the gulf between the Mbeki and Zuma factions. But he was seen precisely as a transitional president, warming the post for Zuma – and it was Zuma who was seen by these Mbeki-loyalists as the mastermind behind the recall of their leader.

There is a tendency of South Africans to see their country as a unique enclosure. But what had happened in the ANC was not dissimilar to the experience of politics everywhere. In the United Kingdom, the revolt against Margaret Thatcher, initiated by Michael Heseltine, was truly bitter. She left Downing Street with tears in her eyes. More recently, the protracted feud between Tony Blair and Gordon Brown, with the arch-Talleyrand figure of Peter Mandelson demonstrating superb and amoral qualities of ruthlessness, cunning, manoeuvrability and service, shuttling his alliances back and forth between the two men, indicated just how divisive and addictively inescapable such power struggles can be.

As soon as Jacob Zuma won Polokwane, however, Mosiuoa Lekota, the powerful Minister of Defence, stood down from his national chairpersonship of the ANC. The Zuma-ites didn't want him and he didn't want any part of them. And, as soon as Mbeki was recalled in September 2008, Lekota resigned from the ANC altogether. His was the cleanest act of principle, but very many were disquieted by the inexorable rise of Jacob Zuma. Not least, there were misgivings north of the border in Zimbabwe. For Mugabe's people had not treated Zuma well when, during the ANC's freedom struggle, the exiled Zuma would visit Zimbabwe often, staying at the home of Joyce Naidoo his fellow exile, and seeking a more positive endorsement from Robert Mugabe of the ANC over its rivals – the PAC (Pan-Africanist Congress), whom Mugabe and ZANU-PF, in the days before the release of Nelson Mandela, preferred. More recently, one of Zuma's many daughters married the son of Welshman Ncube, a key figure in the formation of the MDC and the intellectual animation behind Arthur Mutambara's version of the opposition party. But, if Zuma could not be counted on to be as indulgent towards Mugabe as Mbeki often was, Lekota had for a long time been totally scathing of Mugabe and his right to remain President of Zimbabwe. It seemed, as the South African presidential race counted down, that the Zimbabwean cat-and-mouse game of politics and agreements without movement or enactment might have to come to an end.

The nickname 'Terror' derives from Mosiuoa's prowess on the football field. He was a striker and went forward in a straight line, burly enough to plough through all challenges. He was a student leader of the Soweto generation of the mid-1970s and spent eight years on Robben Island. One of the 'inziles', those who stayed and resisted within South Africa – as opposed to the exiles like Zuma and Mbeki – his liberation credentials were impeccable. He became a member of the ANC National Executive in 1991 and, in 1997, was elected National Chairperson – holding this post for a decade until Polokwane. He was made Minister of Defence in 1999, so his tenure overlapped the arms scandals that surrounded Zuma. No one knows what Lekota's reaction behind closed doors was to these events. No one can accurately ascribe a portion of culpability to him – but procurement of new weapons and systems was a responsibility of his ministry. Somewhere along the line, however – whether because of the way Zuma treated refugees from the Soweto uprising who went into exile, or because of the way Zuma tried to influence decisions within his Ministry, or both – Lekota came to detest Zuma.

But, in order to launch himself and other ANC-dissidents as an independent force, Lekota needed to distance himself from both Zuma *and* Mbeki – despite a record of friendship with Mbeki. He recognised Mbeki's unpopularity and diagnosed its roots as his aloofness certainly, but also the fact that Mbeki had not fought against Apartheid *in* South Africa. His entire liberation career had been conducted, largely comfortably, in exile. Mbeki did not know the South African condition. His African Renaissance, his favoured reading of Afro-American poets and novelists, his intellectual affection for Ngugi wa Thiong'o's work, his need to express a line between the aspiration for freedom and a renaissance of freed history and culture were all very worthy. But little of it resonated in the South African townships like Alexandra, Kliptown and those in the Western Cape. Lekota chose to describe the political malaise that had beset South Africa as the gap between the exile-ANC, with its liberation bases in Lusaka and elsewhere, and the 'inziles', of whom he now sought to claim leadership. Neither Mbeki nor Zuma really understood what had gone on within the country. 'Thabo and Zuma were tongue and saliva,' Lekota said. Parachuting back into high positions and attracting rich friends didn't help the process of reacculturation. The division between exile and inzile was a neat soundbite, but it also allowed Lekota to warn of Zuma's authoritarian style. This man, Lekota implied, was not really a democrat. Without using so many words, Lekota reminded his South African audience of Zuma's interrogation camps where fellow South Africans suffered and died.

'The comrades who were in exile took an almost militaristic approach. Their approach was to want people to be loyal to them all the time. When we criticised certain things, we were seen as almost like challenging their authority.'[2] At the same time, Lekota thought Mbeki had not challenged Robert Mugabe enough. 'We could have taken a much firmer position ... [we] soft-pedalled.' It was an interesting contrast: soft-pedalling abroad while being authoritarian and censorious at home – especially where ANC members were concerned. The vitriol heaped upon William Gumede for his critical biography of Thabo Mbeki was a case in point. Meanwhile, accommodation abroad was desirable, especially if an African Renaissance or African values could be invoked. This was what Mugabe conspicuously and continuously did: he portrayed land and liberation as the hallmarks of a true nationalism, the springboard for renaissance. He knew how to play Mbeki. Zuma, because of past history, and Lekota, because of a genuine attachment to democracy, would be more difficult to handle. Mbeki, kept on as the Zimbabwean mediator after his recall, would no doubt have stressed these points to Mugabe. Strangely, Mbeki was able in some ways to be more effective in Zimbabwe *after* his recall from the presidency. The threat of what *another* president might do was more potent than any effort at a threat he himself might have issued. But, that having been said, Mbeki's problems in the Zimbabwean mediation were not just with Mugabe – whose style of negotiation was intransigent – but with Tsvangirai. In a way, it was in Tsvangirai's interest to force a waiting game, precisely to see whether he could leverage goodwill from the next president. Many of his followers wanted him to do just that. And Tsvangirai was highly conscious that he had accepted too much on good faith alone during the breakthrough discussions that agreed a unity government, and had made too many concessions that he could not publicly admit. He was having difficulty controlling the MDC and, for him, one false move in the Mbeki-led negotiations on problematic details of the agreement could be disastrous. But the state of Zimbabwe was also completely disastrous. Prolonging a waiting game could only impoverish his supporters and the entire country even more. He leaned increasingly upon Odinga in Kenya and Khama in Botswana for advice and support. Khama kept issuing fiery statements about the Mugabe government. These didn't help the negotiations, but they gave Tsvangirai a figleaf of reserve force to bring to the table.

The agreement on a unity or coalition government in Zimbabwe, achieved just before Mbeki's recall as President of South Africa, expressed a clumsy architecture of government. It stipulated which party had how many Cabinet seats. Tsvangirai was confident, or said he was confident, that an outline division of allocations had been agreed. But it was never written down and included in the text of the agreement announced by Mbeki on 15 September 2008. What Tsvangirai wanted was control over the Finance portfolio. Mugabe wanted to give him that, because only Tsvangirai had any chance of persuading the international community to begin reinvestment in Zimbabwe. Simultaneously, Mugabe considered he could checkmate Tsvangirai at any moment if ZANU-PF continued to control the Reserve Bank.[3] Keeping Gideon Gono as Governor of the Bank was a Mugabe priority as he blithely conceded Finance to Tsvangirai.[4] Mugabe demanded control of the Defence portfolio. Tsvangirai conceded that because his information was that 70 per cent of the military rank and file had voted for him in the first and only contested round of the presidential elections. If push came to shove, he reasoned the soldiers would not fire on his supporters. Seeking to pay disgruntled soldiers a liveable wage would also be a key instrument in ensuring they could be detached from the high command. Tsvangirai knew that the senior Generals had a controlling interest in Mugabe, and Mugabe was vital to the Generals. This was something he could only ameliorate with time. He knew there would be no settlement without Mugabe and Defence remaining together. So, in an architecture of government where both major sides were balanced – Mbeki's system of negotiation seemed to be, 'I have given them that, so I am now giving you this' – there was a sub-system of further balances in the key portfolios: Minister of Finance by Bank Governor; military high command and the Ministry of Defence by rank and file. But playing the rank-and-file card could not be guaranteed. There was no automatic chain of command from Tsvangirai. What he needed was a further balancing force. He wanted control of Home Affairs – control of the police. He wanted to be able to field coercion and guns in the face of coercion and guns. Zimbabwe had come to that. And, even if the police were outgunned, they would make any ZANU-PF calculations on the use of force problematic; and they would allow Tsvangirai some leeway in creating a more peaceful environment in the townships, where the police had been feared; they would allow the MDC more freedom to organise its popular foundation, its party branches, without fear of suppression; they would, in short, politically strengthen Tsvangirai. Mugabe was determined this would not happen.

Odinga in Kenya had accepted a distribution of portfolios which left his party with almost none of the powerful ministries. If that was a precedent on how unity governments should work, then Mugabe played it to the hilt. He seemed to say to Tsvangirai: 'Look how your mentor, Odinga, is being successful without having all that you are demanding.' Another important aspect was that, depending on which witness to the negotiations was 'leaking' information, Tsvangirai either did receive some unwritten assurance that he would get Home Affairs, or he actually conceded Home Affairs to Mugabe as the price he had to pay to get the agreement through. On the night of the breakthrough, Tsvangirai was almost delirious with joy. But his supporters immediately told him it was not enough and, in particular, he had to ensure the MDC had Home Affairs. But the Mbeki conviction was that Tsvangirai *had* conceded Home Affairs. The final, vexed negotiations – with the Mugabe side unexpectedly accusing the MDC of bad faith, and the MDC determined to have some sense of counter-vailing coercive force – were almost impossible for Mbeki. He now worked with Motlanthe, his successor as President of South Africa, and Motlanthe held private discussions with Mugabe. Simultaneously, Mbeki worked to detach Khama from his vociferous and uncompromising support of Tsvangirai. He also began to frame the negotiations so that the majority of African presidents would support him. This was to suggest to Tsvangirai that, if he wanted to be taken seriously as a prime minister of an African state, then he needed to appear not unreasonable to other state leaders. He would need their help and cooperation in the future, and he should listen to them now.

Whatever might be said about Mbeki's biases in the negotiations that led to the agreement of a unity government, the subsequent negotiations over details were firmly tilted in favour of Mugabe – not just because Mbeki engaged well with Mugabe, but because Mbeki felt Tsvangirai was negotiating inconsistently. Besides, he knew that Tsvangirai wanted to be Prime Minister – Mbeki had some psychological leverage there – but, also, Mbeki wanted to be finished with the negotiations. He wanted to be far away from South African politics. He did not want the situation to drag on until he was reporting, not to Motlanthe, but to Zuma. If this meant forcing things Mugabe's way, that's what he would do. Although he actually warmed to Tsvangirai by the end of it all, Mbeki was now heartily sick of Zimbabwean politics.

At this time, back in the world of South African politics, movement was rapid and contentious. The decision to name the breakaway from the ANC after the historic Congress of the People was greeted by the ANC as a direct challenge to its legacy. The Freedom Charter, adopted at the original Congress in 1955 had become the binding set of principles under which the ANC, the South African Communist Party, COSATU, exiles and inziles fought. But, in fact, the ANC had taken a year to adopt the Freedom Charter that emerged from the original COPE and, even years later, the exact status of the Charter was a matter of dispute. Was it the defining document, or was it something that would be bypassed by the progress of a more socialist history fulfilling itself? Tom Lodge recounts the debates among the prisoners on Robben Island over this exact issue. Govan Mbeki argued that the Charter was bourgeois and would become irrelevant, that the SACP would emerge as liberation's driving force, and that the future would be Leninist. It was Mandela who argued that the Freedom Charter was seminal and could not be bypassed.[5]

What had happened at Polokwane was that Zuma secured the support of the ANC's radicals, including Blade Nzimande, the leader of the SACP and Julius Malema of the ANC Youth League. In fact, in the lengthy run-up to the deposition of Thabo Mbeki, some of Mbeki's leading supporters – such as Sydney Mufamadi – lost their executive positions in the SACP. These changes were for control of the party's direction, not just a contest of personalities. What Lekota's

COPE articulated was not just a distrust of Zuma, but a continuation of a long debate as to South Africa's direction. By throwing his support behind Zuma, Blade Nzimande had hoped to secure Zuma as a champion of the SACP commitment to the poor – but also for the vision of a future that was not neo-liberal.[6] Getting rid of Mbeki was just part of an historical march. Lekota couldn't stand Zuma, but he had no truck either with the vision of Nzimande. Although clumsily arrived at, the decision to name the breakaway party COPE was a deliberate self-identification with the Freedom Charter and a distancing from the current leadership of the SACP. But it also meant Lekota had no message to take to the poor on his campaign hustings other than what Nzimande already had. All he could say was that COPE stood for equality, as the Freedom Charter had, and that equality was being threatened by high-level corruption. COPE became the party that stood against corruption – and this allowed it to aim a lot of its cannons directly at Zuma – but the anti-corruption message had a flaw. Zuma had been accused of corruption over defence contracts while Lekota had been Minister of Defence. Lekota may have had no knowledge of what was happening beneath him, but the buck stopped at his desk. Many who flocked to COPE's colours asked, 'Who is Lekota to lead us?'

I was in Kliptown on election day, 2009, staying beside the site where the Freedom Charter had been agreed.[7] The Charter itself is laid out in metal tablets inside a conical, shrine-like monument. They look like something Moses would have brought down from Mount Sinai if God had been more verbose than a mere ten commandments. But they were gathered nevertheless under ten principles: the people shall govern; all national groups shall have equal rights; the people shall share in the country's wealth; the land shall be shared among those who work it; all shall be equal before the law; all shall enjoy equal human rights; there shall be work and security; the doors of learning and culture shall be opened; there shall be houses, security and comfort; there shall be peace and friendship. The use of the imperative 'shall' emphasised that here were people who sought to *command* history – not merely await some historical fate. But it is interesting how the descendant groups of the first COPE have selectively emphasised some of the principles more than others. It is not as if Govan Mbeki and Blade Nzimande rejected the People's Charter, but they stressed principles such as 'the people shall share in the country's wealth', which established four subsidiary principles to do with public ownership. COSATU would have found its animation and historic justification in the principle, 'there shall be work and security', one of whose six subsidiary principles mandated the trade union movement as part of the struggle; the impoverished of Alexandra would have demanded of the ANC fulfilment of the principle, 'there shall be houses, security and comfort'. And Thabo Mbeki, in his protracted dealings with Robert Mugabe, could have pointed to the Freedom Charter's final principle, 'there shall be peace and friendship', in which the penultimate subsidiary principle read, 'the rights of all peoples in Africa to independence and self-government shall be recognised, and shall be the basis of close cooperation.' He was not going to tell an independent African state how to live – but would frame his mediation around 'close cooperation'.

The Freedom Charter had socialist leanings but, with its emphasis also on democratic institutions and equality – without any mention of a Leninist vanguard party – it was basically a social democratic document.[8] It was as a social democrat that Lekota took to the polls – and was promptly deposed by his new party as presidential candidate.

But, while COPE began its infancy as a political party, the Democratic Alliance led by Helen Zille was gearing for the elections. Hitherto the official opposition in Parliament, even though it was dwarfed by the ANC, its support base was confined largely to the Western Cape, and those supporters could be stereotyped as largely white and coloured malcontents of the new black dispensation. Zille had great steel in her backbone, and she not only campaigned on a platform of greater efficiency in government and the *delivery* of promises, she had become a

model of administrative efficiency. Look at me, I can do it, she seemed
to say. And, in fact, she could.

It was impossible to write off Zille as some kind of polite, well-
meaning, liberal, white 'madam'. She had all the liberal accoutrements –
the Toyota Prius with the hopelessly messy interior being the most
conspicuous – but no ANC spin doctor could diminish her work against
Apartheid and as a city leader. And she could speak – and sing – in fluent
Xhosa. More than one ANC luminary commented on how good her
language was. They did laugh at her dancing skills. There are some
things she should not have attempted on the campaign trail – but, curiously, her efforts to do something for which she had no natural talent
merely endeared her to friend and many a foe alike. Not every foe: she
did attract serious hatred. But her skin had been thickened long before
she became a politician. She had been at the centre of some celebrated
episodes and movements in South Africa's contemporary history. She
knew what it was like to be nationally vilified at the age of 26. For she
was the young reporter who, in 1977, exposed the cover-up of the causes
of Steve Biko's death. The celebrated black consciousness leader had
been beaten to death in police custody, but the Apartheid authorities had
insisted he had died as the result of a hunger strike. Zille proved this was
false. But it meant her journalistic career was in ruins. She became a full-
blown anti-Apartheid activist instead. She was a member of the famous
Black Sash women's movement in the 1980s, helped lead the anti-
conscription campaign at the time when young South Africans were
being sent to the battlefields of Angola to face the Cubans, and offered
her home as a 'safe house' for hunted activists; and she herself had to go
into hiding for a time in the turbulent last decade of Apartheid.
Basically, she acquired pedigree. And in a 'rainbow nation' of constitutional equalities, no one dared tar her with being white or a woman – not
in public anyway, and not until a year before the elections of 2009.

In 2006, Zille became Mayor of Cape Town. She had already been
elected to both the provincial and national legislatures, but it was as
mayor that she made her name in the majority-rule era.[9] She presided
over huge economic growth and an almost equally huge diminution of

central city crime. Most importantly, she increased capital for 'service delivery' to poorer areas by 15 per cent and slashed 3 per cent off the unemployment rate. And, although housing delivery was theoretically outside the Mayor's scope, by reforming the system of application and waiting lists she helped increase housing delivery from 3,000 to 7,000 units per annum. She got electricity through to the worst parts of Khayelitsha, one of the most derelict townships on the salt flats on the edge of Cape Town.[10] Even her ANC enemies held their breath at what she did.

She became national leader of the Democratic Alliance in 2007 and, at the 2009 elections, Premier of the Western Cape, leading the Democratic Alliance (DA) to ruling party status in the Province. Shortly afterwards she attacked Jacob Zuma's sexism, and the ANC Youth League mounted a national campaign of vilification. She had been through it all before in 1977 but, this time, because it was truly sexist,[11] it served to increase her visibility and support. There were many black women outside Western Cape who were not at ease with Jacob Zuma's becoming their President. The ANC Youth League accused her, among other things, of polyandry – of surrounding herself with male concubines,[12] which was a little rich considering Zuma's polygamy and other amorous habits that must have meant many showers. She had earlier been accused of being a 'Satanist'.[13] Even before these attacks, her character and capacities were clear. The ANC even nicknamed her 'Godzille'. But, just as she was getting the bit between her teeth in readiness for the national election campaign, the last thing Helen Zille and the DA needed was the advent of Terror Lekota and COPE.

Those who have been moving up and down the Western Cape for many years often cannot wait to get out of Cape Town. In Khayelitsha, Table Mountain looks – from where the poor see it – monstrous and oppressive. The Western Cape is truly beautiful. But, even in the vine-yards, where a visitor is greeted with every manner of decorum and invited to pronounce judgement on bouquet and taste, one doesn't have to look very far to see that not all the manual workers look satisfied with their lives. Indeed, some of their wages and living standards are scandalous – partly because they have always been, but now the exploitation of Apartheid has been replaced by the might of the huge international supermarkets who 'capture' suppliers and then mercilessly drive down the prices and operating margins of the producers – who, in turn, drive down the wages and conditions of their workers, who need to work for peanuts rather than have no work at all. It will be interesting to see what Helen Zille, as the new provincial Premier, will do for these people; whether she can repeat her success in Cape Town.

There are 'polite' and not so 'polite' towns in the Western Cape. Towns like Atlantis are so dirt poor and the inhabitants so debt-ridden that they just look hapless. Even in the period after Mandela's release, people would still be incarcerated in a twentieth-century version of a Dickensian debtors' prison in Atlantis. The pretty towns like Stellenbosch, home of the well-known university, have centres that are twee and pretentious. And the towns like Wellington, a mixture of unpretty gentrifications and just down-and-dirty poverty, show what the political contest in South Africa is all about. Wellington has two sides of the track. Those on the wrong side of the track want to move to the other – out of poverty into a semblance of lower (often very lower) middle class. And this is the vision both the Freedom Charter and the ANC held out to people: 'There shall be houses, security and comfort!' The importance of decent housing cannot be exaggerated in South Africa when so many people live in very poor houses, without security and certainly without comfort.

The hopes of the National Party, in its negotiations with the ANC after the release of Mandela, were misguided. The National negotiators wanted to play for time, in order to secure alliances with sufficient non-white communities to give the ANC a run for its money when, finally, elections became inevitable. They thought that they could secure the poor coloured communities of the Western Cape on the grounds that, being neither fully white or black, they had more to fear from a government that was fully black. But race was always only part of the issue. People wanted to migrate from one *class* to another.[14] They wanted to become like the Zimbabweans of Chitungwiza, outside Harare, before Robert Mugabe wrecked the lives of the huge majority of Zimbabweans. And what Helen Zille promised these people was that, because of her efficiency – as evidenced by her track record in Cape Town – she could facilitate this transition. Her appeal was to the educated middle class and those who *wanted* to be middle class – even if only on the lowest borderlands of middle class, but in a housing unit with modern facilities and enough room both for a family and a degree of privacy. As the 2009 election campaign got under way, she and the DA were certain they would capture more black votes than anyone had projected as being possible. And the sensational departure of Terror Lekota from the ANC had seen its early promise and dreams of an equally sensational capture of power slowly seep away.

Terror Lekota had a less successful period as Premier of the Free State than Helen Zille had as Mayor of Cape Town. He was the provincial Premier briefly after Mandela became President. Afterwards, Lekota went on to become Minister of Defence. In the hierarchy of South African government, Cabinet posts are more highly regarded than provincial premierships, and being an MP in the national Parliament more important than holding a provincial ministerial portfolio. The aim is to be at the centre of action. However, the cascading network of national, provincial, municipal and related administrations has meant a multi-layered series of opportunities for patronage, contracts, backhanders and bribes. Having those layers available for patronage has kept the ANC a tight ship. Money and position were coupled with ideology and a history – already a mythology – of having struggled and suffered for freedom. In that sense, the departure of Lekota from the party was viewed as a huge blow. It was seen almost in religious terms as a schism. But, just as in the Christian parable – that God receives more joy in a single lost sheep being found than in the continuing welfare of the settled flock – huge overtures, all publicly denied, were made to lure Lekota back into the fold. The ANC Treasurer, Mathews Phosa, was foremost among those sent to persuade the lost sheep to return. But, by now, Lekota was renegade rather than lost; and his obdurate sense of going forward – as if he were still playing football – also led him to being blindsided by his own new comrades in COPE.

When COPE was formed there was huge national speculation as to whether it could overthrow the ANC or, at the very least, significantly reduce its majority while, at the same time, eclipsing Zille's Democratic Alliance and pushing it into third place. Some thought that, at that stage, Lekota would want to rejoin the ANC, but on terms he dictated – and they would be social democratic terms rather than the socialism Blade Nzimande wanted. Zuma would also have pondered whether he would have to offer Lekota the deputy presidency in such a scenario – for, by now, personal terms had become inextricably linked with philosophical and policy issues in the ANC of the modern millennium. Zuma would have found it as distasteful to work with Lekota as Lekota would have found it to work with Zuma. Thankfully for the ANC, COPE took care of all these problems.

Mbeki was recalled in September 2008. Lekota announced the formation of COPE in October, calling it a serving of 'divorce papers', and was suspended from the ANC in the same month. In December, he was elected unopposed to the first COPE party presidency. However, in February 2009, Lekota was defeated in his bid to be COPE's candidate for President of South Africa.[15] COPE's Deputy President, Mbhazima Shilowa, had manoeuvred to install instead a political tyro, Bishop Mvume Dandala, as the presidential candidate. The choice of Dandala surprised almost everyone. He had been a student leader and was once the senior Bishop of the Methodist Church in Southern Africa. He was totally 'clean' but also, in terms of government experience, totally inexperienced. Zuma had been Deputy President, Lekota had been a provincial Premier and Cabinet minister, Zille had been Mayor of Cape Town and was a Member of Parliament. Dandala had no such experience and was, in addition, almost completely unknown to the electorate. He epitomised the COPE message of anti-corruption – he had bribed no one and no one had bribed him; he had not been in charge of any institution where bribery had occurred. But that was precisely the point. He had not been in charge of any institution except a bishopric; and, although church politics can be vicious in Southern Africa, they are several steps removed from the emotional violence meted out in national government. It is easy to say you are incorrupt if you never have been tempted. The backroom story of why Shilowa moved against Lekota and why Dandala accepted a role for which he was patently ill equipped – although he tried very hard to come up to speed – is still to be told. And it may never be told, especially if COPE fades in importance. Faced with stories that he was disillusioned and that the ANC was attempting to lure him back, Lekota declared, 'There is no way I can return to the company of men and women who are dead set on destroying the constitutional democracy which I gave most of my life to creating. I will go to the grave a member of the Congress of the People.'[16] But whether he meant the new party or the spirit of the original COPE is unclear. After the election, Lekota chose not to enter Parliament.

As a result of such unexpected changes in COPE, its public esteem plummeted. And the new party almost suddenly realised it did not have a national infrastructure with which to fight an election. Mandela had recognised the same problem with the ANC shortly after negotiations for majority rule began, and was content for a time to prolong the negotiations while organisation was put into place. COPE had no such luxury of time, and even though it found sufficient funding for a national campaign – and, to this day, no one can really identify its source – it had to be a sketchy campaign. However, the campaign was festooned with beautiful yellow posters. *Vote for Hope. Vote COPE.* Desperate attempts to gain Thabo Mbeki's endorsement came to naught[17] – although it was said that Mbeki's own mother was determined to vote COPE; and some thought that COPE's finances were at least partly donated by Moletsi Mbeki, Thabo's younger brother, or the businesswoman and feminist, Wendy Luhabe – incidentally the wife of Mbhazima Shilowa. But what it meant was that suddenly, all the early hope did *not* lead to a groundswell for COPE. It was almost a lesson in how not to launch a new party as a fighting force; how not to build on momentum; how not to convince the electorate that you have a consistent message with authoritative personnel who can fit the public imagination of how that message might be enacted. Jacob Zuma was delighted. And so was Helen Zille.[18]

While Terror Lekota was losing his command of COPE, things were moving rapidly in Zimbabwe. On 27 January 2009, the regional presidents in the SADC (Southern African Development Community) announced that there had been a breakthrough in negotiations to enact the unity government in Zimbabwe. Talks on how to do this had been stalemated since the agreement had been signed in September the previous year. The MDC promptly denied that such a breakthrough had been achieved; but, in truth, the executive of the party was suddenly faced with a lack of options. Mbeki had used the assembled persuasion of the Southern African presidents to act upon Botswana's Ian Khama – after the death of Zambia's Levy Mwanawasa, Tsvangirai's sole supporter in the SADC. The SADC message to Khama was that the Zimbabwean issue was going nowhere, people were suffering as a result, so why not try out the unity government and see if it works or not? Khama, although he later issued a public statement decrying the wisdom of the unity government's going ahead,[19] did so more as a face-saving gesture. Behind the scenes, he capitulated to peer pressure. Tsvangirai told his lieutenants that, this time, there really was no choice and, this time, his own hardliners finally, reluctantly agreed. On 5 February, the Zimbabwean Parliament passed a constitutional bill allowing a coalition government and, on 11 February 2009, Morgan Tsvangirai was sworn in – by Robert Mugabe – as Prime Minister. On 22 February, COPE chose Dandala as its presidential candidate and, if Mbeki had ever flirted with the idea of endorsing COPE, he wasn't going to do so now – even with the time to weigh his options after finally putting the Zimbabwe issue to bed, and not with his friend, Terror Lekota, having been subordinated in the vicious young politics of the hopeful new party.

As for vicious politics, Tsvangirai and the MDC were forced to settle on a compromise over the Home Affairs portfolio.[20] This would now be a split or shared portfolio. The only problem was that the part of the portfolio that dealt with the police would go to a ZANU-PF minister. Mugabe and his people would have hoped for the slow incorporation and emasculation of the MDC from this moment on. Tsvangirai knew that he would have to play a political game of manoeuvre as well as, if not better than Odinga had done in Kenya. But Odinga was, by far, the better practitioner of the dark arts; and he had previously worked with Kibaki and knew how to treat his President from the vantage point of being Prime Minister. Coming to know Robert Mugabe would be an education for the new MDC ministers and the new Prime Minister. 'Handling Bob' became a new mantra.[21] Tsvangirai said he was certain he could do it. But, as he was being sworn in as Prime Minister, against a backdrop of assembled ZANU-PF dignitaries and Generals, he could not have been unaware – as he strove to maintain eye contact with the ice-cold Mugabe – that the eyes of all behind him were sceptical, hostile, and saw him as a necessary but temporary impediment. Some very powerful men were looking straight through him. They were determined to make life as difficult as possible for him. This was the time that Zimbabwean inflation hit its most staggering figure, and it is worth repeating it – 6.5 quindecillion novemdecillion per cent – and what it meant was that, for the non-political class, life was a huge daily struggle.[22] But the hard men who had limousined and helicoptered into the ceremony thought little, if anything, about the despair even of their own supporters. For Zuma, with the South African poor to think about, having Mbeki relieve him of the Zimbabwean problem – for now – was a boon. For Mbeki, it had been a close-run thing. After Tsvangirai finally became Prime Minister the South African elections were scheduled for April 2009. Mbeki promptly accepted an African Union invitation to mediate in the Darfur crisis to replicate his 'African solution to African problems' 'success' story in Zimbabwe. On that, at least, he would not have to report to President Zuma.

Although Mbeki and his team were pledged to return to Zimbabwe, if occasion demanded, their transition to the Darfur crisis was swift. Mbeki had discovered that the international 'great and good' had roles of great grandeur and some usefulness to play – without the responsibilities of office and the tiresomeness of rivals. Now he could personify the 'African solutions' rubric under which he had laboured in Zimbabwe. It would seem that he intended to confine such 'greatness and goodness' to Africa – unlike the Jimmy Carters, Tony Blairs and Kofi Annans of the world, often stumbling in where angels fear to tread, carting around their track records and often glib superficialities as entitlements to intervene. But, having said that, Mbeki's amazing patience – epitomised by his capacity to endure, for days at a time, Mugabe, Tsvangirai and their people, eking out a nanosecond's progress into the next day's agenda – was exactly what was required in vexed, complex and almost intractable conflicts like the one in Darfur. An African solution or not, he at least knew that the Western fixation on simple, clean, instant remedies – with one side hailed as victims and therefore the goodies, and the other necessarily as baddies and the progenitors of all evils – would solve nothing, remedy only Western consciences that had sided with the 'good', and possibly render the conflict worse. And, in a way, all those years of struggling for liberation, whether endured in a prison cell or spent jetting about the world organising overthrow that never quite happens, builds immense patience. When the dust clears as to what is good and bad in Mbeki's record and legacy, his future biographers will agree that – whether right or wrong – his patient diplomacy was extraordinary. However, in very different circumstances of course, Kofi Annan delivered an 'African solution' – a power-sharing compromise – in Kenya almost overnight. An African solution does not always have to be slow. There is a strong argument to be made that Mbeki's work in Zimbabwe was too slow. And, in any case, the call of Darfur notwithstanding, he was back in Zimbabwe sooner than he expected – this time for the funeral of a non-political person which, all the same, assumed huge political and psychological importance.

The unity government had begun under vexed conditions, and ZANU-PF set about a complex series of obstructions and tests of MDC resolve and mettle. In a way, they were deliberate distractions to keep the attention on scrub fires while ZANU-PF continued to despoil the forest. Invasions of the handful of farms remaining in white hands occurred; an MDC-nominated deputy minister, Roy Bennett, was imprisoned; other MDC activists already in prison were not released. Tendai Biti, appointed as the MDC Minister of Finance – albeit with no financial expertise whatsoever – soon realised that Gideon Gono, the self-serving ZANU-PF-appointed Reserve Bank Governor, knew all the moves on the financial chessboard; even if he had used them to ensure the prosperity of the ZANU-PF oligarchy and presided over modern global history's most precipitate and dramatic fiscal decline.

By March, the election campaign was in full swing and the phoney war of the preceding months was replaced by the parties fielding their full strength, or as much strength as they could muster. The ANC had a financial war chest of two billion rand, several times that of all its rivals put together. But its newspaper advertising and roadside hoardings were no better than anyone else's. Zuma is a hard man to project in static depictions. So the money was invested in huge rallies and crowded set-pieces where the crowds would be guaranteed to surround the ANC leader with adulation and cheer his dancing, his songs and his promises that he would end poverty. He raised expectations very high. But, all the while, the forced marriage that was the unity government in Zimbabwe smouldered in the background.

Fatal car accidents have long been a favoured form of assassination in Southern Africa. Mugabe's top field commander, Josiah Tongogara, died in a mysterious car crash just before independence. Many thought this was Mugabe ridding himself of a rival,[23] and these rumours lingered right up to the 2000s – when it was said that Mugabe still laid a place at his dinner table every night for Tongogara, in order to placate his *ngozi* or spirit. The rumour was the seedbed for the play, *Breakfast with Mugabe*,[24] which in turn gave Heidi Holland a title to adapt for her book, *Dinner with Mugabe*.[25] In the early 1990s, the death in a car crash of my former colleague Johnson Ndlovu, the Zimbabwean ambassador-designate to South Africa in the wake of the release of Nelson Mandela, and former Speaker of Parliament, was described to me by his friends as an assassination. In Zambia civic action leaders, in the turbulent late 1990s under President Chiluba, would complain bitterly of near misses on the Lusaka roads late at night as being assassination attempts. Given the habits of Lusaka motorists, drunkenness would be an equally likely cause as political disposal – but the discourse of murder by car is embedded in the region. So that when, on 6 March 2009, shortly after Morgan Tsvangirai had finally been able to give his maiden speech in the Zimbabwean Parliament, his car was struck by a lorry and his wife Susan was killed, it looked to all the world like a botched assassination attempt on the new Prime Minister.

Distrustful of the ZANU-PF-dominated police and security commanders, Tsvangirai had refused to travel with official police outriders. It was to cost Susan her life, as these motorcyclist policemen make all oncoming traffic pull over until the official motorcade has passed. Travelling as the centre of a three-car convoy, MDC security personnel in the cars front and back, Tsvangirai's car was struck by a veering truck on the potholed Harare-to-Masvingo road. The impact was enough to roll Tsvangirai's heavy-duty four-wheel-drive three times. If it was not an accident, it was a most precise veering by a full-size truck into oncoming traffic. Morgan Tsvangirai suffered shock and superficial injuries. Susan Tsvangirai was pronounced dead on arrival at a hospital in the town of Beatrice. But everyone at the scene of the accident knew she had died instantly.

Susan Tsvangirai was not a political figure in her own right. She was Morgan Tsvangirai's greatest emotional and personal help. While the wives of the ZANU-PF high command cruised the roads in new Mercedes limousines, she drove a red Japanese pickup, crudely lined with makeshift armour. Her affability, kindness and determination to support her husband were clear. She visited MDC colleagues while they were in jail and in hospital. While the wives of the ZANU-PF oligarchy surrounded themselves with bling behind the closed walls of their Borrowdale Brooke mansions, Susan Tsvangirai ran a soup kitchen from her home in Avondale. In every respect, she fulfilled the requirements of Christ in his peroration on the sheep and goats in the Gospel of Matthew, in which he preached that those who fed and watered the poor, gave hospitality to strangers in their own homes, clothed those in rags, and visited the sick and those in prison, were simultaneously treating the Son of God kindly.[26] In a highly, if often ostensibly, Christian country, this was something genuinely admired – if not necessarily emulated. Everybody knew her kindness. At MDC rallies, the crowds would shout, 'Mother! Mother!', as a great accolade to her. Whether her death was an assassination attempt or a freak accident – and overall consensus, although by a very small margin at first, grew that it was a freak accident[27] – the ZANU-PF hierarchy was shocked, or seriously affected shock. Robert Mugabe and his wife, Grace, hurried to Morgan Tsvangirai's hospital bed and all the hitherto eloquently bitter President could say, while holding his Prime Minister's hand, was 'sorry, sorry . . .'

The funeral was one of those moments when both staged and real reconciliation was attempted. Olive branches were metaphorically handed out like flowers. One of the six Tsvangirai children was so moved that he publicly thanked Mugabe for showing such an unexpected and compassionate face. And the son also said that he saw this as the beginning of a genuine process of cooperation.[28] It was one of those very rare occasions in contemporary Zimbabwe when the great and the good of both ZANU-PF and the MDC were assembled with an injunction against any politics being spoken and any drunken socialisation being attempted.

It wasn't the beginning of a new era. But it was the beginning of slightly greater faith on the part of ZANU-PF in making the unity government work. The change of tone was palpable. And, a few weeks later, albeit after a controversially expensive retreat to a luxury hotel in Victoria Falls, ZANU-PF, Tsvangirai's MDC and Mutambara's MDC announced a common policy platform for the years of unity government ahead. Sometimes it was, and will be, gritted teeth. A forced marriage is a forced marriage. A stolen election is a stolen election. But, in the nature of cohabitation and unavoidable intimacy, even the most stubborn bedfellows must sometimes make a gesture towards each other; then, regretting it, ensure that the regular quota of harassment is enacted, until both learn to live, and operate, under conditions of both cooperation and harassment.[29]

Having said all that, it would be sentimental not to address some harder specific realities that also played their part. Disease stalked the streets and emerged from unmaintained pipes. The infrastructure was, in this case literally, collapsing – and the raw waste was oozing into the poorer suburban streets. Mains drinking water had not been treated for years in any case and now the results of neglect and fiscal incapacity were being felt with a vengeance. Long queues of diarrhoea-ridden Zimbabweans, unable to find or afford medical treatment at home, spilled over the borders into makeshift clinics in South Africa, where they were filmed sprawled emaciated on floors and litters, wearing South African nappies, by a coprophiliac international media. Even the staunchest ZANU-PF diehard knew that the MDC had to be given its chance to restore the nation's financial ability to ensure that adult citizens were spared such mass indignities. It was a very upper-middle-class reaction: not that people were dying or suffering, but that grown men shitting uncontrollably was distasteful.

The curiosity of all this resided in the fact that when these same upper-middle-class supporters of ZANU-PF – the mini-garchs who wanted one day to be oligarchs – spoke about the razing of 'slum' communities like Mbare in 2005's Operation Murambatsvina, their view was that Mbare had become an eyesore. People suffering meant less than how people and their lives *appeared*. There are some very real questions to be asked as to whether such a distorted sense of the world is now pervading the elite echelons of the ANC in South Africa.

Helen Zille can't dance although, when she sings, crowds fall silent, impressed that a white woman, who learnt Xhosa relatively late in life, should sing well and know the words. Jacob Zuma can dance and, when he sings, his crowds sing along. He is a giant karaoke machine made flesh – but he merely continues, and exploits, a very old tradition of resistance and protest expressed in music. And not just in South Africa. Throughout the continent, the antagonism towards colonialism was expressed in song:[30] from the slave ships to the South African rallies in which Jacob Zuma, wearing finely tailored cloth, leaps exuberantly about, song has been a constant articulator of grief, resistance and demands.[31] The crowds are not just singing with Jacob Zuma. They are demanding action from him too. Look, we supported you when you faced trial, we greeted you and sang for you when Judge Nicholson dismissed the case against you, we celebrated in song on your behalf when Thabo Mbeki was recalled, we sing now at your rallies before we elect you. Don't you dare let us down. Song, like the rhetoric at Southern African rallies is all about line and echo. The speaker shouts out a phrase and the crowd shouts back with an answering phrase. It is like a Greek play with a protagonist and a chorus. The chorus can echo, but it can also amplify, and it can also warn.

Even so, from the very start of his troubles under Mbeki, several popular discs were recorded praising Jacob Zuma. One, which was banned by the South African Broadcasting Corporation, declared Zuma was Mandela's heir.[32] The song meant that, like Mandela, Zuma could be understood by the wide spectrum of ordinary people who had no idea, much of the time, what Thabo Mbeki was trying to say. Mbeki's ANC Newsletters were masterpieces of literary erudition. They were showing off to scholars and intellectuals. And, although he could do the gumboot dance when he was young, he was not now going to perform more than a few 'since-I-must' dance steps, emphasising mostly hand gestures and a pallid body sway, at any ANC rally. He couldn't sing either; nor really could Jacob Zuma, but that has never stopped him from bursting full-throated into inhibition-free voice. His 'Bring Me My Machinegun' (*umshini wami*) rendition is his most famous number but, when he was cleared by Judge Nicholson, he sang to the crowd outside the court, *ihubo lempi*, a sad and slow song, musically complex in a non-Western way, about a young man who has come back from the war, and his body is scarred from many deep wounds. This time, not all the crowd sang with him. Many knew that even Jacob Zuma, the man everyone in one way or another has criticised or caricatured, was trying to say that his soul had been pulled apart by Thabo Mbeki's rejection of him.

Jacob Zuma is one of only a handful of world leaders who is a polygamist, but he is alone in his use of songline. But what else apart from song and soundbites about an end to poverty could he deliver to the crowds that greeted him on the campaign trail? What could Dandala and Lekota, campaigning largely separately, promise except that they would not be corrupt? Not so much that they would make people less poor, but that they would ensure that fewer people became improperly rich. What could Helen Zille really do to overcome, even in the brave new rainbow nation, the legacy of white domination and one of its strongest images: the white madam who rules her white and clean home with a rod of iron and makes life hell for her black domestic staff if they misplace an antimacassar by a centimetre? What could the other small, largely regional parties do to gain national credibility? All fought strong campaigns, but all were amazingly short on the details of their platforms. Finally, if it came down to which of the imperfect leaders was best for South Africa, it also came down to which of their parties had the most noble tradition. It was going to be the ANC. The only question was by how much. COPE and the DA were determined to prevent the ANC achieving a two-thirds parliamentary majority. If the ANC fell short of two-thirds, it could not change or dilute the constitution. In some ways, the election became a fight for the equalities of the constitution – but that was not always something that could be explained easily to an impoverished person in his or her slum abode, the weight of breeze blocks and old tyres all that is holding down the unsecured metal sheets of the roof, and maize meal porridge (again) brewing in a pot on the stove (hot-wired into the grid) to be served to an entire family with a tin of pilchards in tomato sauce.

Coming across many such families, I crisscrossed South Africa in 2009, making notes on the election.

What became clear was how migrations of loyalty work in South African politics. Lekota was defeated by Dandala on 20 February 2009 but, just five days before, the writing on the wall had become clear. A frail Nelson Mandela, dressed in a black overcoat while all around him wore open shirts and jackets, appeared on stage with Jacob Zuma at an ANC rally in the Eastern Cape. He said little, thanking the crowd for coming despite the heavy rains, and signed off with, 'Long live the ANC!' Even so, the COPE message was far from obsolete. The very weekend of Mandela's intervention saw the fall from grace of Carl Niehaus, an ANC spokesman and former Member of Parliament.[33] The veteran anti-Apartheid campaigner, who was normally part of Zuma's travelling entourage, had been caught in a string of financial deceptions. He was dismissed as ANC spokesman immediately, but the two sides of the ANC were apparent: the loyalty of those who had fought for liberation within the ANC structures; and the financial self-seeking that had been adopted by so many of its elite members. Even so, Mandela's endorsement of Zuma – for that is what it was, the two seated in armchairs side by side on the same podium – meant that the COPE bandwagon was destined to stall even before Lekota's eclipse.

It was not just Mandela who came to Zuma's side. A whole raft of ANC senior players suddenly forgot they had been friends of Mbeki and went to desperate lengths to display lifelong loyalties to Zuma. One of them, ANC campaign head Fikile Mbalula, even published an open letter repudiating Mbeki and itemising his faults, especially his political interference in judicial processes initiated against Zuma.[34] It was not very savoury, but everyone knew Zuma would win and everyone wanted to get on board because everyone wanted to reap rewards. Power brought benefits. Rather, having a place in the world of power *bought* benefits.

On 6 April 2009, just two weeks before the elections, National Prosecutor Mokotedi Mpshe, plagiarising a Malaysian ruling, dropped the outstanding corruption and fraud charges against Jacob Zuma.

This was an extraordinary reversal from a man who had been brought in as Mbeki's man; someone who, it was thought, would prosecute those whom Mbeki wanted prosecuted and not prosecute others. Now, in fact, Mpshe had grounds to drop the charges. He had been given secret recordings which indicated that the criminal investigators of Zuma's case had abused process and sought to manipulate the application of the law for political purposes. The question however, most pertinently and persistently raised by Helen Zille, was how these recordings reached Mpshe. The campaigning *Mail & Guardian* newspaper revealed the following chain: the tapes were held by the National Intelligence Agency, which had not released them at any earlier stage; it was the NIA's deputy head, Arthur Fraser, who leaked them to Zuma's people (although the newspaper's report was denied by the NIA); Zuma's people then made them available to the National Prosecutor.[35] But, as Zille kept pointing out, this meant that Zuma's people had acquired secret official materials without any legal process involved. The materials had, in short, been illegally obtained. The *Mail & Guardian* boldly claimed that Arthur Fraser was anxious to ingratiate himself with Zuma. So this also was part of the rush to declare or demonstrate loyalty to the new man. But in addition, as Mark Gevisser pointed out in the same edition of the *Mail & Guardian*, Zuma was now using exactly the same sort of access to supposedly independent organs, and using them for his own political purposes, that Zuma's people had accused Mbeki of doing.[36] At the top of South African politics, the separation of functions is a blurred line of convenience; it is blurred to curry or disburse patronage and favours; patronage, by way or appointment or retention in high office – or, depending where you are in the food chain, any office – will buy the recipient power and lifestyle. The ANC was a liberation organisation and is now a benefits club. Lekota was right.

However, it is not right to caricature the ANC as being only this. It is, simultaneously, the only mass agency in South Africa that can, however clumsily and with however many leaks of funding, do something to improve the lives of ordinary people. It is a repository of faith. And its senior club members have adopted a schizophrenic morality whereby the benefits are just reward for previous suffering – or, increasingly, mere association with suffering; or kowtowing to someone who suffered. The percentages stolen change with habituation and enjoyment.

Even so, Zuma and the ANC had not yet won the election. It was one thing to have all the remaining ANC-loyalists lined up as fawns and courtiers, it was another altogether to minimise the opposition vote. COPE was self-destructing, so that meant the big guns could be turned on Zille and the DA. The ANC's intelligence had predicted that the ANC would almost certainly lose Western Cape, so the effort was to minimise the DA's margin of victory. The smaller the turnout for the DA, the more chance the ANC had of gaining the two-thirds national parliamentary majority it craved: if not to change the constitution, at least for its symbolic value in declaring and acting as if South Africa was a dominant-party state. The days of single-party states in Africa had gone. With dominant-party states it is possible to be democratic and have as much power as you need, if not exactly the amount you might want.

In order to minimise the DA vote, Zuma made an extraordinary speech calling the white Afrikaners – the former bedrock supporters of Apartheid – the only true white South Africans. It was a curious form of ethnic divide-and-rule. It was an effort to separate the descendants of the Boers from the polite English-speaking society of Cape Town – to cede Cape Town proper to Zille, and to erode her white support in the countryside. But it was a clunky old-fashioned analysis of the modern South Africa. Since majority rule, it has been the Afrikaans-speaking white population, even if from a low base, that has made huge efforts to acculturate to the new realities. The Cape Town liberals want to retain their existing privileges. There is a renaissance of sorts in Afrikaner culture and the Afrikaans language. And the 'new Boer' is not as he or she was. The acclaimed detective fiction of Deon Meyer, written in Afrikaans, celebrates black detective heroes.[37] It is Batman who is now black, and Robin the Boy Wonder is the pallid hanger-on. And who, in fact, is a pure-line Afrikaner anyway? In the Western Cape, it seems the huge majority are like Helen Zille – fluent in English and Afrikaans, with an African language like Xhosa thrown in.

And what, in any case, is a South African? A South African is part of a nation of historic divisions and exploitations. Not just black and white, but Asian,[38] various hues of coloured and many types of black – and, as Jacob Zuma tried to exploit, formerly separate identities for whites. Is the nationalist project of South Africa complete? If it is, or is nearly, then it is the ANC that has been the glue that has joined together an improbable bunch of squabbling and often morally destitute peoples. They don't have a nice history. To do that in less than 20 years since the release of Nelson Mandela is phenomenal. Although the ANC might pause and reflect: it cannot take its support for granted. Throughout the Western Cape I met many whom I would call the 'ANC irregulars', people who made a stand against Apartheid without being part of the ANC resistance. They were unknown to the ANC – and still are – but took it upon themselves to act as if under the name of the ANC. Mothers lost children and people lost spouses to the struggle – and the ANC has recognised and rewarded them not at all. It bequeaths rewards to those it remembers as having been part of it, as if it were a club, and not a national movement.

Perhaps the ANC is like a teenager, not quite 20 in its years of legal existence, borrowing the car keys and irresponsibly trashing the car. But that is a metaphor too far. The ANC is populated by some very serious and intelligent and mature people. It has done very much. It could do better. Now it will try to do so under Jacob Zuma.

Election day was noteworthy for its good organisation and calm. Only in a small part of KwaZulu-Natal was there momentary difficulty and a local effort at rigging. This was quickly discovered. Otherwise, it was the fairest possible conduct of a poll I have seen in Africa. Thabo Mbeki showed up to vote, pursued by cameras. The reporters wanted to know whether he had voted for COPE. He gave them his practised noncommittal smile and gentle manner of public evasion. Then he flew off for Darfur via Ethiopia. The results would have been counted while he was conferring with his African Union colleagues in Addis Ababa. All through the period of counting the projections veered now one way, then the other, as to whether the ANC would get its two-thirds majority. At one stage it seemed almost certain it would get 66.7 per cent. But, when the dust cleared, the ANC had just missed out on its two-thirds. It got 65.9 per cent. The opposition had done it. Helen Zille's DA got 16.66 per cent, COPE 7.42 per cent, and an assortment of minority parties the remainder. The DA also won the provincial contest for Western Cape and Zille was set to become Premier there, as well as again Leader of the Opposition nationally.

The ANC's vote had fallen from the 70 per cent it won in the first majority rule elections of 1994 – but if, in 15 years of power, it had lost only 4 per cent of its vote, this was still an extraordinary achievement. Helen Zille could not claim to have deprived the ANC of its two-thirds by herself. The DA vote was as high as anyone could have expected – and it definitely attracted a small but discernible slice of the black vote nationally. The critical final few percentage points were owed to COPE. To that extent, Lekota's adventure had been worthwhile.

Turnout was 77.3 per cent, a staggering figure when placed alongside turnout in British and American elections. Voting still means something in South Africa. The franchise was hard won and it has not been treated lightly.

One message of congratulations stood out. It was from Kenyan Prime Minister Raila Odinga. He said the victory resonated well beyond South Africa's borders. 'After many dubious elections, undemocratic transfers of power and even coups in some African countries in recent days, it is refreshing to see one clean election and a clean victory on the continent.'[39]

One clean election and one clean victory. Odinga had in mind how the Kenyan election was stolen from him. He had in mind how the Zimbabwean election was stolen from Morgan Tsvangirai. And there was a barb in his comments. He might have been sincerely congratulating South Africa, but he thought it was also South Africa – through

Thabo Mbeki – that facilitated an undemocratic transfer of power in
Zimbabwe. Unity government or not, and whether in Kenya or
Zimbabwe, these paled beside the one clean election and clean victory
for the ANC. Critics can say all they like about Jacob Zuma. He won
fair and square.

CHAPTER 13

WHAT IS THE FUTURE OF IT ALL?

The defining aspects of recent South African and Zimbabwean history have been elections and how democracy is not always expressed in those elections – or expressed only as part of a multi-faceted process that has key decision-making elements hidden from public view. In this process, old treacheries and new deceits play leading roles. Even so, in South Africa, the first year of Jacob Zuma passed with very little real difference to the years and policies of Thabo Mbeki. In a sense, it is Mbeki – not Mandela – who dominates South Africa. Mandela was not a good administrator or techno-crat. Those skills were difficult to learn in an adult lifetime spent in prison. He allowed Mbeki to have considerable, not total, say in the way the country was governed and the policies implemented – so that, when Mbeki became President, there was a seamlessness from one regime to another. Mbeki, in dealing with the needs of development, established policies and procedures based on South Africa's being a part – he hoped an important part – of the global and liberal economy. Zuma, coming to power in the midst of a global recession, has no choice but to continue Mbeki's policies. But the poor of South Africa are restless, and it remains to be seen how well Zuma's administration sees out its full term. Mbeki's stamp is also all over

Zimbabwe. There, power-sharing or 'inclusiveness' has had a mixed record. Zuma's mediation has been less tolerant of Zimbabwean politics and ideologies than Mbeki's – but just as private. The country that recovers from the Zimbabwean meltdown will not be the Zimbabwe of old, and the outlook for democracy uninflected by power plays is not high. Power plays and democracy are bedfellows in South Africa, but the constitution has survived, and the liberties of the people have been sustained. People's lives have not always got better, but they have only to look across the border to Zimbabwe to see how much worse they could get. But, even in South Africa, the generation of old treacheries is coming to its end. Newer deceits, and a new generation, will be necessary for the future. Whether that new generation will be within a self-serving, oligarchic and patronage-driven ANC, or whether other forces will emerge, is an open question. South Africa might long be like the Football World Cup it hosted in 2010. Beautiful stadiums were envisaged and built. But the national team went out in the first round, and its supporters couldn't always get to the stadiums. But the vuvuzelas certainly made a lot of noise.

This book has concentrated on South Africa and Zimbabwe, the two most intimate partners of Cecil Rhodes' original dream. A road runs through them. There has been little escaping this. Geographical contiguity, historical formation and political complementarity – the two have always been close siblings. Not Siamese twins, but each has always been in the other's thought as something natural and something done. What one did has always affected the other. Each has always denied this. The closest parallel I can think of is also from the southern hemisphere. Zimbabwe is New Zealand to South Africa's Australia. There are deadly rivalries and separable identities, but the two understand each other with an intimacy that is uncanny. Whether Ian Smith and P.W. Botha, or Robert Mugabe and Thabo Mbeki, the two have been wittingly and inextricably linked. Like all good siblings, they have hated this and cannot live without it.

There is more to Southern Africa than these two. And there is much more to the democratic movements in Southern Africa and, indeed,

Africa as a whole than these two. In 2009, when the Zimbabwean power-sharing landscape was finally settled, when Jacob Zuma won elections to become President of South Africa, there were elections also in Botswana, Malawi, Mozambique and Namibia. Scheduled Angolan elections were delayed. Some were more fraught than others, but some species of democracy is, for now, here to stay. The exact species of that democracy is a key question – and it is not a question of whether democracy is endangered. There are democracies and democracies, and Southern Africa might yet yield a prototype of something new. The lessons of 2009 will have to be digested. But 2009 was also the year of the continent's most 'successful' Western-style democratic contest, with Atta Mills winning the Ghanaian elections, overturning the long-serving, military-descendant ruling party without a whisper of complaint or hindrance. But not all democracy has to be under a Western stamp. Southern Africa, innumerable British 'ethical foreign policies' about a certain form of democracy notwithstanding, may have its own path and its own discoveries to make.

Although COPE did not fare nearly as well as Terror Lekota had first hoped, it did establish itself, tentatively, as an important minor force in South African politics – not so much in the national configuration as in provincial legislatures. It became the main opposition party in five provinces – but capturing that status from the DA, not the ANC. Even so, it meant both a pluralism within opposition politics – which Helen Zille would wish to coordinate – and that COPE had something of a continuing voice. However, it is likely that some of COPE's new provincial legislators will be tempted back into the ANC because of patronage networks. Very few experienced people came to COPE without a political past: they came from the ANC, and the ANC will seek to woo them back. COPE fought these elections without much of a grassroots organisational base, and the sense of party cohesion that the ANC manifests – people buy into its liberation rhetoric – will not be easily manufactured. And building an organisational base in the poor townships is, frankly and literally, a bruising business. Political turf and complex forms of gangland turf live uneasily, if often within a well-negotiated politesse. Newcomers need to fight their way in. Finally, despite capturing leading opposition status from the DA in some legislatures, the overall provincial capacity of the DA is higher, Zille is leader of the national opposition, and the abilities of Lekota will be missed in Parliament. Shortly after the election, the underlying tensions between Lekota and those who had sponsored and supported Dandala, particularly Mbhazima Shilowa, began to surface, so that COPE witnessed much internal manoeuvring and chaos in the first year of Jacob Zuma. This culminated in a fiasco at its first elective conference in May 2010, and the bitter feuding that erupted into the open badly damaged the credibility of the party.[1]

The national level saw the retention of several of Lekota's friends in Cabinet, and the reintroduction of others. Two in particular stand out, and both owed their position – at least in part – to Zuma's need to repay the support he had received at Polokwane or shortly after Polokwane. To an extent, the nature and configuration of 'friendship' had been altered to accommodate the inevitability of Zuma as South Africa's President. In the ANC, Lekota said this didn't have to be inevitable and took the challenge to Zuma. Others became the political equivalent of Zuma's bosom buddies and, although that shift and development of 'friendships' is common in any government anywhere, in the ANC they reinforced the hegemony of the party as a hermetically sealed unit. More than that, political elite and financial oligarchy could both be embraced and deployed under the ANC 'family of liberation friends' umbrella.

The most outstanding example of this was the appointment to Zuma's Cabinet of Tokyo Sexwale. It was his phantom candidature for the ANC presidency at Polokwane that deceived Mbeki's people into thinking that Zuma didn't have enough votes; then Sexwale abruptly put his weight and supporters behind Zuma. He had once been rumoured to be preparing to contest the ANC presidency against Mbeki – and Mbeki had ensured Sexwale left national politics for the duration of his time as leader of South Africa. Sexwale had become extraordinarily rich as a businessman, but he not only wanted back into politics, he wanted revenge upon Mbeki, and he still harboured thoughts of the presidency for himself. Zuma owed him and, even though Sexwale was both wealthy and the darling of the corporate world,[2] Zuma made him Minister of Human Settlements – basically in charge of the townships. Sexwale had been born in poverty in a squatter camp on the edge of Soweto, Orlando West, just a little north of Kliptown. Many of the ANC liberation generation had been born in comparable circumstances, but few had made a comparable fortune for themselves. Much of Sexwale's wealth may have been invisibles that lost value in the credit crunch and global recession of 2008–10, but it was still an odd choice to place a far-from-impoverished oligarch in charge of so much that was to do with poverty. Nevertheless, not even a year after the beginning of Zuma's presidency, Sexwale was already being touted as his successor.[3] He was appointed to the same Cabinet as Blade Nzimande, the SACP boss who had been prominent in the recall of Mbeki.

As reward for his efforts, Nzimande was given none of the economic, financial or planning portfolios he wanted. Instead he was made Minister of Higher Education and Training. In some respects it is a nothing portfolio, a Blade-can't-get-up-to-mischief portfolio. In other respects it is vitally important. The nation's universities are in a serious mess. Forced amalgamations have conspired to water down the standards of eminent universities as they have had to absorb technical and community colleges. Where it has worked, as in the case of the University of Johannesburg, it has owed more to local good management than to the original national plans; where it hasn't worked, as in the case of the University of KwaZulu-Natal, the results are a dishevelled example of why ministers who have never run anything should not presume to think efficiency can be gained from macro-units comprised of unequal parts. Nzimande has to get all this up and running again, and make some pretty poor Apartheid-era universities into decent places. These are not just the former Bantustan universities; some of the Afrikaans-speaking universities are enclosures with far from global relevance. Nzimande has to do this and live with the spectacle of Sexwale, a billionaire, working with those in poverty. He also has to share a place in Cabinet with the much more powerful Trevor Manuel.[4]

If the appointment of Sexwale is replete with ironies, the effective consolidation of Manuel in Zuma's Cabinet is the result of intense lobbying and pressure. In a debate featuring Moletsi Mbeki and Mathews Phosa, immediately after the South African elections and held in the Palace of Westminster, Phosa point-blank denied that Manuel would become Zuma's planning tsar. Some thought this was because Phosa, a recidivist presidential-aspirant himself, didn't want a possible future rival so close to all the big national decisions. But it reflected the intense currents of debate within the ANC. A huge number of local actors did not want Manuel to have any kind of economic portfolio: they wanted an end to what he and Mbeki had wrought in terms of a neo-liberal South Africa. But the South African corporate community and powerful Western governments had made it clear to Zuma that Manuel had to be retained in some senior economic or financial capacity. The contest was between those who wanted a new departure from the Manuel method, a method that had not centralised the poor, and those who thought that only globally related stability and neo-liberal prosperity would provide the foundations for helping the poor. That the neo-liberal world was in recession and had to await recovery, while the poor of South Africa were determined to wait no longer – hoping their new billionaire Minister of Human Settlements would remember what their lives were like – was an exercise in explosive frustration waiting to happen. Finally, Manuel got the post he wanted because he campaigned hard for it, campaigned better than those who opposed him, and won the ear of Zuma. He became Minister in the Presidency in charge of the National Planning Commission. Effectively, the Minister of Economic Development and the Minister of Finance would be subordinated to him. As it was, the new Minister of Finance, Pravin Gordhan, was also fiscally cautious.[5]

Otherwise, the Cabinet was a quite remarkable mixture of races and both genders. As is habitual in cabinets around the world, the Minister of Sport and Recreation, Makhenkesi Stofile, was a stout individual who would be beaten by Robert Mugabe in a sprint across a sports field. But there was someone who was not an HIV-dissident, Dr Aaron Motsoaledi, as Minister of Health – some things had finally moved on from the Mbeki years – and, for the junior grab-bag portfolio, where everything inconvenient could be marginalised, Noluthando Mayende-Sibiya became Minister of Women, Youth, Children and People with Disabilities. It does take gross insensitivity and insensibility to contrive such a portfolio – but South Africa has always mixed the wonderfully aspirational with the ponderously marginal. Now it also had the Great Contradiction as its President.

Less than one hundred days after Jacob Zuma's inauguration, riots swept through many townships. This time there were no 'straw men', no Zimbabweans and other migrant communities who were the surrogate targets. It was the ANC, particularly both its lack of 'service delivery' – meaning mostly housing units, electricity and water – and the fact that prestige projects such as the stadiums and infrastructure for the 2010 Football World Cup were costing so much.[6] In fact, a lot of ANC strategy seemed to be seeking to contain unrest until after the World Cup. A successful event of this globally televised magnitude would send out a priceless image of South Africa as capable and modern. And, unlike Thabo Mbeki's bemusement by rugby, no besuited BMW-driving minister would fail to appreciate football – hopeful all the while that the national team would do well enough for a national feel-good factor to buy, yet again, more time for a service delivery that will, in fact, never fully come.[7]

People know this. They would rather have jobs than await state provision of things they would like to buy for themselves. They hope only for the state to do better at providing the things it promised and, amidst chaotic administration and incompetence at all levels, failed to deliver. The ANC was being accused of incompetence, lack of transparency, lack of consultation, and corruption. The World Cup was simply a symbol of maladjusted priorities. In fact almost everyone was looking forward to it – while complaining bitterly about its cost. Other resonant symbols would be the sudden new limousines acquired by ministers, and the huge bonuses corporate bosses and boards awarded themselves – while measuring out meanly small salary increases for those lucky enough to be in their employment. The wealth gap is growing faster than under Apartheid. On 25 July 2009, after two weeks of rioting, Jacob Zuma pleaded for patience. But, in the townships, some very old practices were being resurrected: the burning tyres as barricades, the police firing rubber bullets into the angry and screaming crowds.

To be fair to the ANC, since Mandela's time it has built 2.6 million homes but, at the time of the July 2009 riots, was 2.1 million behind schedule. Service delivery at only 55 per cent of promise and expectation is a disaster. Moreover – and no one has accurately calculated this, so the estimates vary and are anecdotal – the number of housing units completed that are substandard means that delivery of liveable and utility-connected housing units is probably just 40 per cent of target. The number of units with flush toilets in areas completely without sewerage pipes is a triumph of planning.

In the first week of August 2009, Tokyo Sexwale went into the townships. One was Diepsloot, north of Johannesburg, and home to 150,000 people, many of whom live in amenity-free shacks. He went with a budget slashed by the recession by almost 10 per cent. He pleaded it would be a long journey because of the recession. There was no magic wand, he said. In effect he, like Zuma, begged for patience. But what he said in Diepsloot was extraordinary. He stood on ground that, as in the streets of Harare – the capital of a country in meltdown – oozed raw sewage. But this was South Africa. He said he had come on a 'sincere listening campaign'. He said, 'if we didn't love you, we would not be here'.[8]

But why does it take a minister, since majority rule one of the country's most powerful political or financial voices, a doyen of everything he has touched, to say he has come to listen sincerely? Why did the huge numbers of ANC municipal officials, councillors, managers, provincial legislators and national parliamentarians not sincerely listen before Sexwale? Why did they award contracts to their friends – often as unqualified as themselves – under BEE and BBBEE conditions without sufficient quality controls and late-delivery penalties? The barely muffled words from the townships spoke of nepotism, cronyism and corruption. To be a member of the ANC, to hold any official position – however minor – under ANC auspices, is an escalator to influence, an escalator to the middle class, an escalator out of poverty. They will leave behind thousands who had no foot upon the ANC escalator. The officials didn't have to be qualified. They didn't have to be experienced. They often did not have to be honest. You bought your way upwards by supporting others who were higher. In the end, you support Jacob Zuma at Polokwane. Perhaps Mbeki's analysis of why he lost there was correct. Zuma's votes came from this kind of grass roots. Everyone has the rhetoric of freedom and provision. But they will be, in the residual Leninist terms of the SACP, the beneficiary vanguard.

But the beneficiary vanguard is itself under threat. The visits of Sexwale to the impoverished and disadvantaged were not enough. Zuma had to do the same in May 2010; visiting the inappropriately named Sweetwaters, he said 'I really feel almost like crying' when confronted by the dreadful sanitation and lack of facilities. Here, he finally castigated municipal authorities, but he seemed to have no remedy.[9] And it was a case not only of too little too late, but of floodgates suddenly bursting open. Shortly after the end of the World Cup, South Africa was swept by huge public sector strikes. They became so bitter that some feared that, under a Zuma presidency, the ANC would lose its trade union support for good.[10]

The ANC Youth League firebrand, Julius Malema, saw the deteriorating situation as the perfect environment for his rhetoric. His penchant for violent antics and abusive language makes the headlines but in the increasingly bitter struggle behind the scenes for the succession, many think that Malema is being 'run' by ANC plutocrats who covet the presidency, and that he is being used to test the waters to find out how much populism will be needed as candidatures are launched.[11] But, if that is the case, those being used have a habit of demanding their prices. The rumours in Johannesburg are that both Mathews Phosa and Tokyo Sexwale fund Malema. But they cannot both be president. The open feud within COPE between Lekota and Mbhazima may, in due course, pale by comparison to the tussle between Sexwale and Phosa – with Malema perhaps eyeing, in a spectacular rise, the deputy presidency as reward for services rendered. Meanwhile, Zuma has work to do on the economy.

In the absence of increased budgets, Jacob Zuma and Tokyo Sexwale – not to mention the planning tsar, Trevor Manuel – could learn from what Helen Zille did in Cape Town. By rigorous reform of the administrative systems involved, she impressively increased the delivery of housing units. But to do this nationally would entail some root and branch reform of provincial and municipal appointments and promotions, quality assurance, administrative capacity, and answerability. It would either mean the crash course training of by now thousands of largely untrained administrators – or their dismissal. Neither is likely to happen. What could act as the spur for self-education is answerability. One of the things conceded by Nelson Mandela in the protracted negotiations that led to majority rule was a first-past-the-post electoral system. Although the compromise was a relatively simple form of proportional representation it meant that, at all levels, people gained positions by being on party lists. Getting on to the party list meant everything. This is within the gift of more senior people – although, ostensibly, members are meant to be selected by party organs. Some of the ministers who resigned when Mbeki was recalled, and who refused reappointment under Motlanthe, were offered places on the 2009 parliamentary list by Zuma. This was a goodwill gesture of reconciliation – but the gesture was not by and large taken up. This means that a successful candidate's answerability is to the party: not directly to a designated and specific part of the electorate. It is hard to see a nationally integrated system of patronage being reformed – still less being brought to an end.

If anything, list-based proportional representation seems set to increase throughout Africa as a result of the political compromises engineered by Thabo Mbeki and Kofi Annan in places as diverse as Democratic Republic of Congo, Kenya and Zimbabwe. And, in fact, the African 'model' that answers the Western demand for democracy may simply be an extension of what is found in parts of the West, and not anything dramatically new at all. It may have nothing to do with community-level deliberations that, Athenian-like, arrive at common if local ways forward – as proposed by some constitutional visionaries who have, as yet, not yet worked out how a cascading upwards of often different local commonalities can be transparently and, in turn, democratically facilitated at national level.[12] Sometimes the desire to be more 'African' is fanciful nostalgia for an imaginary romantic communal past. For all the talk of Jacob Zuma's traditional ways – and these seem, like polygamy, to be self-indulgences as much as cultural self-expressions – the nation over which he now rules wants to be modern. It wants modern delivery of modern habitats and utilities. It wants schools and universities of formal learning. It wants clinics, hospitals and medicines that are accessible and that work. And there is no traditional virtue in poverty. What Thabo Mbeki pulled off, first in Democratic Republic of Congo and then Zimbabwe, and what Kofi Annan quietly and authoritatively bullied through in Kenya were wrong in terms of who became President in the Kenyan and Zimbabwean cases. Both Odinga and Tsvangirai, in a fair electoral count, would have been President. Instead they are prime ministers under the losers' presidencies. But the idea of power-sharing in Cabinet, according to proportion of electoral support, is not undemocratic. In some ways it is more democratic than most Western models. In close-run Western elections, what happens to the policy preferences and personnel choices of over 40 per cent of those who voted? They are swamped by those of narrow winners.

However, in systems of proportional representation, where party seats in Parliament are calculated by percentage of votes won, why not extend this so that seats in Cabinet are also calculated by percentage of votes won? And the leading party chooses the President and the second-largest party, within an acceptable margin, chooses the Prime Minister? It is wholly democratic, it ends exclusion; more cynically, it allows the continuation of patronage systems and, because it does so, it is not a disincentive to playing clean. Even those on the 'losing' side have not lost everything. If something like this emerges, will it be the great legacy of Mbeki and the African legacy of Annan? It may not necessarily work at municipal levels where the interface between expectation and delivery often resides; but it could end an awful lot of reruns of the forgery that passed as the re-election of Robert Mugabe in 2008.

As for the problematic power-sharing government that eventuated from those elections, there was far from universal buy-in from any of the parties. Every inch of progress was accompanied by harassment, testings of nerve and ill will. Many in ZANU-PF hated the very idea of cooperation with the MDC and, at the increasingly poverty-stricken grassroots level, competition for scarce resources could often be fought out along party lines. But, despite assassination threats and persecution of their activists, the senior members of Morgan Tsvangirai's party not only worked hard as ministers, they began to live alongside the great-if-not-good of ZANU-PF.

An illustrative case occurred at the turn of July and August 2009. The MDC-appointed Minister of Finance, Tendai Biti, received a 9mm bullet in an envelope delivered to his house, together with a written instruction to prepare his will. In fact, Biti was not someone whom any element within ZANU-PF would have wanted to assassinate at that time. His relative stabilisation of the economy by then – ensuring dire did not become direr – was to the long-term benefit of ordinary citizens and oligarchs alike. The MDC milked the publicity from the bullet – and also the fact that Biti's gardener had been assaulted by soldiers as he passed the senior army commander, General Phillip Valerio Sibanda's house. The gardener ran to Biti's house where he sought refuge, but was caught by the soldiers at the gate and beaten there.[13] The gardener was well enough to tell his tale afterwards – but this meant that Biti and Sibanda were living in the same elite neighbourhood. The new MDC ministers have been gifted the same sorts of facilities – Mercedes limousines for instance – as the ZANU-PF ministers. Only the MDC-Mutambara Minister of Education, David Coltart, refused his. Lifestyle will tell how long and how well this power-share will last.

However these processes play out, one thing is certain. Just as Nelson Mandela is living his last frail days, so also the liberation generation in Zimbabwe is dying. On 5 August 2009, the ZANU-PF-appointed Vice-President, Joseph Msika, died at 85 – the same age as Mugabe. Almost all those who held leadership positions in the struggle are now at least in their seventies or close to it. Even the dazzling young field commanders aged, say, 30 at the elections that followed the Lancaster House talks would be over 60 at the time of this book's publication. But there is a 'get in line' ethos in ZANU-PF. 'Youngsters', even at 60, have to wait their turn. The senior oligarchy is becoming a gerontocracy as well. And the gerontocracy is, in critical part, a 'securotocracy', given the immense power of the Generals and security forces. The advantage of the MDC is comparative youth. The equivalent generation in ZANU-PF, those who never stopped following Simba Makoni, at least philosophically, are closer to the MDC in some ways than to their ZANU-PF seniors. If the Mutambara/Ncube faction were to rejoin Tsvangirai, there would be added inducement for a merger of the technocratic talents of all groupings. However, at the time of writing, MDC Mutambara might also be splintering, with Ncube at odds with Mutambara.[14] Notwithstanding the problems of the MDC, the ZANU-PF gerontocracy will lumber on and, like Msika, might be determined to die with their boots on. However, even despite the seniority accorded age in what passes as traditional politesse, Zimbabwe is not a hermetic enclosure. The youth of Obama and Sarkozy in the West, the masculine vigour of Putin in Russia, even the astonished fact that the Chinese leadership is younger than the ZANU-PF gerontocrats will tell.

Meanwhile, until age and the demand for generation renewal take their toll, it is well to remember that constitutional negotiations and an initial form of power-share between Mandela's majority ANC and De Klerk's minority National Party took four years to complete. Although the formal power-share collapsed two years after the first democratic elections, lifelong bonds had formed between the negotiators of the two parties – Cyril Ramaphosa and Roelf Meyer in particular – and the National Party subsequently joined the ANC. There may yet, in time, be a dominant party state in Zimbabwe – only not the sort many currently imagine or prefer. The unholy alliance that many see as the unity government in Zimbabwe is not unlike the spectacle that used to afflict the Italian navy – where, in the Cold War years, there were two admirals for every vessel. It gave, I suppose, an authentic meaning to the term, 'Rear Admiral' but, even with admirals front and back, the ship can only go forward. In Zimbabwe though, any future government will almost certainly give amnesties or immunities to those who looted the country. It will be the price of a form of peace and progress. The dishonest oligarchs will live out their gerontocratic years in freedom and splendour. Their children will turn the ill-gotten fortunes of their parents into capital for new businesses that will regenerate key sectors of the economy and, albeit on a Zimbabwean scale, a new lineage of corporate giants and philanthropists will arise – unless the bulk of the Zimbabwean revival is captured by South African investors already circling the scene like predators.

What might be the foundation for any Zimbabwean economy revival? During the dark days of worst meltdown, and while it was being excoriated by ZANU-PF, the West paid for emergency food aid and at least a modicum of essential drugs. Despite collapse of production, loss of market and foreign disinvestment, Zimbabwean exports still brought in US$2 billion annually (although that would not have been enough to rescue even a single small bank in the British credit crunch of 2008). No one has accurately estimated the amount of money involved in remittances from the Zimbabwean diaspora. Working on a modest calculation of some four million Zimbabweans abroad, about one million of those in Europe – mostly in Britain – and three million in South Africa, and supposing that the diaspora in Europe sent home US$30 per month, and the disapora in South Africa managed to send home US$10 per month (and the figures in both cases were almost certainly much higher), then the annual remittances into Zimbabwe came to US$360 million each from Europe and South Africa. Let us round the combined total up to roughly US$1 billion.[15] Those remittances were the critical variable for keeping untold numbers of families alive. The South Africans are letting the Zimbabweans stay – even if a periodic 'xenophobic riot' encourages some to return home. Presuming the British Home Office, in its anxiety to reduce migrant numbers, does not wish to cause a national catastrophe in Zimbabwe by repatriating huge numbers of remittance-senders, we should assume that the remittance figures will be at least stable; and the export revenues should grow. Gradually, following the early Australian and Chinese examples, official bilateral financial assistance packages should help balance-of-payments – replacing humanitarian aid – and that, together with slowly rising productivity and the continuation of a US dollar and South African rand-based currency system, should see a discernible if slow regrowth of the economy. When that happens, what will also happen will be an influx of 'chancers' and fly-by-night investors. There will be many former East European concerns as well as Indian and Chinese corporations, and they will buy, asset-strip and sell on. The productive sectors may have to go through more than one stage of regeneration. The estimates in this paragraph have not included unofficial earnings, i.e. monies made by plunder outside Zimbabwe or by theft from such bilateral financial aid as is still being rendered. It is impossible to say how much of such income is exported to foreign bank accounts via circuitous processes and intermediate institutions, and how much is reinvested in Zimbabwe. Curiously, if the fiscal situation begins to improve in Zimbabwe, the possibility of some of these funds being invested locally will also improve. It will be the corrupt, possibly even before their children, who will have the wherewithal to enter joint ventures with external investors, for instance. Just as it will be those who stole the largest farms who will be in a position to help revitalise large-scale agro-industry. The new peasant class, if it stays on the land, will become in terms of export crops marginal producers once again. Many new farmers, lured by Mugabe's romance of land for all, will return to the cities. But, there, the middle-class dream will have died for a huge number.

There will be no widespread renaissance of the Chitungwiza Buddhist Society that prays for the souls of cockroaches. The demeanour of Zimbabwean society will become harder. But there is a redeeming factor, and this means that there will not be the slums and shanties that characterise the Western Cape in South Africa, or Cato Crest and parts of Cato Manor in Durban; not even Alex in Johannesburg. Zimbabwe is too small for such extremes. And, just as with the phenomenon of remittances from the diaspora, the practice of caring for extended families and friends will mean that scarce monies have coverage. If anything, Zimbabwe will become like Zambia. This is a suitable irony for, in its days of prosperity, Zimbabweans looked down upon the hapless Zambians – for whom nothing seemed to go right and whose feats of misorganisation and over-bureaucratisation meant that everything that was not stolen smouldered into dust. But that country held together – not just politically, but in terms of a form of economic cohesion. Kenneth Kaunda's tribal balancing act – in some ways easier to accomplish with so many tribes than with a few – and the recent rise in copper prices has allowed a comparative prosperity to sweep Zambia.

Chilenje, on the eastern side of Lusaka, is lower-middle-class. Even with the emphasis on 'lower', the denizens build locking gates and walls. Anything unbolted is stolen. Cars don't stop at traffic signals at night for fear of car-jackings. You know you are physically safe if, when you are forced to get out, your car-jackers fan out like a police formation. They *are* a police formation out moonlighting. If they're not, you're going to get a gratuitous beating and, because the attackers are untrained, the beating can be fatal. There is a perfect symbiosis between the formal and informal sectors in Zambia, with classes of professionalism and expertise.

This will happen in Zimbabwe. Chitungwiza will become like Chilenje – hardened lower middle-class, fighting the constant advent of collapse. The visual signs will be when seven-foot walls and steel gates spring up around every property. And Epworth, already an early shanty on the outskirts of Harare, will become like George Compound in Lusaka, where amazing forms of recycling (others') wealth sit alongside an incredible if street-hardened form of cooperation amidst squalor. But the water runs and the electricity works (more or less) in George. Nothing in Harare will become like the Mathare Valley in Kenya where, a short ride from tourist Nairobi, acres of slums stretch from your eye to the horizon. In short, Zimbabwe will be *bearably* poor in many of its parts that once were or aspired to be lower-middle-class. Macroeconomic recovery will be very different from sector to sector and the class of oligarchs will grow, not just from dishonesty but from the profiteering that will come from recovery, adding to the foundation generation of the corrupt. For the nation as a whole, nothing homogeneous will occur again. It will be different again in South Africa.

Mbeki's dream of an African Renaissance is alive and well in Hillbrow – only it is practised by a rainbow nation unenvisaged by Mandela. All of Southern Africa's migrant workers seem to live in or hang out in or near Hillbrow. This, despite his scholarly interest in such things, is not the Renaissance Mbeki had in mind. His was contradictory and high-minded, but its future realisation will be by urban congestions and miscegenations, by meltdowns and recoveries, by misrule and the resistance of citizens to misrule.

Even so, it means that South Africa is host, not only to a huge number of Zimbabwean economic refugees, some of whom have had no choice but to turn to criminality, but to a massive influx of skilled and qualified professionals who are the black role models for instance in the nation's universities. Academic salaries are too low to attract a local black high-flyer, but are massive compared to those in Nigeria and Zimbabwe. Johannesburg in particular has become a melting pot. But it means that the 'South African question' is now far from black and white; it has its own provincial and some would say ethnic considerations; it has huge gaps in wealth and class; it has diasporic influx; and it has both gangsterism and the ever-present possibility – if the government fails to provide – of informal 'civic associations' reforming from their late-Apartheid manifestation into vehicles for community organisation that simply bypass the state. The question may be, in the absence of a comprehensively national political opposition – and, despite all her gains, Helen Zille and her DA are not yet that – whether there will be a contest between the ANC and what it will term lawless localisms. The riots in the townships will not take long to organise themselves.

Will South Africa have such extremes of wealth that it will become like an African version of Brazil – home of all things beautiful and all things brutally ugly; home of every ecological wonder and every ecological despoliation, home of urban 'cleansings' by death squads and rural 'sanitisations' by the clearing out of bothersome Indians. Brazil does slum clearances too. In South Africa, the razings of suburbs like Sophiatown under Apartheid have begun to happen again under the ANC – just as Robert Mugabe's Operation Murambatsvina razed so much of Mbare to the ground because it contained 'unauthorised' buildings – and Tokyo Sexwale's August 2009 visit to Diepsloot came on the heels of riots that protested about forced relocation of the residents there. The ANC planners' answer to crumbling sewerage pipes was to shift everybody out so they wouldn't have to live amidst liquid shit oozing from the ground – but to a new location where they would have to 'self-build'. They would not receive new homes. Repair of their community infrastructure meant homelessness. Under such conditions people would riot. They would join with their colleague rioters and draw up a Rioters' Charter. Then they would form a local citizens' group and threaten to firebomb the local ANC office. It may come to such things. But it will not come to be like Brazil; not even Lagos; and it will not be as extensive as Nairobi's Mathare Valley. It will not be like those places because, unlike Kenya, South Africa has a greater number of big cities – so huge slums are not all concentrated around one or two places. It will not be like Lagos because, despite everything, there is still sufficient working and administrative infrastructure to address problems, even if clumsily and sometimes stupidly. And it will not be like Brazil because the population is not as vast. The population is larger than that of Zimbabwe, so the kind of close familial-support networks there cannot be as extensive and inclusive in South Africa; and, again, the population is spread across, not only great cities, but a huge network of towns and small urban settings. Roads and communications work, so travel and escape are possible. There is not a hemming in of the population. But what this all means is that South Africa will work and be successful only if provincial and municipal government work and are successful. And this is the Achilles heel of the ANC's rule of South Africa.

Even so, it might be worth recounting the assessment of someone who was running South Africa even before Mandela's walk to freedom. F.W. de Klerk was the white leader who began the process that brought a negotiated end to Apartheid. Sometimes he is the forgotten man in the contemporary history of the country, yet he was the joint winner of the Nobel Prize alongside Mandela. Commenting on the first year of Jacob Zuma, and the years of ANC rule that led to it, de Klerk made 11 positive points:[16]

- There had been 14 years of uninterrupted economic growth and, even with the advent of the global recession, the economy was not expected to shrink more than 1 per cent in 2010.
- The South African GDP, on a purchasing power parity basis, was US$600 billion, about the same as those of the Argentinian and Polish economies.
- South Africa's was by far the largest of Africa's economies. With only 6.5 per cent of sub-Saharan Africa's population, it produced a third of its gross economic product and two-thirds of its electricity.
- South Africa was a viable and valuable member of the G20.
- There were more foreign embassies in Pretoria than in any other nation's capital city – with the exception of Washington, DC.

- South Africa were the rugby world champions and were hosting the 2010 Football World Cup.
- Tourism was a huge feature of the new South Africa and the tourism sector now produced more than 8 per cent of GDP, more than gold.
- South Africa produced 600,000 motor vehicles in 2009, and produced cars at the high end of the market, including BMW and Mercedes vehicles. As part of a diversified economy, the automobile industry now accounted for 8 per cent of GNP.[17]
- Cape Town, Johannesburg and Port Elizabeth had made the top 100 best cities-in-which-to-live list.
- Millions of black South Africans have joined the middle class, thus enhancing the internal market as well as social stability.
- Seventy per cent of all households now received water and electricity; 13 million children and pensioners now received state allowances; and millions of housing units had been built.

Curiously, the list would not have been out of place in an ANC apologia or self-vindication. The ANC, however, would be less enthusiastic about de Klerk's four key negative points:

- South Africa has the highest number of HIV-infected people in the world. He attributed that directly to the 'AIDS denialism of former President Thabo Mbeki'.
- Almost 50 per cent of South Africans lived in poverty.
- At least 30 per cent of South Africans were unemployed. This had been aggravated by poor education, rigid labour laws, and 'the influx across our porous borders of uncounted millions of economic refugees from other African countries'.
- Unemployment and poverty are the main causes of the high rates of South African crime.

The de Klerk assessment would be disputed by R.W. Johnson. His 2009 book was despondent and critical of almost everything South

Africa had accomplished.[18] Its subtitle was *The Beloved Country since the End of Apartheid*, but that's precisely the point: if you love the country too much, it can only disappoint you because you expect too much. The de Klerk assessment is a judicious one. But his four negative points are huge ones.

At the time of writing, I do not know how long Robert Mugabe will live or how long-lived Morgan Tsvangirai's political career will be. I do not know the future political careers of Arthur Mutambara or Simba Makoni. I do not know how successful Jacob Zuma will be or how the power struggles within the ANC will develop – with Mathews Phosa, Kgalema Motlanthe and Tokyo Sexwale all rumoured to be seeking the presidency after Zuma. I do think it is time the ANC introduced some very much younger people into its seniority. The idea of yet another 'liberation generation', as in Zimbabwe,[19] eking out its grip on power while exhausting its imagination and capacity is appalling. But youthful leaders like Julius Malema of the ANC Youth League behave like wild young men, undisciplined by learning or proper roles in politics. The way the ANC is 'developing' such younger generation as it has is not always encouraging.

However, I have tried to give some long-term indications and to reflect some of the colour, vibrancy and aspirations of life beyond the realms of politicians who live in Borrowdale Brooke or who buy watches in Sandton City; life beyond the vanities of Zimbabwean Reserve Bank Governor, Gideon Gono, whose two doctorates include one honorary award from the University of Zimbabwe when he was chairman of its governing council, and one from an unaccredited American university of neither consequence nor reputation, but a man whose wristwatch – if I identified and priced it correctly from his photo portrait in the Zimbabwean government newspaper – was worth US$65,000. There is a world of difference between those who rule and those who, for now, consent to be ruled.

A road was meant to run from Cape Town to Cairo. It reached the north of Zambia and links South Africa with Zimbabwe. Once, South

Africa sought to destabilise Zimbabwe, and then Zimbabwe held itself up as a beacon of majority rule to South Africa. Times change, but the linkages remain. At present, two old men rule these countries – with the President of Zimbabwe 18 years the senior. The younger man is still manifestly virile, even if that has added to his problems, and he has continued to marry. The older has a younger wife and lives in a Chinese palace on the outskirts of his capital. They are a strange couple. And, before the much-married Zuma, there was the scholarly and aloof philosopher-king who despite all his faults was, with his dreams of Renaissance, one of the last great idealists of Africa.[20] And, before him, was history's only modern saint – or, at least, we made him so, despite our governments' signally failing to have him released from prison for decades – who, all the same, was wily and cunning and knew the dark arts of politics and symbols. Who else but Mandela would contemplate having a rugby jersey tailored for a symbolic moment? And, if these are the leaders, what tales will the millions of ordinary citizens have to tell of how they rejoiced and despaired and how, with unremitting patience and courage, lawlessly as much as lawfully, they struggled?

The story of Zimbabwean Joseph at the beginning of this book is in fact a true one. His real name is not Joseph but his condition was real. He sent enough money home to pay for a private operation and medicine for his mother and she is alive because of this. He has saved enough money to build a small but comfortable house in the Harare suburb of Waterfalls. He will shortly return to Zimbabwe to live in it with his family. He will not miss South Africa, but he will miss the many friends he made who all, like him, tried to do something hard and good. I wanted to write this book for Joseph and so that Joseph's story would have a context that transcended the borders of the separate but linked countries of Southern Africa with their old treacheries, new deceits – and new hopes.

NOTES

Introduction

1. Mark Gevisser, *Thabo Mbeki: The Dream Deferred*, Johannesburg: Jonathan Ball, 2007.
2. William Gumede, *Thabo Mbeki and the Battle for the Soul of the ANC*, London: Zed, 2007.
3. Stephen Chan, *Robert Mugabe: A Life of Power and Violence*, Ann Arbor: University of Michigan Press, 2003.

1 The Great North Road

1. Andrew Hurrell, 'The Politics of South Atlantic Security: A Survey of Proposals for a South Atlantic Treaty Organisation', *International Affairs*, 59:2, 1983; Christopher Coker, 'South Africa and the Western Alliance 1949–81', *RUSI Journal of Defence Studies*, 127:2, 1982.
2. Gerald Horne, *From the Barrel of a Gun: The United States and the War against Zimbabwe, 1965–1980*, Chapel Hill: University of North Carolina Press, 2001, pp. 154–7; Michael Charlton, *The Last Colony in Africa: Diplomacy and the Independence of Rhodesia*, Oxford: Blackwell, 1990, pp. 1–4.
3. For a superb 'damn by faint praise' account of Rhodes, see Bertrand Russell's *Freedom and Organisation*, now out of print but excerpted as 'A Bad Man in Africa', *New African*, May 2010.
4. See Robert Ross, *A Concise History of South Africa*, Cambridge: Cambridge University Press, 1999, Chapters 2 & 3.
5. Dan Wylie, *Myth of Iron: Shaka in History*, Oxford: James Currey, 2008.
6. Gregory Fremont-Barnes, *The Boer War 1899–1902*, Oxford: Osprey, 2003; Martin Dugard, 'Farmers at Arms: The First Modern Insurgency – and how the British Crushed it', *Military History*, 27:1, 2010.
7. T.R.H. Davenport, *South Africa: A Modern History*, London: Macmillan, 1987, Chapters 8 & 9.

8. David Birmingham, *Kwame Nkrumah*, London: Cardinal, 1990, pp. 100–12.
9. Paul Foot, *The Politics of Harold Wilson*, Harmondsworth: Penguin, 1968, pp. 259–70.
10. David Birmingham, *A Concise History of Portugal*, Cambridge: Cambridge University Press, 1993, Chapters 6 & 7.
11. For a contemporary edition of his works, see David Birmingham, *Frontline Nationalism in Angola and Mozambique*, London: James Currey, 1992.
12. See the moving, barely fictionalised account that opens Alexander Kanengoni, *Echoing Silences*, Harare: Baobab, 1993.
13. Much to the consternation and anger of the presidents of independent Southern African states: Martin Meredith, *Mugabe: Power and Plunder in Zimbabwe*, Oxford: Public Affairs, 2002, p. 3.
14. Lord Carrington, *Reflect on Things Past*, London: Grafton, 1988, Chapter 13.
15. Ibid., pp. 254–5.
16. John Newhouse, 'Profiles – A Sense of Duty: Lord Carrington', *New Yorker*, 14 February 1983.
17. Commonwealth Observer Group, *Southern Rhodesian Elections 1980*, London: Commonwealth Secretariat, 1980.
18. Cited in Ibbo Mandaza, 'The State in Post-White Settler Colonial Situation', in Ibbo Mandaza (ed.), *Zimbabwe: The Political Economy of Transition 1980–1986*, Dakar: CODESRIA, 1987, p. 42.

2 The armed trek

1. Victor de Waal, *The Politics of Reconciliation: Zimbabwe's First Decade*, London: Hurst, 1990.
2. See, e.g., the measured analysis of Richard Hodder-Williams, which recognised but greatly underestimated the nature and scale of the government response, *Conflict in Zimbabwe: The Matabeleland Problem*, London: Institute for the Study of Conflict, Conflict Studies 151, 1983.
3. Richard Werbner, *Tears of the Dead*, Edinburgh: Edinburgh University Press, 1991. Richard Werbner, 'In Memory: A Heritage of War in Southwestern Zimbabwe', in N. Bhebe and Terence Ranger (eds), *Soldiers in Zimbabwe's Liberation War*, Vol. 2, Harare: University of Zimbabwe Publications, 1995.
4. Jocelyn Alexander, 'Dissident Perspectives on Zimbabwe's Post-Independence War', *Africa*, 68:2, 1998. See also Jocelyn Alexander, JoAnn McGregor and Terence Ranger, *Violence and Memory: One Hundred Years in the 'Dark Forests' of Matabeleland*, Oxford: James Currey, 2000.
5. But not without grave problems within the ANC. See Hugh Macmillan, 'After Morogoro: The Continuing Crisis of the African National Congress (of South Africa) in Zambia, 1969–1971', *Social Dynamics: A Journal of African Studies*, 35:2, 2009; Thula Simpson, 'The Making (and Remaking) of a Revolutionary Plan: Strategic Dilemmas of the ANC's Armed Struggle, 1974–1978', *Social Dynamics: A Journal of African Studies*, 35:2, 2009.
6. Deon Geldenhuys, *The Diplomacy of Isolation: South African Foreign Policy Making*, Johannesburg: Macmillan, 1984.
7. Victoria Brittain, *Hidden Lives, Hidden Deaths: South Africa's Crippling of a Continent*, London: Faber & Faber, 1988.
8. Kenneth W. Grundy, *The Militarization of South African Politics*, Oxford: Oxford University Press, 1987. Also see Phyllis Johnson and David Martin (eds), *Destructive Engagement: Southern Africa at War*, Harare: Zimbabwe Publishing House, 1986. Thomas G. Weiss and James G. Blight (eds), *The Suffering Grass: Superpowers and Regional Conflict in Southern Africa and the Caribbean*, Boulder: Lynne Rienner, 1992.
9. Laurent C.W. Kaela, *The Question of Namibia*, London: Macmillan, 1996.

10. Moises Venancio, 'Angola and Southern Africa: The Dynamics of Change', in Paul B. Rich (ed.), *The Dynamics of Change in Southern Africa*, London: Macmillan, 1994.
11. Paul L. Moorcraft, *African Nemesis: War and Revolution in Southern Africa 1945–2010*, London: Brassey's, 1990, Chapter 10.
12. Joseph Hanlon, *Apartheid's Second Front: South Africa's War against its Neighbours*, Harmondsworth: Penguin, 1986.
13. The complete text of this treaty can be found in *Accord: An International Review of Peace Initiatives*, 3, 1998.
14. There is a very interesting fictional recreation of the assassination, involving South African corporations, in Deon Meyer, *Blood Safari*, London: Hodder & Stoughton, 2009.
15. Lloyd M. Sachikonye, 'Unita and Renamo: "Bandit" Social Movements?', *Southern African Political & Economic Monthly*, 3:7, 1990.
16. Tom Young, 'The MNR/Renamo: External and Internal Dynamics', *African Affairs*, 89, 1990.
17. There are almost no fully reliable accounts. My own is derived from regional military personnel. However, among the accounts is a largely unknown, lengthy essay by Fidel Castro himself, that somehow years later was published in Zambia: Fidel Castro, 'The Battle of Cuito Cuanavale', *Saturday Post* (Lusaka), 15 March 2008.
18. Chester Crocker, *High Noon in Southern Africa: Making Peace in a Rough Neighbourhood*, New York: Norton, 1992.
19. J.E. Davies, *Constructive Engagement? Chester Crocker and American Policy in South Africa, Namibia and Angola, 1981–8*, Oxford: James Currey, 2007.
20. For the extensive background to this, see Vivienne Jabri, *Mediating Conflict: Decision-making and Western Intervention in Namibia*, Manchester: Manchester University Press, 1990.
21. Paul Rich, 'The United States, its History of Mediation and the Chester Crocker Round of Negotiations over Namibia in 1988', in Stephen Chan and Vivienne Jabri (eds), *Mediation in Southern Africa*, London: Macmillan, 1993.

3 The rainbow bridge

1. Human Rights Watch, *Abdication of Responsibility: The Commonwealth and Human Rights*, New York: Human Rights Watch, 1991.
2. Not least his own account of his life: Nelson Mandela, *Long Walk to Freedom*, Johannesburg: Macdonald Purnell, 1994. For a curious but touching series of tributes, see Xolela Mangcu (ed.), *The Meaning of Mandela: A Literary and Intellectual Celebration*, Cape Town: Human Sciences Research Council, 2006.
3. David James Smith, *Young Mandela*, London: Weidenfeld & Nicolson, 2010.
4. For accounts of his rise to power, see his own autobiography: Kenneth Kaunda, *Zambia Shall be Free*, London: Heinemann, 1962; and the accounts by Philip Brownrigg, *Kenneth Kaunda*, Lusaka: Kenneth Kaunda Foundation, 1989; Richard Hall, *The High Price of Principles: Kaunda and the White South*, London: Hodder & Stoughton, 1969; and John Hatch, *Two African Statesmen*, London: Secker & Warburg, 1976. These were flattering accounts, but even critical ones focused on difficulties in class as opposed to race relations: Douglas Anglin and Timothy M. Shaw, *Zambia's Foreign Policy: Studies in Diplomacy and Dependency*, Boulder: Westview, 1979.
5. See David Welsh and J.E. Spence, *Ending Apartheid*, Harlow: Longman Pearson, 2011, Chapter 5.
6. R.W. Johnson and Lawrence Schlemmer (eds), *Launching Democracy in South Africa: The First Open Election, April 1994*, New Haven: Yale University Press, 1996.
7. Hasu H. Patel, 'Zimbabwe's Mediation in Mozambique and Angola, 1989–91', in Stephen Chan and Vivienne Jabri (eds), *Mediation in Southern Africa*, London: Macmillan, 1993.

8. Cameron Hume, *Ending Mozambique's War: The Role of Mediation and Good Offices*, Washington, DC: US Institute of Peace, 1994, pp. 15–18; Dinis S. Sengulane and Jaime Pedro Gonclaves, 'A Calling for Peace: Christian Leaders and the Quest for Reconciliation in Mozambique', *Accord (The Mozambican Peace Process in Perspective)*, 3, 1998; Riccardo Chartroux, 'Interview with Matteo Zuppi, Community of Santo Egidio', in Stephen Chan, Moises Venancio et al., *War and Peace in Mozambique*, London: Macmillan, 1998. The final full agreement is published as *General Peace Agreement of Mozambique*, Amsterdam: African-European Institute, 1993.

9. Paul Moorcraft, *African Nemesis: War and Revolution in Southern Africa 1945–2010*, London: Brassey's, 1990, Plate 12.3.

10. Chan et al., *War and Peace in Mozambique*.

11. Robert Ross, *A Concise History of South Africa*, Cambridge: Cambridge University Press, 1999, pp. 198–9.

12. Mandela had to intervene personally to quell resentment by his own ANC colleagues in KwaZulu-Natal at a settlement with Inkatha: *Guardian*, 7 June 1994. See also Chris McGreal, 'Inkatha Deal – the Price of Peace in Blood-soaked Land', *Guardian*, 7 May 1994; and Richard Dowden, 'How the Peace Was Won', *Independent*, 20 April 1994.

13. Paul B. Rich, *White Power and the Liberal Conscience*, Manchester: Manchester University Press, 1984; Paul B. Rich, *Hope and Despair: English-Speaking Intellectuals and South African Politics, 1896–1976*, London: I.B. Tauris, 1993.

14. Sachs was a reasoned but staunch critic from an early stage: Albie Sachs, *Justice in South Africa*, Berkeley: University of California Press, 1973.

15. John Carlin, *Playing the Enemy: Nelson Mandela and the Game That Made a Nation*, New York: Atlantic, 2008. See also the Clint Eastwood movie, *Invictus* (2009), starring Morgan Freeman and Matt Damon. It is based on Carlin's account, but nobody seems to know how to play rugby properly in this film.

16. Mark Gevisser, *Thabo Mbeki: The Dream Deferred*, 3rd and 4th pages of photos immediately prior to Chapter 13.

4 The formation of Thabo Mbeki

1. John Hatch, *Two African Statesmen*, London: Secker & Warberg, 1976.

2. *Saturday Post* (Lusaka), 20 December 2003.

3. Thabo Mbeki's ANC Newsletters were serialised regionally. I cite their appearances in Zambia. 'We'll Resist the Upside-down View of Africa', *The Post*, 9 January 2004.

4. Henry Kissinger, *Diplomacy*, New York: Simon & Schuster, 1994.

5. Probably his greatest works: Ngugi wa Thiong'o, *Petals of Blood*, London: Heinemann, 1977; and the play that led to his imprisonment (with Ngugi wa Mirii), *Ngaahika Ndeenda: Ithaako ria Ngerekano* (I Will Marry When I Want), London: Heinemann, 1982. His latest novel is *Murogi wa Kagogo* (The Wizard of the Crow), New York: Knopf, 2006.

6. Ngugi wa Thiong'o, *Decolonising the Mind: The Politics of Language in African Literature*, London: James Currey, 1986.

7. He tries to address this: Ngugi wa Thiong'o, 'Europhone or African Memory: The Challenge of the Pan-African Intellectual in the Era of Globalization', in Thandika Mkandawire (ed.), *African Intellectuals: Rethinking Politics, Language, Gender and Development*, Dakar: CODESRIA, 2005.

8. As in his early books of essays: Ngugi wa Thiong'o, *Detained: A Writer's Prison Diary*, London: Heinemann, 1981; *Writers in Politics*, London: Heinemann, 1981; *Barrel of a Pen: Resistance to Repression in Neo-Colonial Kenya*, London: New Beacon, 1983.

9. Thabo Mbeki, 'Nobody Knows My Name', *The Post*, 10 September 2004.

10. Hatch, *Two African Statesmen*.

11. There is an hilarious account of such in Caryl Phillips, *The Atlantic Sound*, London: Vintage, 2001.
12. Despite the fame of these books in the US, I take as key examples of the homogenisation of Africa in the name of blackness: Molefi Kete Asante, *The Afrocentric Idea*, Philadelphia: Temple University Press, 1987; Marimba Ani, *Yurugu: An African-Centred Critique of European Cultural Thought and Behavior*, Trenton: Africa World Press, 1997.
13. Ali Mazrui, *Cultural Forces in World Politics*, London: James Currey, 1990, pp. 132–7.
14. Thabo Mbeki, 'Is There Anybody There?' *The Post*, 14 October 2005.
15. William Gumede, *Thabo Mbeki and the Battle for the Soul of the ANC*, London: Zed, 2007.
16. He wrote an early book: Govan Mbeki, *Transkei in the Making*, in 1939; it was published by a house called Verulam but is out of print; and journalism in organs such as *New Age*.
17. After his release, he wrote two further books: Govan Mbeki, *Learning from Robben Island*, Cape Town: David Philip, 1991; and *The Struggle for Liberation in South Africa: A Short History*, Cape Town: David Philip, 1992.
18. Some have seen this as a form of continuity from Kwame Nkrumah. See Adekeye Adebajo, *The Curse of Berlin: Africa after the Cold War*, London: Hurst, 2010, Chapter 11.

5 The degeneration of Zimbabwe

1. See the account in Martin Meredith, *Mugabe: Power and Plunder in Zimbabwe*, Oxford: Public Affairs, 2002, Chapter 8.
2. Clive Foss, 'Cuba's African Adventures', *History Today*, 60:3, 2010.
3. Meredith, *Mugabe*, Chapter 9.
4. For detailed studies of the Zimbabwean trade union movement: Brian Raftopoulos and Ian Phimister (eds), *Keep on Knocking: A History of the Labour Movement in Zimbabwe, 1900–97*, Harare: Baobab, 1997; Brian Raftopoulos and Tsuneo Yoshikuni (eds), *Sites of Struggle: Essays in Zimbabwe's Urban History*, Harare: Weaver, 1999; Brian Raftopoulos and Lloyd Sachikonye (eds), *Striking Back: The Labour Movement and the Post-Colonial State in Zimbabwe, 1980–2000*, Harare: Weaver, 2001.
5. See Mugabe's comments in Michael Charlton, *The Last Colony in Africa: Diplomacy and the Independence of Rhodesia*, Oxford: Blackwell, 1990, p. 80. For a detailed consideration of the land issue: Sam Moyo, *The Land Question in Zimbabwe*, Harare: SAPES, 1995.
6. *New African*, 441, June 2005, p. 6.
7. E.g. Blessings-Miles Tendi, 'Zimbabwe's Third Chimurenga: The Use and Abuse of History', unpublished Oxford D.Phil. thesis, 2008, Chapter 4.
8. As expressed even by someone like Alexander Kanengoni, who had written about the horrors of war, when he received a parcel of confiscated land. See Terence Ranger, 'Herbert Chitepo: Assassination, Confession, Narrative', *Journal of Southern African Studies*, 29:4, 2003, p. 1001. Kanengoni, after seeming to criticise Mugabe's regime in his fiction, went on to publish an apologia for Mugabe, making a romance even of him: Alexander Kanengoni, 'One Hundred Days with Robert Mugabe', *Daily News* (Harare), 12 April 2003.
9. For an account: David Blair, *Degrees in Violence: Robert Mugabe and the Struggle for Power in Zimbabwe*, London: Continuum, 2002, Chapters 4 & 9.
10. For accounts of how behaviour in this group could differ: Blair Rutherford, *Working on the Margins: Black Workers, White Farmers in Postcolonial Zimbabwe*, London: Zed, 2001.
11. For a brief but precise rendition of what this meant in terms of land and possible future recovery, see Sam Moyo, 'Then and Now', in Gugulethu Moyo and Mark Ashurst (eds), *The Day after Mugabe: Prospects for Change in Zimbabwe*, London: Africa Research Foundation, 2007, pp. 76–7.

12. On the spiritual qualities of land: Terence Ranger, *Peasant Consciousness and Guerrilla War in Zimbabwe*, London: James Currey, 1985; David Lan, *Guns and Rain*, London: James Currey, 1985; Terence Ranger, *Voices from the Rocks: Nature, Culture and History in the Matopos Hills of Zimbabwe*, Oxford: James Currey, 1999; Billy Mukamuri, *Making Sense of Social Forestry: A Political and Contextual Study of Forestry Practices in South Central Zimbabwe*, Tampere: Acta Universitatis Tamperensis, 1995; M.F.C. Bourdillon, *Where Are the Ancestors? Changing Culture in Zimbabwe*, Harare: University of Zimbabwe Publications, 1993.

13. Joseph Chaumba, Ian Scoones and William Wolmer, 'New Politics, New Livelihoods: Agrarian Change in Zimbabwe', *Review of African Political Economy*, 98, 2003.

14. Recounted to me by (1) a senior Commonwealth Secretariat official, (2) a senior South African official, and (3) a senior Nigerian official, all differing only in the emphasis placed on the word 'not'.

15. Summarised by Mandy Rossouw, 'Mbeki's Prescient Warning to Bob', *Mail & Guardian*, 27 June 2008.

16. Thabo Mbeki, 'The Mbeki–Mugabe Papers: A Discussion Document', *New Agenda*, 2nd quarter, 2008 – although it should be pointed out that the publication was not mandated or approved by Mbeki.

17. I am grateful to David Moore for providing me with a copy of the original.

6 How Morgan Tsvangirai formed himself

1. Stephen Chan, *Citizen of Africa: Conversations with Morgan Tsvangirai*, printed in Cape Town by the Fingerprint Cooperative, 2005, with no acknowledged publisher or ISBN. Pirate US edition by the same title, from Palo Alto: Academia Press, 2006, but with registered ISBN. There is now a new, updated and above-ground edition, *Citizen of Zimbabwe*, Harare: Weaver, 2010. The Tsvangirai quotes in this chapter derive from the 2005 edition.

2. Interviews excerpted in Stephen Chan, 'Commonwealth Residualism and the Machinations of Power in a Turbulent Zimbabwe', *Commonwealth & Comparative Politics*, 39:3, 2007, pp. 70–3.

3. Ngugi wa Thiong'o, *Decolonising the Mind*, London: Heinemann, 1986.

4. Chan, *Citizen of Africa*, p. 40.

5. Ibid., p. 41.

6. Morgan Tsvangirai in a 1990 edition of *Southern African Political & Economic Monthly* (full citation unobtainable), cited in Richard Saunders, 'Life in Space – The New Politics of Zimbabwe', *Southern African Review of Books*, 5:1, 1993, p. 19.

7. Chan, *Citizen of Africa*, p. 38.

8. Ibid., pp. 45–6.

9. His own account: Olusegun Obasanjo, *My Command*, London: Heinemann, 1980.

10. Martin Dent, 'Military Government in Perspective (The Murtala Regime)', in Keith Panter-Brick (ed.), *Soldiers and Oil*, London: Cass, 1978.

11. *Mission to South Africa: The Commonwealth Report – The Findings of the Commonwealth Eminent Persons Group on Southern Africa*, Harmondsworth: Penguin, 1986.

12. *South Africa: The Sanctions Report – Prepared for the Commonwealth Committee of Foreign Ministers on Southern Africa*, London: Penguin, 1989.

13. This quality alone led to hagiographies, e.g. Sarah Hudleston, *Face of Courage: Morgan Tsvangirai*, Cape Town: Double Storey, 2005.

7 How can a car go forward with two different speeds on only one gear?

1. I benefited greatly from the narrative of Brian Pottinger, *The Mbeki Legacy*, Cape Town: Zebra, 2008, Chapter 6.

2. South Africa had also always been part of the Western neo-liberal order, and remains so: Merle Lipton, *Capitalism and Apartheid*, Aldershot: Gower, 1985; Merle Lipton, *Liberals, Marxists, and Nationalists: Competing Interpretations of South African History*, New York: Palgrave Macmillan, 2007.

3. And neither state nor market provided for the concept of, and widening gaps in, class relations: Jeremy Seekings and Nicoli Natrass, *Class, Race and Inequality in South Africa*, New Haven: Yale University Press, 2005; Adam Habib, 'Economic Policy and Power Relations in South Africa's Transition to Democracy', *World Development*, 28:2, 2000.

4. I benefited also from the rendition offered by Richard Knight, from whom the figures above are gleaned: 'South Africa: Economic Policy and Development', http://richard-knight.homestead.com/files/sisaeconomy.htm

5. See Jonathan Ball, *Making Mistakes, Righting the Wrongs: Insights into Black Economic Empowerment*, Johannesburg: KMM Review, 2006; Nicholas L. Waddy, 'Affirmative Action versus Non-Racialism in the New South Africa', *African Issues*, 31:1/2, 2003–4; Omano Edigheji, *The Evolution of Black Economic Empowerment in South Africa from the Lenses of Business, The Tripartite Alliance, Community Groups, the Apartheid and Post-Apartheid Government, 1985–1999*, Johannesburg: National Labour and Economic Development Institute, 2000.

6. See Johannes Fedderke, 'Social Welfare: Social Stasis', *Focus*, 55, 2009.

7. Adam Heribert et al., *Ethnic Power Mobilised*, New Haven: Yale University Press, 1979; Mohamed Adhikari, *Not White Enough, Not Black Enough*, Cape Town: Double Storey, 2005; Michael MacDonald, *Why Race Matters in South Africa*, London: Harvard University Press, 2006; and Seekings and Natrass, *Class, Race and Inequality*.

8. Cited in Seekings and Natrass, *Class, Race and Inequality*, p. 345.

9. Although the courts could still block enrichment deals that were too blatant: Linda Ensor, 'BEE Deal Linked to Malema Blocked', *Business Day*, 19 May 2010.

10. E.g. 'Buthelezi Slams Affirmative Action', *Mail & Guardian*, 1 February 2007.

11. See the special issue, *China in Africa* of the *South African Journal of International Affairs*, 13:1, 2006. For extensive work on the overall profile of China in Africa: Chris Alden, Daniel Large and Ricardo Soares de Oliveira (eds), *China Returns to Africa: A Rising Power and a Continent Embrace*, London: Hurst, 2008. For the best summary: Chris Alden, *China in Africa*, London: Zed, 2007. But for a Chinese view: *The Symposium of China–Africa Shared Development*, Beijing: Chinese Academy of Social Sciences, 2006.

12. It was a key ingredient embedded in the Blair-inspired *Our Common Interest: Report of the Commission for Africa*, London: Commission for Africa, 2005.

13. Mandela actually delivered several variations of this same speech over the years, tellingly before the Zimbabwean Parliament on 19 May 1997; as early as the Organisation of African Union summit in Tunisia in 1994; at the Assembly of Heads of States and Government of the Non-Aligned Movement in Durban, September 1998; and at the African Renaissance Festival, Durban, March 1999.

14. For early visions of this: Gavin Maasdorp and Alan Whiteside (eds), *Towards a Post-Apartheid Future: Political & Economic Relations in Southern Africa*, London: Macmillan, 1992; Nancy Thede and Pierre Beaudet (eds), *A Post-Apartheid Southern Africa?*, London: Macmillan, 1993.

15. Antoinette Handley, *Business and the State in Africa: Economic Policy-making in the Neo-Liberal Era*, Cambridge: Cambridge University Press, 2008, Chapter 2.

16. For a fine disquisition on the wax and wane of educational development in South Africa, see Julia de Kadt, 'Education & Injustice in South Africa', *Focus*, 55, 2009.

17. Nana Poku, 'The Crisis of AIDS in Africa and the Politics of Response', in Nana Poku (ed.), *Security and Development in Southern Africa*, Westport: Praeger, 2001.

18. Mark Gevisser, *Thabo Mbeki: The Dream Deferred*, Johannesburg: Jonathan Ball, 2007, Chapter 41.

19. Ibid., p. 727.
20. Ibid.

8 The long electoral trek

1. I was regularly in Zimbabwe during the period of this chapter, and attended the 2005 elections, so that the data represented in this chapter were gathered at first hand.
2. Jonathan N. Moyo, *Voting for Democracy: Electoral Politics in Zimbabwe*, Harare: University of Zimbabwe Publications, 1992.
3. Figures from the *Independent*, 16 February 2000.
4. *The Times* (London), 16 February 2000.
5. For accounts: David Blair, *Degrees in Violence: Robert Mugabe and the Struggle for Power in Zimbabwe*, London: Continuum, 2002, Chapters 9–12; Martin Meredith, *Mugabe: Power and Plunder in Zimbabwe*, Oxford: Public Affairs, 2002, Chapters 11–12.
6. See the special issue, *Reflections on the Commonwealth at 40*, of *The Round Table*, 380, 2005.
7. W. David McIntyre, *The Significance of the Commonwealth, 1965–90*, Christchurch, NZ: Canterbury University Press, 1991, especially Part II.
8. Even writers antipathetic to Mugabe wrote lyrically about the meaning of land: Chenjerai Hove, *Bones*, Harare: Baobab, 1990. For his later criticisms about Mugabe and the meaning of land: Chenjerai Hove, *Palaver Finish*, Harare: Weaver, 2002.
9. Figures from the *Guardian*, 28 June 2000.
10. Zimbabwe Electoral Commission figures. For critical views on the 2002 elections: Henning Melber (ed.), *Zimbabwe's Presidential Elections 2002*, Uppsala: Nordiska Afrikainstituet, 2002.
11. Although see the views also of Norma Kriger, 'ZANU-PF Strategies in General Elections, 1980–2000: Discourse and Coercion', *African Affairs*, 104:414, 2005.
12. Ibbo Mandaza (ed.), *Zimbabwe: The Political Economy of Transition, 1980–1986*, Harare: CODESRIA, 1987; Ibbo Mandaza and Llyod Sachikonye (eds), *The One Party State and Democracy: The Zimbabwe Debate*, Harare: SAPES, 1991.
13. My calculations are derived from my studies of earlier voting patterns, with allowances made for boundary changes, and adjustments made for size of electorate, percentage turnout, interviews and direct observation.
14. This is discussed below. (See pp. 176–8.)

9 The return of the Zulu king

1. I visited South Africa often during the period discussed in this chapter.
2. The best available biography is Jeremy Gordin, *Zuma: A Biography*, Cape Town: Jonathan Ball, 2008.
3. Right up to a few days before polling, COPE was claiming Mbeki would make a dramatic last-minute switch to the new party: *The Times* (Johannesburg), 17 April 2009.
4. *The Freedom Charter 50th Anniversary Celebrations 1955–2005*, Gauteng Provincial Government, 2005, pp. 12–13. For the only full-length scholarly study of South African Chinese and their political and social manoeuvres: Yoon Jung Park, *A Matter of Honour: Being Chinese in South Africa*, Johannesburg: Jacana, 2008.
5. Tom Lodge, 'Spectres from the Camps: The ANC's Commission of Enquiry', *Southern Africa Report*, 8:3–4, 1993.
6. Cited ibid.
7. See the Truth and Reconciliation Commission Report, Volume 12, Chapter 4, http://www.doj.gov.za/trc/report/finalreport/volume%204.pdf

8. Alistair Boddy-Evans, '14 April 1990 – ANC Admits to the Use of Torture', http://africanhistory.about.com/b/2007/04/14/14-april-1990-anc-admits-it-used-torture

9. 'Tutsis Boycott Burundi Talks', BBC, 27 July 2004. http://news.bbc.co.uk/2/hi/africa/3929519.stm

10. For one account, among several differing accounts, of the political manoeuvres of the time: William Mervin Gumede, *Thabo Mbeki and the Battle for the Soul of the ANC*, London: Zed, 2007, especially Chapter 2.

11. The following timeline is that of the BBC: http://news.bbc.co.uk/go/pr/fr/-/hi/world/africa/7153378.stm

12. 'Many faces of Schabir Shaik', reported on 21 February 2005: http://www.news24.com/News24/South_Africa/Shaik_trial

13. The most forthright coverage of this was in *The Star*. See 'The Story of the State v. Schabir Shaik and Others', *The Star*, 7 October 2004.

14. 'The Schabir Shaik trial story in short', http://www.armsdeal-vpo.co.za/special_items/schabir_shaik_trial/story_short.html; 'Schabir Shaik on Trial', http://www.sabcnews.com/features/schabir_shaik_trial/index.html For full text of the judgment: http://www.iol.co.za/html/static/shaik.php

15. 'SA's Zuma Showered to Avoid HIV', http://news.bbc.co.uk/1/hi/world/africa/4879822.stm

16. 'Zuma's Rape Accuser Questioned', http://news.bbc.co.uk/1/hi/world/africa/4781440.stm

17. For all the documents and resolutions of this conference: http://www/anc.org.za/ancdocs/conf/conference52/index.html

18. But there was also a real battle between ideological persuasions, identified simplistically as between free-marketeers and socialists: George Ogola, 'The Battle for the ANC's Soul', *News Africa*, 31 August 2007.

19. ANC 'will be more divided' after Polokwane, *Mail & Guardian* (Johannesburg), 6 December 2007; Mariette Le Roux, 'ANC on Knife Edge ahead of Polokwane', *Mail & Guardian*, 13 December 2007.

20. Mandy Rossouw, 'Deputy President Sexwale?', *Mail & Guardian*, 5–11 October 2007.

21. See Sibongakonke Shoba, 'Gauteng ANC Vote Gives Sexwale Early Poll Lift', *Business Day*, 8 October 2007.

22. Gumede, *Thabo Mbeki and the Battle for the Soul of the ANC*, p. 416.

23. Jonathan Clayton, 'Power Struggle Pushes ANC Factions to Naked Hostility', *The Times*, 18 December 2007.

24. The *Mail & Guardian* devoted a great deal of investigative journalism to this. See the reports of 5–11 October 2007. See also Alec Russell, 'Arrest Warrant Fuels S. Africa Political Crisis', *Financial Times*, 6–7 October 2007.

25. Adriaan Basson, 'Of Arms and Brave Men', *Mail & Guardian*, 5–11 October 2007.

10 The elections of no election: the prelude to vexed compromise in Zimbabwe

1. I observed both rounds of the 2008 elections within Zimbabwe and my projected percentage outcome of the first round, related later in this chapter, has been compared to those of others by the South-African-based political scientist, David Moore, as 'probably the most accurate' (although, in the frenzied world of those elections, nothing escaped brushes with sheer conjecture): David Moore, 'An Academic's Journalism in the Zimbabwean Interregnum', 25 June 2008, http://concernedafricascholars.org/an-academic%e2%80%99s-journalism-in-the-zimbabwean-interregnum/

2. See the work of Simon Bekker of Stellenbosch University. I found Bekker's seminar at the University of Johannesburg, 15 April 2009, very helpful. Simon Bekker, *Xenophobia and Violence in South Africa*, lecture handout at the University

of Johannesburg Anthropology and Development Studies Wednesday Seminar, 2009.

3. Brian Chikwava, *Harare North*, London: Jonathan Cape, 2009.

4. The MDC launched an inquiry, *Commission of Enquiry into Disturbances at Party Headquarters (Draft Report)*, December 2004.

5. *Report of the Management Committee of an Inquiry into the Disturbances and Beatings at Harvest House, Bulawayo Provincial Office and in Gwanda at the Late Masera's Funeral, 2005*. Harare: MDC, 2005.

6. See the 25 July 2005 BBC report: http://news.bbc.co.uk/2/hi/africa/4715635.stm

7. Brian Raftopoulos, 'Reflections on the Opposition in Zimbabwe: The Politics of the MDC', in Ranka Primorac and Stephen Chan (eds), *Zimbabwe in Crisis: The International Response and the Space of Silence*, London: Routledge, 2007. As the mediator between the two factions, Raftopoulos provides excellent material on the background to and surrounding the split in the MDC.

8. Raftopoulos in a discussion with the author.

9. See Peta Thonycroft's 2009 description: 'All you need to know about Arthur Mutambara', http://www.newzimbabwe.com/pages/senate141.13789.html

10. Personal ZANU-PF reports to the author.

11. Alone among Zimbabwean senior politicians, Makoni has a personal website: www.simbamakoni.co.zw

12. His first book in post-independence Zimbabwe effectively set the tone for all debate that followed: Ibbo Mandaza (ed.), *Zimbabwe: The Political Economy of Transition 1980–1986*, Dakar: CODESRIA, 1987.

13. His revealing early rationales for this: Ibbo Mandaza, 'The One Party State and Democracy in Southern Africa: Towards a Conceptual Framework', in Ibbo Mandaza and Lloyd Sachikonye (eds), *The One Party State and Democracy: The Zimbabwe Debate*, Harare: SAPES, 1991.

14. In the single issue of this election tabloid, *Mavambo/Kusile/Dawn* (undated), he declared – notwithstanding all the preceding manoeuvres – that he had quit ZANU-PF as 'a matter of principle'.

15. Fay Chung wrote a revealing memoir of ZANU-PF, *Reliving the Second Chimurenga: Memories from Zimbabwe's Liberation Struggle*, Uppsala: Nordic Africa Institute, 2006.

16. When Dongo left ZANU-PF, it was a sensation. She was the cover story, under the banner 'Fair Play Finds a Star in Dongo', of *Horizon*, September 1995.

17. Rudo Gaidzanwa's election leaflet for the Chisipiti Senatorial Constituency was revealing. 'As a Land Committee member, I became convinced that the land reform had gone wrong.' The dissent was not so much about Mugabe's philosophy, as about the operationalisation of the policies that emanated from it.

18. So much so that, despite an almost ritual warning against unaccredited observers and journalists, almost everyone who wanted to cover the elections was able to enter Zimbabwe: George Chollah and Kingsley Kaswende, 'Zim Warns "Illegal" Journalists', *The Post* (Lusaka), 18 March 2008.

19. Mabasa Sasa, 'President Tipped to Win by 57pc', *The Herald*, 28 March 2008.

20. Ed Davey in a discussion with the author.

21. Catherine Philip, ' "Military Coup" in Zimbabwe as Mugabe is Forced to Cede Power to Generals', *The Times*, 9 June 2008.

22. This probably also saved Bonyongwe's job as, even two weeks before, there were rumours of his dismissal for his Makoni sympathies. See the Zambian report: *The Monitor & Digest*, 14–17 March 2008.

23. Personal South African and US State Department information to the author.

24. Personal testimony to the author by one of the abductees.

25. Some of this scandal-mongering became salacious, and only really stopped with the tragic death, later, of Susan Tsvangirai.

26. *New York Times*, 1 July 2008.

11 The legacy of mixed legacy: Mbeki breaks through on Zimbabwe, Zuma breaks through on Mbeki

1. Much of the information in this chapter was secured from senior ANC sources.
2. Not that Mbeki fully escaped suspicions surrounding the scandal of the naval ships. This haunted him as late as the eve of Polokwane: Stefaans Brummer, Sam Sole and Adriaan Basson, 'Arms: Germans Squeeze Mbeki', *Mail & Guardian*, 5–11 October 2007.
3. Chris McGreal, 'How Did It All Go So Wrong?' *Guardian*, 23 September 2008.
4. Andrew Feinstein, *After the Party: A Personal and Political Journey inside the ANC*, Johannesburg: Jonathan Ball, 2007.
5. Para. 210 of Nicholson's judgment.
6. Ibid., para. 220.
7. See Sydney Mufamadi, 'Lessons from African Diplomatic Intiatives in the Democratic Republic of Congo, Sudan and Zimbabwe, *The Round Table*, 99: 411, 2010.
8. Adam Hochschild, *King Leopold's Ghost*, London: Pan Macmillan, 1998; and Dave Renton, David Seddon and Leo Zeilig, *The Congo: Plunder and Resistance*, London: Zed, 2007.
9. Filip de Boeck and Marie-Françoise Plissart, *Kinshasa: Tales of the Invisible City*, Ghent: Ludion, 2004.
10. Clive Foss, 'Cuba's African Adventures', *History Today*, 60:3, 2010 – complete with a sentimental cover photograph of Che cuddling a Congolese baby.
11. For the problems ahead: Anthony W. Gambino, *Congo: Securing Peace, Sustaining Progress*, New York: Council on Foreign Relations, 2008.
12. Michaela Wrong, *It's Our Turn to Eat: The Story of a Kenyan Whistle Blower*, London: Fourth Estate, 2009; and Paul Collier, *War, Guns and Votes: Democracy in Dangerous Places*, London: Bodley Head, 2009.
13. There is a vast literature of competing schools of thought on conflict resolution. 'Founding fathers' include Adam Curle, John Burton and Herman Kelman; while currently influential 'harder' and 'realist' scholars include I. William Zartman and Francis Deng; and there is a 'critical philosophy' group which includes Vivienne Jabri. Only one seriously sustained and applied body of work has emerged from Africa itself: H.W. van der Merwe, *Peacemaking in South Africa: A Life in Conflict Resolution*, Cape Town: Tafelberg, 2000.
14. Nkosana Moyo in a discussion with the author.
15. For details: http://news.bbc.co.uk/1/hi/world/africa/7617731.stm
16. George Shiri, senior ZANU-PF operative in London, in discussion with the author.
17. *Financial Times* figure for that month.
18. For his resignation speech: www.politicsweb.co.za/politicsweb/view/en/page71619?oid= 103889&sn=Detail
19. The ANC also seemed to be dominated by those who sought to be close to Zuma by making, during the 2009 elections, the most extraordinary attacks on Mbeki – very recently their own leader: Carien du Plessis, ' "Mbeki Betrayed ANC but We Won't Kick Him Out", says Mbalula', *The Star*, 15 April 2009.
20. For a summary and report: http://allafrica.com/view/group/main/id/00010086.html
21. Mbeki took it as a vindication: *The Star*, 13 January 2009.
22. T.R.H. Davenport, *South Africa: A Modern History*, London: Macmillan, 1987, pp. 78–82.

12 A divorce, a forced marriage, and an historic election

1. I attended the South African elections of 2009 and spoke to senior figures from both the ANC and COPE.
2. *Financial Times*, 30 January 2009.

3. By which control, ZANU-PF continued the enrichment of its oligarchy: Greg Mills, 'How Mugabe & Co. Prosper', *International Herald Tribune*, 12 June 2007.

4. Gideon Gono has written a fascinating book of self-vindication (and advertisement), *Zimbabwe's Casino Economy: Extraordinary Measures for Extraordinary Challenges*, Harare: Zimbabwe Publishing House, 2008.

5. Tom Lodge, *Mandela: A Critical Life*, Oxford: Oxford University Press, 2007, pp. 131–3.

6. Innocent Sithole, 'ANC at the Crossroads', *News Africa*, 28 February 2009.

7. For the vexed tale of Kliptown and efforts to capture its legacy: Christa Kuljian, 'The Congress of the People and the Walter Sisulu Square of Dedication: From Public Deliberation to Bureaucratic Imposition in Kliptown', *Social Dynamics: A Journal of African Studies*, 35:2, 2009.

8. For its full text: www.freedomcharter.co.za

9. She won the 2008 World Mayor Prize: www.worldmayor.com/contest_2008/world-mayor-2008-results.html

10. See   http://www.polity.org.za/article/da-zille-extract-from-a-speech-by-the-leader-of-the-democratic-alliance-at-bela-bela-in-limpopo-11092009-2009-01-11

11. See Robert Morrell, 'Our Sexist Ways', *The Witness*, 20 May 2009.

12. *The Sowetan*, 12 May 2009.

13. Ibid., 10 March 2009.

14. Mohamed Adhikari, *Not White Enough, Not Black Enough*, Cape Town: Double Storey, 2005; Jeremy Seekings and Nicoli Natrass, *Class, Race and Inequality in South Africa*, New Haven: Yale University Press, 2005.

15. Chris McGreal, 'Bishop Chosen to Fight Zuma in Election', *The Guardian*, 23 February 2009.

16. From Lekota's own Facebook site.

17. Dominic Mahlangu and Nkululenko Ncana, 'Cope: "Mbeki is our Trump Card" ', *The Times* (Johannesburg), 17 April 2009.

18. S'thembiso Msomi, 'Battle for Western Cape', *The Times*, 21 April 2009.

19. Tom Burgis, 'Zimbabwe Power-sharing Comes under Fire', *Financial Times*, 9 March 2009.

20. Tony Hawkins, Richard Lapper and Tom Burgis, 'Lifeline for Mugabe as Tsvangirai Settles on "Forced Marriage" ', *Financial Times*, 31 January–1 February 2009.

21. Although, just a little later that year, senior MDC personnel were expressing surprise at Mugabe's demeanour of cooperation. Tendai Biti was one such: David Smith, 'Mugabe is a Typical Victorian Gentleman, Says Tsvangirai Ally', *The Guardian*, 2 June 2009. For other recollections of Mugabe, all recounting his complexities but making him far from a unidimensional person of 'evil': http://news.bbc.co.uk/go/pr/fr/-/hi/world/africa/7899057.stm

22. The literature on Zimbabwe's financial meltdown is multivarious and uneven. For a catalogue, see Brent Cloete and Greg Mills, 'Scan of Zimbabwe Economic Recovery Literature', in *The African Century*, Johannesburg: Brenthurst Foundation, 2009.

23. Mark Olden, 'This Man Has Been Called Zimbabwe's Che Guevara. Did Mugabe Have Him Murdered?', *New Statesman*, 12 April 2004.

24. *Breakfast with Mugabe*, a play by Fraser Grace, premiered in London's Soho Theatre in 2006.

25. Heidi Holland, *Dinner with Mugabe: The Untold Story of a Freedom Fighter Who Became a Tyrant*, London: Allen Lane, 2008.

26. Matthew 25:32–45.

27. 'Tsvangirai Says Crash an Accident': http://news.bbc.co.uk/1/hi/world/africa/7932463.stm (9 March 2009).

28. http://newzimbabwe.com/pages/primeminister30.19507.html

29. That the West should recognise such a vexed arrangement was nevertheless the argument of Greg Mills and Jeffrey Herbst, 'Bring Zimbabwe in from the Cold', *New York*

Times, 27 May 2009, building on the call inaugurated some years earlier by Richard Dowden, 'Engaging with Mugabe', *The Times*, 16 May 2005. See also Greg Mills, 'Regime Change *or* Change within the Regime?', *RUSI Journal*, June 2005.

30. LeRoy Vail and Landeg White, 'Forms of Resistance: Songs and Perceptions of Power in Colonial Mozambique', in Donald Crummey (ed.), *Banditry & Social Protest in Africa*, London: James Currey, 1986.

31. Liz Gunner, 'Jacob Zuma, the Social Body and the Unruly Power of Song', *African Affairs*, 108:430, 2009.

32. 'Msholozi' by Izingane ZoMa.

33. Barry Bearack, 'Party Rally Is Buoyed by Presence of Mandela', *International Herald Tribune*, 16 February 2009.

34. *The Star* (Johannesburg), 13, 14, 15 April 2009.

35. 'The Spy who Saved Zuma', *Mail & Guardian*, 9–16 April 2009, p. 2.

36. Mark Gevisser, 'How Zuma Became Mbeki', *Mail & Guardian*, 9–16 April 2009, p. 4.

37. E.g. Deon Meyer, *Heart of the Hunter*, London: Hodder, 2003.

38. Including Chinese. See Yoon Jung Park, *A Matter of Honour: Being Chinese in South Africa*, Johannesburg: Jacana, 2008.

39. *Financial Times*, 25 April 2009.

13 What is the future of it all?

1. Christelle Terreblanche, 'Make-or-break Time for Cope', *The Star*, 24 May 2010.

2. Immediately before the elections, he was already seen as a highly controversial character: Buddy Naidu and Marcia Klein, 'Meet the New Pariahs', *Sunday Times* (Johannesburg), 12 April 2009, had three subsidiary headlines, 'In with the new, out with the old: change of guard brings in new black elite', 'Zuma Loyalists can now cash in', and 'Sexwale in' – a boxed headline over his photograph.

3. Sue Cullinan and Sello Mabotja, 'Tokyo Sexwale: The Apprentice', *The Africa Report*, 22, April–May 2010.

4. Pippa Green, *Choice Not Fate: The Life and Times of Trevor Manuel*, Johannesburg: Penguin, 2008.

5. Richard Lapper, 'Zuma Appointments Help Ease Business Fears', *Financial Times*, 11 May 2009.

6. Alex Duval Smith, 'Zuma Plea as Protests Sweep the Townships', *Observer*, 26 July 2009.

7. But the protests against the World Cup continued for more than a year. See the *Guardian*'s photograph of thousands of Oukasie residents marching for housing, water, electricity and toilets, and threatening to disrupt the Cup, 11 March 2010.

8. Richard Lapper, 'S. Africa "Listening" to Voice of Poor', *Financial Times*, 5 August 2009.

9. Xolani Mbanjwa. 'How Do We Explain their Misery, asks an Angry Zuma', *The Star*, 19 May 2010.

10. Simon Mundy, 'Strike Shows Fragility of South Africa's Coalition', *Financial Times*, 27 August 2010; David Smith, 'South African Unions on Verge of Break with ANC as Strike Hardens', *Guardian*, 27 August 2010.

11. Steven Friedman, 'Malema just a Pawn in the Battle for ANC's Soul', *Business Day*, 19 May 2010.

12. E.g. Issa G. Shivji, *Fight My Beloved Continent: New Democracy in Africa*, Harare: SAPES, 1992.

13. David Smith, 'MDC Finance Minister Fears for his Life after Bullet in the Post', *Guardian*, 7 August 2009.

14. Dumisani Sibanda, 'MDC-M Wrangle Sucks in Grassroots', *News Day*, 11 August 2010.

15. For alternative calculations on remittances: France Maphosa, *Rural Livelihoods in Zimbabwe: Impact of Remittances from South Africa*, Dakar: CODESRIA, 2009; and for more anecdotal accounts: Norbert Musekiwa, ' "State Failure" in Provision of Education and Health Services in Zimbabwe: Adjustments, Adaptations and Evolving Coping Strategies of Rural Communities, 2000–2007', unpublished Ph.D. thesis, University of Cape Town, 2010.

16. F.W. de Klerk, 'The Recent Election and the Zuma Presidency', *The Round Table*, 99: 406, February 2010.

17. For the most detailed description of this, see Fholisani Sydney Mufamadi, 'Crossing the River by Groping for Stones: Statist Fostering of the Automotive Industry in China, South Africa and Thailand, 1994–2008', unpublished University of London Ph.D., 2009.

18. R.W. Johnson, *South Africa's Brave New World: The Beloved Country since the End of Apartheid*, London: Allen Lane, 2009.

19. And with its ownership of so-called 'patriotic history' being used, for decades after, as its rallying banner: Robert Mugabe, *Inside the Third Chimurenga*, Harare: Department of Information and Publicity, 2001; Blessings-Miles Tendi, 'Zimbabwe's Third Chimurenga: The Use and Abuse of History', unpublished D.Phil. thesis, University of Oxford, 2008; Terence Ranger, 'Nationalist Historiography, Patriotic History and the History of the Nation: The Struggle over the Past in Zimbabwe', *Journal of Southern African Studies*, 30:2, 2004; Terence Ranger, 'The Uses and Abuses of History in Zimbabwe', in Mai Palmberg and Ranka Primorac (eds), *Skinning the Skunk – Facing Zimbabwean Futures*, Uppsala: Nordiska Afrikainstitutet, 2005.

20. But already there is a debate as to the future role of intellectuals no longer within an Mbeki shadow: William Gumede and Leslie Dikeni (eds), *The Poverty of Ideas: South African Democracy and the Retreat of Intellectuals*, Johannesburg: Jacana, 2009.

INDEX